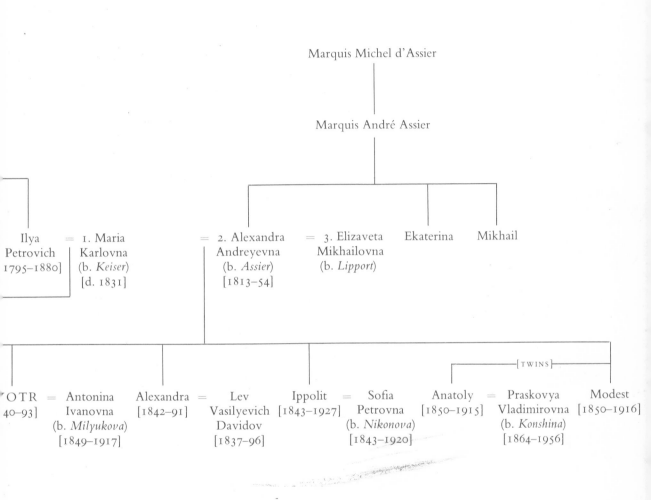

Marquis Michel d'Assier

Marquis André Assier

Ilya
Petrovich
1795–1880]

= 1. Maria
Karlovna
(b. *Keiser*)
[d. 1831]

= 2. Alexandra
Andreyevna
(b. *Assier*)
[1813–54]

= 3. Elizaveta
Mikhailovna
(b. *Lipport*)

Ekaterina     Mikhail

[TWINS]

OTR
40–93]

= Antonina
Ivanovna
(b. *Milyukova*)
[1849–1917]

Alexandra
[1842–91]

= Lev
Vasilyevich
Davidov
[1837–96]

Ippolit
[1843–1927]

= Sofia
Petrovna
(b. *Nikonova*)
[1843–1920]

Anatoly
[1850–1915]

= Praskovya
Vladimirovna
(b. *Konshina*)
[1864–1956]

Modest
[1850–1916]

# Tchaikovsky

*John Warrack*

CHARLES SCRIBNER'S SONS
*NEW YORK*

This book was designed and produced by
George Rainbird Ltd, Marble Arch House,
44 Edgware Road, London W2, England

House editor: Penelope Miller
Designer: Brian Paine
Indexer: F. T. Dunn

COLOR PLATES
Reverse of frontispiece: costume design for The Sleeping Beauty
Frontispiece: Tchaikovsky's piano

Text printed and book bound by Jarrold & Sons Ltd, Norwich, England
Color printed by Westerham Press Ltd, Westerham, Kent, England

Printed in England

Library of Congress Catalog Card Number 73–7216
SBN 684–13558–2

To Lucy

# Contents

# List of Color Plates

# Preface

The purpose of this book is to give the general reader an introduction to Tchaikovsky's life and work, and to discuss the relationship between them. I have not assumed any musical knowledge beyond that which most concert-goers may be expected to possess, nor even the ability to read music. There are therefore no technical terms except the most familiar and the most essential to the argument, no music examples and no footnotes: those interested in seeking further are invited to consult the Bibliography, where the most important sources are cited. Over the still-vexed question of transliteration I have tried to strike a reasonable balance between familiarity and consistency: Tchekov has nowadays become Chekhov, but it seems too late for Tchaikovsky himself to become Chaykovsky. I have avoided the, to us, cumbersome use of patronymics except in special circumstances or when it is necessary in order to make distinctions. Dates are given in New Style, that is to say in concordance with our Gregorian calendar; in the nineteenth century this was twelve days ahead of the Julian calendar used in Russia up to the Revolution.

I have incurred substantial debts of gratitude to kind and learned friends. Dr Gerald Abraham, whose knowledge of Russian music is as deep as his generosity in sharing it, provided insistent encouragement and solved a number of problems for me. Sir John Lawrence gave me the benefit of his encyclopedic knowledge of Russian history and life, and carefully checked some of the new translations I have found it necessary to make throughout. Mme Xenia Davidova, of the Tchaikovsky House-Museum at Klin, was helpful with information and material. Mme Galina von Meck kindly gave me much information about her family history. I am also grateful to Mr Victor Kennett, for answering a number of queries but chiefly for his beautiful and sensitive photographs; to Dr David Brown, who checked my worklist and made some useful suggestions; to Felix Alexeyev, of Novosti, for supplying many rare original photographs from Russian archives; to Mrs Penelope Miller, for her work with the illustrations; and to the patient and erudite staffs of the B.B.C. Music Library, the Central Music Library and the London Library. Particularly I am grateful to my wife, who read the typescript with a sharp eye and made a large number of helpful suggestions.

*Rievaulx, 1973*                                                                                         JOHN WARRACK

*The Decembrist rebellion in Senate Square, St Petersburg*

Opposite *Nicholas* I

When Tsar Nicholas I opened his reign by hanging the ringleaders of the 1825 Decembrist conspiracy, there were few in Russia with the optimism to see the event as the first act in the long drama of revolution. Despite the reforms and the crowning liberal achievement which Nicholas set in motion, the emancipation of the serfs, the keynote of his reign was one of reaction and repression. Nikolay 'Palkin', 'Ramrod Nick', turned Russia into a parade ground; and if the writers, artists and poets of his kingdom absented themselves from the muster or showed any inclination to step out of line, Nicholas's notorious Third Section, the political police, was at hand to seize them. Abroad, he embodied the spirit of reaction in European politics in the years following Napoleon; at home he treated his subjects like wayward children who must keep silent and trust obediently in the concern of their strict paternal Tsar to see that matters were efficiently run. To the Marquis de Custine's remarks about constitutional monarchy, the Tsar retorted, 'I can conceive of a republic. It is a proper and sincere form of government – or at least, it can be. I can also conceive of an absolute monarchy since I am, after all, the head of such an arrangement. What I cannot conceive of is a constitutional monarchy. It is a government of the lie, of fraud, of corruption; and I would rather retreat as far as China, if need be, than ever adopt it.'

The effect of Nicholas's exile of over a hundred Decembrists to Siberia was to drain society of many of its ablest minds. Upon those who remained there settled a sense of despair and apathy. While the rest of Europe was looking forward, Russia had her gaze forcibly turned inwards; and those who, headed by the brilliant critic

*Vissarion Belinsky* (1811–48)

Vissarion Belinsky, seized with enthusiasm upon the new German philosophers, Schelling and Fichte and then especially Hegel, found that part of the effect of their reading was to intensify their feelings of isolation. It is this sense of separation from the rest of Europe, and in turn of separation from the mass of their own countrymen, that most sharply marks the plight of intelligent Russians during these years. The censorship, described by one of its functionaries as 'a police station in which ideas were treated like thieves and drunkards', saw to it that even arithmetic textbooks and pieces of music were scrutinized for deviations and for secret codes; and like-minded men with ambitions for the country's intellectual life could only meet with a sense of belonging to a special class and in an atmosphere on the verge of conspiracy. The amiable apathy into which many Russians sank was epitomized by Goncharov's Oblomov, whose descendants were Turgenev's figures of *poshlost*, of complacent and indolent inferiority; while those who, sensitive and intelligent but chafing at their frustration and inability to act, found themselves without a role became, in a phrase put into currency by the title of one of Turgenev's earlier stories, 'super-fluous men': such are Pushkin's Eugene Onegin and Turgenev's brilliant but ineffectual Rudin with, as their elder brother, Lermontov's Pechorin, the so-called Hero of Our Time.

Both Pushkin and Lermontov were to die young as a result of duels which owed their real origins to the writers' separateness from the society of which they should have formed part, Pushkin hounded into an absurd challenge and Lermontov, it is said, forced into an issue over *A Hero of Our Time* and dying in the same way as his own Grushnitsky. Another group, emerging from traditional backgrounds with intellectual aspirations but unable to set these effectively to work, formed itself into what inevitably became a new social class, soon named, with a word that the

Russian language has given to English, the *intelligentsia*. It comprised both thoughtful members of the aristocracy and more radical and vehement recruits from the professional, merchant and even peasant classes, known as the *raznochintsy*. Some Russians, impelled by the uncomfortable presence among them of the intelligentsia, reacted by attempting a fundamental renewal of what they believed to be essential Russian ways of thought and conduct. Against these conservative, nationalist Slavophiles, motivated by a mystic sense of Russianness, were the Westernizers, claiming an equally honourable ancestry in the ideas of Peter the Great, and believing that the only hope for Russia lay with the European community of nations. It was a polarization, brought about by a particular historical situation, of elements that coexist in every thinking Russian. As Herzen was to observe, Slavophiles and Westernizers were like the imperial eagle, whose two heads faced in opposite directions but in whose breast there beat one heart. Few questions have so concerned Russia during the last 200 years as the problem of her relationship with the rest of Europe, and none of her important writers or composers has failed to reflect it.

Yet though the Tsar seems to have regarded the arts as having no impact upon life – so much so that, to Gogol's despair, he was able to roar with laughter at the production of *The Inspector General* – he was quick to pounce upon apparently seditious activities. Pushkin was frequently summoned for reproof by Count Benckendorff, the head of the Third Section, and was (unsuccessfully) invited to rewrite *Boris Godunov*; Pyotr Chaadayev was punished for his trenchant analysis of Russia's schism from European thought with the now familiar device of pretending that he must be mad and shutting him up; and in 1849 Nicholas went so far as to stage the sadistic sentencing and last-minute reprieve of a group that included Dostoyevsky, whose crime had been to possess Belinsky's famous letter to Gogol in which he asserted his stand for a literature committed to the highest human ideals and values. Yet it was in these conditions of gloom and apathy, lit only by fitful bursts of revolt, that there was created the public for the poetry, the novels and the music of the great nineteenth-century flowering of the Russian arts. Forbidden to think, Russians were not shut off from the arts which their autocrat Tsar saw as at the least a kind of *divertissement*, at the most a safety valve which his police could regulate. Denied the right of public debate, they were obliged to turn for a critical portrait of their society to the writers who had heeded Belinsky's inspiring call for a literature identified with life, vivid in tone and sharp in comment. This is not only the age in which the Russian novel rose to its supreme heights, it is also one in which, for all the troubles with the censorship, Gogol, Turgenev and Ostrovsky brought new themes and new methods into the young but thriving tradition of the theatre, and in which opera developed from a grafted foreign tradition into a vigorous, nationally rooted art concerned with real issues and new truth of expression that had produced by the end of the century a body of distinctive work and a handful of masterpieces.

If the writers who sought to act as a new voice for their countrymen felt themselves in a state of isolation, that of the musicians was even more acute. To some extent this served to make their lives easier: music – and especially opera – had long been subject to the personal whim of Russia's rulers, from the enthusiastic participation of Catherine the Great to Paul I's restrictions on opera and Nicholas's capricious interference, but it was relegated to a position of entertainment beyond the serious attention of the censors and the police. On the other hand, composers were faced with the problem not only of formulating a musical language that was distinctively Russian but of making music for the first time move beyond its roles as either courtly entertainment or folk activity and become capable of engaging with the issues that absorbed other artists. Only if this could be achieved would the ardently cultivated new tradition be worthy of consideration alongside the rest of European music.

It is easy to forget how short was this tradition into which Tchaikovsky was born in 1840. Catherine, who dominates the musical life of Russia in the second half of the previous century as she dominates everything else, had turned to the standard Italian models for her opera and encouraged the century-long dynasty of Italians who came to the Russian court as official composers, though her own interests, as an admirer of the Encyclopedists, lay with *opéra comique* and the drama of social comment. This much is evidenced in the propaganda content of the librettos she wrote for her composers. The long-enduring Russian fascination for all things French (satirized in one opera of the 1770s) was at least as crucial as the Italian influence, and proved easily able to survive its sharp interruption in 1812 – the more so since the pursuit of the French to their capital brought numbers of young Russian aristocrats into direct contact with French art and ideas and with ordinary people of all classes involved in the arts. Philidor, Dalayrac, Monsigny and Grétry had become, literally, household names by virtue of the number of private performances in noblemen's homes; and Russian music of the first decade of the new century owed an incalculable amount to the presence of Boieldieu as conductor and composer at the Imperial Opera in St Petersburg.

However, in the early stages the opera was Italian in origin and form, with local colour in the shape of folksongs and Russian types and subjects being gradually introduced by Russian composers whose models were still Italian. There were limits to what could be achieved by composers feeling their way with a novel medium, and with performers who were actors willing to sing rather than properly trained singers. There were limits, too, to how securely the art could root itself in a country still more or less feudal in structure, still lacking an informed middle class and still without any but the most primitive communications. The development of concert life in Russia dates from the last third of the eighteenth century, but was even then severely hampered by difficulties of travel: not until Tchaikovsky's own lifetime was the railway between Moscow and St Petersburg laid or a telegraph established. From these closing decades of the eighteenth century, too, date the first journal of

*Catherine the Great*

printed music, the first music publisher, the first folksong collections and the first music club.

By the early decades of the nineteenth century there was a steady flow of musical visitors, all of whom found a ready market for the Western music they brought with them and for the instrumental and vocal techniques they had to display. Those who settled included Catterino Cavos, who arrived in 1798 and founded by his teaching a school of singing that substantially helped to pave the way for a national opera, and John Field, who was to create a school of piano-playing of such vigour and character as to cause St Petersburg to be nicknamed 'Pianopolis'. But inevitably the stimulus and propagation of ideas about music through informed criticism was slow to follow in a society which was unused to handling them. Not until the 1820s was any kind of a start made. Prince Vladimir Odoyevsky brought a more professional training and an enthusiastic patriotism to bear upon the subject in the 1830s; and the fruitful influence of Belinsky even upon music began to be felt with the work of Botkin, for whom music was, in a phrase to be nearly echoed many years later by Tchaikovsky, 'the art of those secret movements of the human soul, for the expression of which neither form nor word is adequate'. The first great Russian critic of music, however, and one whose work can still be read with profit, is Vladimir Stasov. That the seeds scattered by Belinsky had taken root was shown in a letter Stasov wrote his father on New Year's Day 1844, on the eve of his twentieth birthday, in which he claims for criticism the role of insisting upon the meaning and the allotted task of works of art, of showing how they utter their thought and what is its meaning for the world. He stresses the inseparable connection between the history of the human race and the arts which it has produced, and he draws his letter towards a close with the significant remark, 'The greater the artist, the more he is a man, the more he feels himself connected with the world and his fellow men.'

The first half of the century was for Russia a period, rapidly accelerated because of its belatedness in European terms, of imitation and assimilation; and through the haste with which its leaders, both creative and theoretical, were forced to construct it, there shows in the music great unevenness of achievement and a proneness to swallow powerful influences without fully digesting them. As late as 1835 Verstovsky was supporting his published arguments in favour of German Romantic opera with heavy doses of Weber in his music, in *Askold's Tomb* translating to a new context all the most famous effects of *Der Freischütz*. The importance of Glinka, who was born in 1804 and died in 1857, is that he was the first composer to gather together all the threads and make of them a pattern that was instantly recognizable as authentically and independently Russian. Just as Lomonosov (who died in 1765) is credited with having created the modern Russian language by amalgamating Church Slavonic with spoken Russian, thus making possible the emergence of a great literary tradition, so Glinka can take credit in *A Life for the Tsar* and *Ruslan and Lyudmila* for having brought together European influences with native folk music to formulate a musical language that was distinctively Russian and the basis for major creative achievements. But he was also a great artist. And again, just as Russians regard the novels of their great tradition as the broad river whose pure spring is Pushkin, so they hold Glinka in scarcely less honour as the source of their authentic musical tradition. It is a river that divides as sharply as that of any other Russian artistic tradition, with the Slavophile branch paradoxically flowing north to St Petersburg and the *moguchaya kuchka* – the 'mighty handful' of Mussorgsky, Borodin, Cui, Balakirev and Rimsky-Korsakov – and the Westernizer branch flowing into Moscow, where Nikolay Rubinstein and the circle around him provided Tchaikovsky with shelter and encouragement. Tchaikovsky, in a famous phrase, called Glinka's music the acorn from which the oak of Russian music grew; but it was Tchaikovsky himself whom Stravinsky, looking back over all those who had worked for the formation of a national music, called 'the most Russian of us all'.

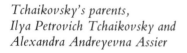

*Tchaikovsky's parents,*
*Ilya Petrovich Tchaikovsky and*
*Alexandra Andreyevna Assier*

The first historical Tchaikovsky of whom we hear is Fyodor Afanasyevich, a Cossack officer who left on his death a widow and two children. One of these, Pyotr Fyodorovich, became a civil servant and rose to be Chief of Police successively in two towns in the Vyatka Province, some 600 miles east of Moscow. His wife, Anastasia Stepanova Posokhova, had been orphaned in the Pugachev rebellion. She bore her husband no fewer than twenty children before his death in 1818. The youngest, Ilya Petrovich, born in 1795, chose a career in the Department of Mines, in which he proved capable and hardworking; he seems to have been well liked by his colleagues, and though (in Modest's description) of only moderate culture and intelligence, to have played the flute as a young man and to have taken an interest in the theatre. At thirty-two he married Maria Karlovna Keiser, a girl of German descent who died only two and a half years later, leaving him a daughter, Zinaida.

Ilya Petrovich remained a widower for only two years. In 1833 he married Alexandra Andreyevna Assier, a girl of twenty whose forebears had come to

Russia from France at the Revocation of the Edict of Nantes in 1685 and whose father, the Marquis André d'Assier, was a state councillor; thus was brought into the family not only French blood but the nervous temperament which Alexandra inherited from her father together with, from her grandfather, a tendency to epilepsy. She spoke French and German, and played the piano and sang, perhaps more as the normal accomplishment expected of educated young ladies than out of any marked gift, though her sister Ekaterina made a modest musical career in St Petersburg. When Ilya Petrovich finally achieved, at the age of forty-two, the rank of lieutenant-colonel in the Department of Mines, he was given with it the position of Chief Inspector of the mines and metallurgical works at Votkinsk, on the borders of the Vyatka Province. Settled here securely, the couple began their own family; and here were born to them Nikolay in 1838, Pyotr – whom his mother liked to call Pierre – on 7 May 1840, Alexandra in 1842, Ippolit in 1843 and the twins Anatoly and Modest in 1850.

Votkinsk was, in the middle of the nineteenth century, a mining town of considerable standing, important chiefly for its manufacture of heavy machinery and engines. Ilya Petrovich's post brought him not only the means with which to run a comfortable house – at one time he owned ten serfs – but a leading position in the society of people of his own kind, many of them craving, after the manner reflected in so much contemporary literature, civilized company in what seemed a

*An old photograph* above *and a painting* right *of the house in which Tchaikovsky was born in Votkinsk*

Overleaf, left *Ivan Turgenev, by Ilya Repin, and Alexander Ostrovsky, by Vasily Perov*

Overleaf, right *Vladimir Stasov, by Repin*

Right *Fanny Dürbach,
Tchaikovsky's governess*

Left *Mikhail Glinka, by Repin*

burdensome exile from Moscow or St Petersburg. He himself appears to have been an agreeable, hardworking if somewhat stolid man, well liked by his children though not producing the emotional stimulus of his more gifted and unpredictable wife. His house contained a piano and also an orchestrion, a kind of mechanical organ, popular at the time, controlled by a wooden cylinder and capable of playing quite elaborate pieces in imitation of orchestral effects. The repertory included excerpts from operas by Rossini, Donizetti and Bellini, and – which Tchaikovsky always remembered with gratitude as his introduction to his beloved Mozart – from *Don Giovanni*. His own musical efforts began with attempts to improvise at the piano; and when in September 1844 his mother paid a visit to St Petersburg, he and his sister devised a song called 'Our mama in Petersburg'.

Alexandra Andreyevna returned from St Petersburg having achieved at least one of the objects of her journey. To Votkinsk in November came a French governess to begin the education of Nikolay and his cousin Lydia, who also lived in the house. Fanny Dürbach was then twenty-two, evidently a sensible and intelligent girl who quickly became part of the family; she retained an affectionate interest in the Tchaikovskys all her life, eventually outliving Pyotr and leaving some vivid reminiscences of him. Hardly had she begun lessons when Pyotr was begging to join them; and he did so with such good effect that, if we may trust the memory of a governess proud of a famous and certainly precocious charge, he was reading French and German fluently by the age of six. Certainly at seven he was writing verses in imperfect but very creditable French, as his first effort, a poem on Joan of Arc, a subject that was to fascinate him all his life, shows. Fanny was clearly much taken with her youngest pupil. She found him slovenly and grubby, and

*The Tchaikovskys in 1848: Pyotr is on the left, Zinaida and Nikolay at the back, Alexandra leaning on her mother and Ippolit sitting on his father's knee.*

reluctant to take the bracing exercise she thought proper, but responsive and sensitive to such a degree that she called him 'a porcelain child'. Once, when she delivered a lecture to the children on working harder to justify all their poor papa's efforts on their behalf, Nikolay merely waited until she had finished and then went back to his toys, while Pyotr remained morose and silent until bedtime when, to the astonishment of Fanny (who had by now forgotten the incident), he burst into floods of tears and protested his love and gratitude to his parents.

Worried by such hypersensitivity – for Fanny had clearly been producing no more than a piece of routine French seriousmindedness about lessons – she tried to restrain his interest in music, which she regarded as morbid, especially when he formed the habit of slipping away from her improving talks and tinkering with his beloved piano. When he could not get to the piano, he would stare absently out of the window, tapping out tunes on the pane; once, carried away, he broke the glass and cut himself. After playing the piano himself, he was often upset and unable to sleep. Following a party at which there had been music, she found him sitting up in bed crying, 'Oh, this music, this music! Take it away! It's in here' (striking his forehead) 'and it won't let me sleep.' She tried to direct his interest to poetry and painting, but without much success. His greatest delight of these first years was when a Polish visitor introduced him to Chopin's mazurkas, a couple of which he was soon able to manage to play himself. Fanny naturally regarded with suspicion the appearance of a piano teacher, a freed serf named Maria Markovna Palchikova. Tchaikovsky

*The Schmelling School in St Petersbu*

himself later recalled with some amusement that he was soon able to match his teacher in sight-reading, and that her knowledge of music was narrow. His devotion to Fanny never swerved: as a child he was once found patriotically kissing the map of Russia and spitting on the rest of Europe, having (as he pointed out to the reproachful Fanny) first carefully covered France with his hand; and in the last year of his life he paid a visit to her in France, finding the old lady full of spirit and unchanged in her warmth.

In February 1848 Ilya Petrovich resigned from the government service with the rank of major-general, and began to contemplate a move to Moscow. Pyotr's older half-sister Zinaida had joined the family on her graduation two years previously, to no pleasure on his behalf: she seems to have been, even for her age, difficult and self-centred, and Pyotr made little contact with a girl who inhabited her own world, coloured by growing up in the city, and showed no interest in treating him gently. A further shock was the parting from Fanny, who left to take up another position shortly before the Tchaikovskys departed for Moscow in October. Ilya Petrovich had been led to expect a good appointment; but the family arrived only to find that a friend who knew of the vacant position had taken it himself. Disappointed, and alarmed by the cholera epidemic in the city, the Tchaikovskys moved on to St Petersburg. Pyotr was at first left in Zinaida's care while his mother busied herself with arranging the moves, and then dispatched with Nikolay to the Schmelling School as a boarder. Provincial, nervous, ill equipped for the strict lessons and still less for the rough-and-tumble of boarding-school life, Pyotr quickly became ill. Fanny Dürbach must have been distressed by the hysterical letters from her former pupil and the more measured but still worrying accounts of his behaviour from Alexandra Andreyevna. In December both brothers caught measles; Nikolay made a normal recovery, but Pyotr remained mysteriously ill.

A doctor spoke of a spinal brain disease and prescribed six months' rest, which gave him a chance to recover though it cut him off from the one school activity he had enjoyed, piano lessons from a musician named Filippov. He was, however, occasionally taken to the opera by his parents, though the only work he remembered from this youthful opera-going was *A Life for the Tsar*.

By the end of this time, in June 1849, Ilya Petrovich had secured another appointment, this time at Alapayevsk, near Nizhni-Novgorod on the further side of the Urals from Votkinsk. Separated from Nikolay, Pyotr became still more morose, nursing a sense of loss and loneliness and irritating his mother by his idleness. She was by now pregnant again, and less able to take an active hand in his education; a new governess, Anastasia Petrova, was engaged, and Fanny Dürbach was soon to learn from her former pupil that he was reading vigorously and, from his relieved mother, that he was settling to his work again. He would still tell Fanny that he was often sad, though comforting himself with the piano; but he was entranced with the arrival, on 13 May 1850, of the twins Anatoly and, the brother to whom he remained devotedly close all his life, Modest. A plan to enter him, together with Nikolay, in the School of Mines was abandoned in favour of the School of Jurisprudence. Almost as soon as she was able to travel, Alexandra Andreyevna set off with him to St Petersburg, and there in October he passed his exam into the preparatory class in one of the first places. A week later he was to be handed over to Modest Alexeyevich Vakar, a family friend who had agreed to act as his guardian. At the prospect of parting from his adored mother and having to face life away from his family, Pyotr became frantic. No amount of encouragement or consolation would calm him, and when eventually the day of departure came and Alexandra Andreyevna stepped into the waiting carriage, Pyotr broke from those who were trying to restrain him and flung himself at the turning wheels to try and stop them. He never forgot the horror of that moment of parting, and always regarded it as the most terrible event of his childhood.

A long period of intense loneliness followed. Pyotr and Nikolay were still boarders, though Vakar kept in touch with them and did his best to watch over their well-being; indeed, when scarlet fever broke out in the school he immediately removed the delicate Pyotr to his own home. Pyotr did not catch the disease; but he must have been in some way a carrier of the germs, for Vakar's own son caught it, and, after a short illness, died. Despite his grief Vakar nobly tried to conceal the nature of the fatal illness from Pyotr, but without success; Pyotr miserably blamed himself for having caused the death of a boy of whom he had grown fond, declared that he wished he had died himself instead, and besought his mother to have him removed since he could not bear to face the bereaved father. But Vakar seems to have found in the unhappy Pyotr nothing but an object of affection, the more so in the gap left by his own son. As soon as the period of mourning was over, Vakar took Pyotr to the opera for a treat; and with either kindly good judgment or an

*A contemporary print of St Petersburg*

inspired stroke of luck, the choice fell upon *Don Giovanni*. It was for Pyotr a turning point. *Don Giovanni*, he later wrote, was the first music that really overwhelmed him, that decided him to devote himself to music. He went on to describe his excitement at Donna Anna's recognition of Giovanni and her succeeding aria, 'Or sai chi l'honore': 'I tremble with horror; I long to shout, to weep, to groan, crushed by the violence of my impressions.' Mozart was never dislodged from the position in his affections as 'the Christ of music, in whom are quenched all his predecessors, just as rays of light are in the sun itself'.

Life otherwise continued uneventfully. Pyotr worked at his lessons; and though his letters were full of the usual complaints, he seems to have settled to a routine in which he was able to obtain reasonable marks in most subjects. His happiest time was a six-week summer holiday in 1851 spent in the country, which he already loved with the intensity of one who associated it with earliest memories and lost happiness. Ilya Petrovich visited him in St Petersburg in September and October; they enjoyed each other's company, for their relationship had always been comfortable and affectionate, lacking the intensity that had caused the scenes when

*No. 41 Sergevskaya Street, St Petersburg, where the Tchaikovskys moved in the autumn of 1852*

Alexandra Andreyevna left for home. When the time came for Ilya Petrovich to return to Alapayevsk, Pyotr resumed his studies without demur: he was, of course, older and had learned a degree of self-sufficiency, and there was the chance in the winter holiday of concentrating his interest on music and his piano. His twelfth birthday that May was the occasion of great happiness, for it coincided with the arrival of the entire family to take up residence in St Petersburg. By the end of the month it seemed clear that, although one of the youngest students, he was certain to pass into the School of Jurisprudence itself from the preparatory class. A happy summer followed on the estate of some friends in the country. The large family gathering included a musical aunt, with whom Pyotr sang his way through a duet from *Semiramide* and who played through the score of *Don Giovanni* with him. Back at school in the autumn, he progressed steadily from class to class; he began to make friends, with a musical boy, Vladimir Adamov, who was to follow a legal career, and with the precocious young Alexander Nikolayevich Apukhtin, whose verses were among the first he set and to which he returned for texts for songs throughout his life. He seems to have retained his untidy habits, which Fanny Dürbach evidently failed to correct, and to have been still a gentle, oversensitive boy with nevertheless sufficient liveliness of mind and charm to make him well liked by his fellow pupils; his miseries he had learned to keep to himself.

The School of Jurisprudence gave him ample opportunity to develop his love of music. Founded by the Tsar's nephew, Prince Peter of Oldenburg, it was really a school for the civil service; and its founder's enthusiasm for music was reflected in the class activities. Stasov (whose architect father had actually built the school) had been a pupil in the days when the piano was taught by Adolf Henselt, and the orchestra, in which everybody was expected to play, was good enough to accompany concertos by the best piano pupils and included players of sufficient skill to form chamber groups capable of performing quite difficult works at school concerts. Pyotr was later to take full advantage of this interest; and he was passed on from a disciplinarian, Ivan Alopeus, to Edgar-Prosper de Baccarat, a French *émigré* who stimulated his pupils' interest in Romantic poetry and encouraged a handwritten periodical, edited by Pyotr, entitled *The School Messenger*. Despite this, the school was never suited to Pyotr's temperament. Like all similar institutions in the Russia of the day, it was run on lines scarcely less authoritarian than those of the military academies, with a retired army officer named Zhazikov at its head. The only musical memory of it we have from the composer is a march dating from 1885, of formidable solemnity and dullness.

Then in June 1854 Alexandra Andreyevna contracted cholera. The disease had always been endemic in India, and from there it crossed through Russia to Europe in successive great waves throughout the nineteenth century. The third of these, probably a recrudescence of the particularly deadly epidemic of 1847 in which one of the Tchaikovskys' servants had died, entered Russia in 1853 and, through the poor sanitary standards then prevailing, proved difficult to eradicate. Hardly anything was then known about the disease, either about its origin or its prevention; its treatment consisted of little more than attentive nursing. Alexandra Andreyevna received every care; and with it she passed through the crisis into the deceptive stage of the disease in which recovery seems to have begun. But there was a relapse, and the doctors had recourse to the long-enduring method of relieving the patient's intense cold and the dryness of the skin that accompanies it by immersion in a very hot bath. It was without effect: on 25 June, so quickly as to have no time for words, she died.

The effect upon Pyotr was devastating. Not for two years did he feel able to write and tell Fanny Dürbach of the event; and for the rest of his life he remembered the day of his mother's death, noting it in his diary with usually a sorrowful comment. For all the friendly relationship he had with his father, it was his mother who provided the most powerful attachment of his childhood, who responded sympathetically to the nervous temperament she was probably chiefly responsible for bequeathing him, who encouraged his musical interests and who set the atmosphere of his home life by the greater strength of her personality than that of her husband as well as through her normal maternal role. One would need to know a great deal at first hand about Tchaikovsky's psychology, to say nothing of a great deal more about the causes of homosexuality, before attributing his subsequent sexual disposition to any definite origin, but we need not be too surprised to find it developing in an extremely sensitive, vulnerable boy with a childhood dominated by a powerful, and powerfully returned, affection for the mother.

There was, moreover, the influence of the School of Jurisprudence, at that time well known for the homosexual tendencies among its students. The fact that Modest was to share these confirms or denies nothing. For all the private tolerance which homosexuality received, society was not ready to accept it openly, and in a situation of intense social stigma there were for someone of Tchaikovsky's temperament all the attendant agonies of guilt, of furtive liaisons and the threat of blackmail, of remorse and fear of gossip and exposure, of feeling hopelessly cut off from the world of normal men and women. All his life Tchaikovsky wrestled with the problem, discussing it freely with Modest, recording in letters or in his diary frequent references to 'This' or 'Z', often accompanying his allusions to particular incidents with miserable resolves to overcome the condition that obsessed him with its demands and its burden. It is the central emotional fact of his life, and hence was to be a powerful formative influence on his art and the particular expression it took. Lonely, desperately unhappy and, for all the fictions he consciously assumed, fundamentally honest with himself, he turned to composition for consolation and delight, and gradually, as his art grew to maturity, for the release into music of his frustrated personality. It is not until we understand his threefold isolation – a man feeling himself cut off emotionally from the ordinary world, an exceptional talent projected into a young musical tradition struggling to form itself, and a Russian of intense patriotism ambitious for his isolated country's artistic and intellectual maturity – that we shall fully appreciate the scope of his achievement.

Tchaikovsky's immediate reaction to the loss of his mother was to turn to music: within a month of her death he was making his first serious efforts at composition. In July 1854 he wrote to Zinaida's brother-in-law, Viktor Olkhovsky, about a libretto for a one-act opera to be called *Hyperbole*; nothing came of the project, since the text consisted largely of recitatives and arias and the would-be composer wanted more concerted numbers. In the following month Ilya Petrovich, who had himself caught cholera but recovered, took the family for the remainder of the summer to Oranienbaum, on the Gulf of Finland; and here Tchaikovsky composed a little 'Valse dédiée à m-lle Anastasie' for his former governess. Back in St Petersburg in the autumn, he started singing lessons with Gavril Lomakin, the distinguished conductor and teacher who was later to found, with Balakirev, the Free School of Music; he is said to have had a good treble voice, though we can assume that it was beginning to break from the fact that Lomakin gave him the alto part in a trio. As a pianist, he continued improvising in private and playing for his friends' amusement and for dancing; he had lessons from one of the Becker piano firm, and later from Rudolf Kündinger. But when Ilya Petrovich consulted Kündinger about the prospects of a musical career for his son, the reply was discouraging. 'If I had had any idea,' Kündinger was later to write,

> of what he was to become, I should have kept a diary of our lessons, but I must admit, to my great embarrassment, that at no time did the idea occur to me that Tchaikovsky had in him the stuff of a musician . . . Certainly he was gifted, he had a good ear and memory, an excellent touch, but apart from that there was nothing, absolutely nothing, that suggested a composer, even a fine performer . . . Nothing remarkable, nothing phenomenal . . .

Kündinger's honesty does him credit. Probably there was indeed nothing in the Tchaikovsky of these years to indicate exceptional gifts; he was a very slow developer, from beginnings that were at this stage hardly more than a disposition towards music, and Kündinger was obviously right to recommend that he should not attempt the very arduous life of a musician in contemporary Russia. He was told to complete his course and then to try for a post in the Ministry of Justice.

Tchaikovsky was now almost fifteen, growing more independent of a family that had begun to move apart with Zinaida's marriage and Ippolit's enlistment in

*The School of
Jurisprudence in
St Petersburg*

Left *Luigi Piccioli,
an Italian singing-teacher*

the Navy, and that was broken further by Alexandra Andreyevna's death. Ilya Petrovich was to live for twenty-six more years, and to marry for a third time, but though he remained in contact with his children, and though they in turn showed every respect and affection for him, he was never again to be firmly at the centre of the family circle. Upon Tchaikovsky himself there now devolved greater emotional responsibilities: to Alexandra, two years younger than him and now going to school, he remained devoted all his life and upon her he was to lean in his many emotional crises, and he grew no less fond of the four-year-old twins Modest and Anatoly, who in turn always remembered his warmth and kindness.

The family was taken in by Ilya Petrovich's brother, Pyotr Petrovich, an elderly ex-soldier recluse who seems to have made little impression on them, although his wife did her best to take Alexandra Andreyevna's place with her nephews and niece. The household was further augmented by some Schobert relations; and through them Tchaikovsky came to know a Neapolitan singing-teacher, Luigi Piccioli. A grotesque figure, probably nearly in his sixties though claiming fifty, with painted cheeks, dyed hair and a weird device at the back of his head to tighten the wrinkles on his face, Piccioli was devoted to Italian music to the exclusion of all else: Glinka was anathema to him, Beethoven and Mozart treated with pity. Tchaikovsky can hardly have taken these opinions seriously, but he was fascinated by the Italian's wide knowledge of operatic lore and his understanding of the human voice. Whatever the effect on his private life of his friendship with the older man, he found his love of opera stimulated and his understanding of it given more systematic encouragement than he could achieve unaided by his visits to the Italian opera. An outcome was his first printed composition, a song for soprano or tenor and piano entitled 'Mezza Notte', which he later had printed at his own expense. He continued his opera-going, though like other young musicians of the day he could only come to know orchestral music through piano transcriptions; these were difficult to obtain, and not until he was grown up did he even know how many symphonies Beethoven had composed. A further family upset came with the loss of Ilya Petrovich's money in an unwise venture; at the age of sixty-three he was obliged to find new work, and was fortunate to be appointed director of the Technological Institute. But the crowded household remained together throughout Tchaikovsky's

*Graduates of the law school, 1859. Tchaikovsky is in front of the man with the bow tie.*

school years, and finally, just after his nineteenth birthday in 1859, he graduated, thirteenth in the class, with the rank of government clerk.

To enter the government service was no longer so secure or so respectable as it had been during Tchaikovsky's training. With Nicholas I's death in 1855, restrictions on ordinary life began to ease; his son, Alexander II, no less conservative but more realistic, rebuffed from interference in European affairs by Russia's defeat in the Crimean War in 1856, saw it as his task to put forward as smoothly as possible the internal reforms that were inevitable. Chief among them was the great question of the emancipation of the serfs; but quietly the censorship was relaxed, newspapers and, more crucially in so vast a country, magazines such as Herzen's famous *The Bell* began to circulate more freely, and a new generation in the universities began debating not so much the Slavophile-Westernizer question as whether the coming change should be gradual or violent. The foundations of the administrative system were to be permanently altered by the emancipation; but already in the early years of the new reign, the novel whiff of freedom let in through Alexander's cautiously opened window blew coldly upon the officials who had been controlling matters.

*Alexander II (1818–81) in his study*

[33]

In the absence of any tradition of enlightened public service, officialdom could hardly be more than merely bureaucratic; and to be an official became a matter of reproach.

It is hardly surprising, then, that even if his interests had not lain elsewhere, Tchaikovsky should have proved an undistinguished member of the Ministry of Justice to which he was attached. Though he rose through several ranks, his devotion to his career may perhaps be measured by the story that once, when talking to someone, he absently tore an important document to shreds and chewed up the pieces. His life was not here, but in the theatres he went to in the evenings, where he learned more about opera and about the technique of classical ballet, in the ballrooms and at the parties where his gifts as a pianist made him popular. In 1860 Alexandra married Lev Davidov, son of one of the Decembrists, and left St Petersburg to make a new home at one of his family properties at Kamenka, in the Government of Kiev; possibly this served to draw Tchaikovsky closer to his father, who had clearly been observing how matters had been going. One night he raised again the question of a musical career. 'At dinner they spoke of my musical talent,' Tchaikovsky wrote to Alexandra in March 1861:

> Father declared it was not yet too late for me to become an artist. If only that were really true! But it's like this: even if I actually had any talent, it can hardly be developed now. They've made an official of me, though a poor one; I'm doing my best to improve and attend to my duties more conscientiously; and at the same time I'm to study thoroughbass.

Nevertheless he remained at the Ministry; he formed new friendships and continued to be close to Apukhtin, with whom he read poetry and discussed literature. But despite his interest in the public reaction to the declaration of the emancipation of the serfs, read out in all the churches of the Empire on 17 March, he took no

*Lev and Alexandra Davidov*

part in political activity and showed no sympathy with the Nihilist views given expression that same year by Turgenev in *Fathers and Sons*. Neither an Oblomov nor a Rudin, he was still less a Bazarov.

In the summer a foreign trip was proposed by a friend of Ilya Petrovich, Vasily Pisarev (who is not to be confused with the Pisarev whose extreme views lay behind the Nihilists). Tchaikovsky was to act as companion and interpreter; and in July they duly set off. Berlin soon bored him, as did Hamburg, Antwerp and Brussels; London somewhat depressed him, and he was unenthusiastic about the young Patti; but like many a Russian before him and after him, he fell into the arms of Paris with delight. Six happy weeks followed, in which his letters were filled with accounts of opera performances that he enjoyed while loyally finding them inferior to those at home, before a quarrel with Pisarev cut the trip short. Returning to St Petersburg alone, he bewailed his mistake in making the trip to Alexandra:

> If ever I started on a colossal piece of folly, it was this journey . . . I spent more money than I ought to have, and got nothing useful out of it . . . You know I have a weakness: as soon as I have any money I squander it on pleasure; it's vulgar and silly, I know, but it seems to be in my nature. Where will it take me? What can I hope for? It's awful to think of it. I know that sooner or later I shall no longer have the strength to battle with life's problems; till then, I mean to enjoy it and to sacrifice everything to enjoyment. For the past fortnight I have been pursued by misfortune; my work has gone badly; money goes up in smoke; no luck in love.

But to this self-reproachful outpouring, of a kind with which the ever-sympathetic Alexandra was to grow very familiar, he adds a postscript: 'I am studying thorough-bass and am making good progress. Who knows, perhaps in three years you'll be listening to my operas and singing my arias.' Six weeks later, his resolve to take up a musical career has strengthened, though it is accompanied by characteristic self-doubt: 'With my quite respectable talent (I hope you won't think this is boasting)

*The Alexandrinsky Theatre, St Petersburg,*
*where several of Modest Tchaikovsky's plays were first given*

Right *Nikolay Zaremba*
*(1821–79),*
*Tchaikovsky's first*
*important teacher*

Left *Herman Laroche*
*(1845–1904),*
*one of the first critics to*
*appreciate Tchaikovsky*

it would be silly not to try my luck in this direction. I'm only afraid of my own spinelessness. In the end my idleness will win, but if it doesn't I promise you something will come of me. Luckily it's not yet too late.'

The classes where Tchaikovsky was studying thoroughbass were held by the Russian Musical Society, formed in 1859 with the intention of raising the standard of music in the country and disseminating musical education. His teacher was Nikolay Zaremba, under whom he was required to work at a traditional German training. Modest later recalled that as a boy he was surprised not only to discover his elder brother really working but to learn that together with pleasant music went a very boring kind that for some reason seemed the more important. Zaremba was a well-schooled pedagogue, and his training did Tchaikovsky nothing but good; he spent most of his spare time working at harmony and counterpoint, seeing fewer friends and visiting the theatre less often. In 1862 he learned of a better position in the Ministry, and set himself to achieve it by hard work at his office; but music came into the foreground again when news reached him of the intended opening of the new Conservatory.

Though this step was the natural outcome of the work of the Russian Musical Society, it was not universally welcomed. Even so enthusiastic a propagandist for Russian music as Stasov opposed the move on the grounds that it was a weak copy of European example, and that conservatories tended to be breeding-grounds for mediocrity. But the day was carried by the energy of two remarkable people. One was the Grand Duchess Elena Pavlovna, an aunt of the Tsar, an energetic and intelligent woman of liberal sympathies and keen musical interests; the other was her protégé, the young pianist and composer Anton Rubinstein. Together they had originally discussed the then startling project of the Russian Musical Society. The Grand Duchess had obtained the somewhat grudging approval of the Tsar, who was cautious about the establishment of new institutions, and Rubinstein, having prepared the public with an article in the magazine *Vek* (The Age), opened proceedings with a concert at which he played one of his own piano concertos. Classes were then established in the Grand Duchess's house, the Mikhailovsky Palace; and further approval and subsidy having been won from the now impressed Tsar, a regular Conservatory was opened in September 1862 in a house on the Neva. Rubinstein was director, and his youthful staff included Wieniawski, Leschetizky and the cellist Karl Davidov. Among the earliest pupils to join was Tchaikovsky.

Committed now more fully to music, he found his capacity for work rising with his hopes of a career. Within two days he was writing to Alexandra asserting that sooner or later he was determined to give up his present job for music: 'I only want to do the work for which I feel I have a vocation. Whether I become a famous composer or merely a struggling teacher, it's all the same. My conscience will be clear and I'll no longer have the depressing right to grumble. Of course I shan't resign my position until I'm certain that I'm not an official but an artist.' He worked busily at Zaremba's exercises, studied the piano and the flute and had a few organ lessons. Much encouraged by a new friend, the future critic Herman Laroche, who quickly came to believe in his gifts, he was further strengthened in his eagerness to abandon his job by one of his teachers reproving him for not working when he had so much talent (Laroche and another contemporary and future critic, Nikolay Kashkin, disagree as to whether it was Zaremba or Rubinstein himself).

Late in 1863 he entered Rubinstein's class, and within a few months he was being excused compulsory piano so as to give more time to theory and composition. He flung himself into the work with enthusiasm. Once, Rubinstein recalls, having been told that quantity as well as quality was important in working variations on a theme, he produced instead of a dozen or so, over a hundred. Zaremba had been for him merely an instructor, whose dislike of Mozart and Glinka annoyed him and whose admiration for Beethoven and Mendelssohn he found unsympathetic. But

*The building, later to be the Conservatory,*
*in which music classes were held in St Petersburg*

between Rubinstein and Tchaikovsky, who never came to like each other's music, there was a powerful relationship: until well into middle life he would have valued Rubinstein's praise more than anybody's, and never really received it. However, Rubinstein was willing to help by arranging some private pupils for him; and by economizing on theatre visits and living simply in a small bed-sitting-room, he hoped to be able to make his way as a musician. 'The professors are all satisfied with me and say that with hard work I shall do very well', he told Alexandra. 'I'm not boasting – that's not my way – but saying this to you frankly and without false modesty. I long to come to you for a year when my studies are finished and compose a big work in your quiet surroundings. Then – out into the world.' The once rather dandified young man who had delighted smart parties and spent most of his evenings at the theatre had now reverted to his childhood shabbiness, with a threadbare coat and artistically long hair to match Rubinstein's. He was engaged as an accompanist in public concerts and found pupils; and when he failed to obtain the expected promotion at the Ministry, he resigned. The future was far from secure, for so far from having the honoured status they enjoy in modern Russia, musicians were not officially accepted as having a profession at all. But he was, Modest tells us, happier than at any other period of his life.

Materially, of course, he was considerably worse off. He managed to scrape a living by teaching, by accompanying, by making pot-pourris of Italian operas, but he was also obliged to borrow. Yet he was happy not only in his work but in his friends. In the autumn of 1863 Alexandra's mother-in-law, Alexandra Ivanovna Davidova, settled in St Petersburg with her children Vera and Elizaveta. Tchaikovsky was not only interested to make friends with these members of his sister's new family, but was fascinated by Alexandra Ivanovna's stories of how the Decembrists had met at Kamenka, how Pushkin had written part of *The Prisoner of the Caucasus* there (perhaps she drew a tactful veil over her sister-in-law Aglaya's advances to Pushkin, whose poem to her is tersely outspoken about her lovers) and by her daughter Elizaveta's memories of Gogol. The younger daughter, Vera, was attracted to Tchaikovsky himself, but when his sister, perhaps encouragingly, suggested that Vera might be falling in love with him, he drew sharply back.

Apart from any disinclination to return her feelings, he was deep in the hardest work he had yet known in his life. He continued his technical exercises, and in addition to his instrumental studies he had his first experience of conducting, an occupation which long filled him with alarm. Laroche was his companion at many concerts, and together they met Serov, Rubinstein's enemy but the composer of an opera, *Judith*, which Tchaikovsky greatly admired; it was on this occasion that, Laroche recalled, 'Dostoyevsky talked at length, and very foolishly, about music in the way of literary men who do not understand it at all.' Tchaikovsky was also busy with his first real efforts at composition – a scene of Pushkin's *Boris Godunov*, an oratorio and some instrumental and piano pieces, among the latter a Theme and Variations in A minor. But his first important work, written as a holiday task set by Rubinstein during the summer of 1864 spent with a friend at Trostinets, near Kharkov, was the overture on *The Storm*. Ostrovsky's play, later to be the source of Janáček's *Kat'a Kabanová*, had come out in 1859, when its portrayal of a sensitive nature destroyed by a rigid and uncomprehending society had much moved Tchaikovsky; and upon the subject he now lavished his fullest imagination. Falling ill just before he was due to return to St Petersburg, he sent the score to Laroche, asking him to take it to Rubinstein so that the great man's opinion should be sought as soon as possible. It was Laroche who received it: confronted with not the academic exercise he expected but an elaborate piece of programme music after the descriptive overtures of Henri Litolff – Tchaikovsky's new enthusiasm – and scored for an orchestra that included such 'forbidden' instruments as harp, cor anglais and tuba and such devices as divided and tremolo strings, and including a Russian folk tune (which Mussorgsky was later to use in *Khovanshchina*), Rubinstein exploded in fury. Though episodic and somewhat self-indulgent in effects of colour, *The Storm* remains a remarkably powerful work for so inexperienced a composer; and already

Right *Alexander Serov* (1820–71)
Left *Fyodor Dostoyevsky, by Perov*

in it can be detected not instrumental extravagance, as Rubinstein believed, but the flair for instruments, alone and in novel combinations, that was to be part of Tchaikovsky's genius. In that Tchaikovsky was to lean heavily upon this gift, and to lack the mastery of form that comes from an ability to think in extended musical paragraphs, Rubinstein was right, and he may have felt justified in reproving a student composer for being lured by a love of colour and failing to work at the real basis of his art. But it is difficult to avoid the suspicion, especially in view of Rubinstein's own music, that his irritation sprang at least in part from seeing his own principles set aside in favour of such vigorous invention.

At all events, Tchaikovsky was not put off by what was to be the first of many such incidents. Nor did Rubinstein wash his hands of his troublesome pupil: he produced a much needed, and perhaps rather pointed, task in the shape of translation of the eminent Belgian theorist François Auguste Gevaert's *Traité Général d'Instru-mentation*, which had appeared in 1863. Having observed, with approval, his father court and marry a third wife, a widow, Elizaveta Mikhailovna Alexandrova, Tchaikovsky went to the Davidov estate at Kamenka to set to work on further orchestral compositions. These included two rather more 'correct' overtures, in C minor (using a reworking of the opening of *The Storm*) and F, and a set of charac-teristic dances, the *Dances of the Serving Maids* which were later to be used in the opera *The Voyevoda*. In September they were included in an outdoor concert in the Pavlovsk Park given by none other than the Waltz King himself, Johann Strauss the younger; and enough of a success did this first real public performance prove, to encourage Tchaikovsky to feel that it was worth continuing along his own lines.

However, he was still a long way from earning his living by composition. He was compelled to move from one set of rooms to another; his eyes were troubling him; he even contemplated returning to government service. Rescue came in the form of an invitation from Moscow. In 1860, helped and encouraged by his brother Anton, Nikolay Rubinstein had founded a Moscow branch of the Russian Musical Society in his own house, and so successful was he – no doubt in part due to Musco-vite anxiety not to be outdone by the rival city – that he was eventually able to move into larger premises and expand his work. His chief harmony instructor was to be Serov, a gifted man whose intelligence had impressed Wagner but whose violent opinions and cutting pen had won him many enemies. When Moscow showed no immediate sign of welcoming his second opera, *Rogneda*, which had triumphed in St Petersburg in November 1865, Serov abruptly refused to take up a post in so obtuse a city. Nikolay turned to his brother for advice about a replace-ment, and was recommended Tchaikovsky – an act which says more for Rubin-stein's real view of his talent than all the reproofs and criticisms of his music.

But before the post could be taken up, Tchaikovsky still had to finish his own studies. He had been busy on various works. One was a String Quartet in B flat,

*The Rubinstein brothers, Nikolay (1835–81) and Anton (1829–94)*

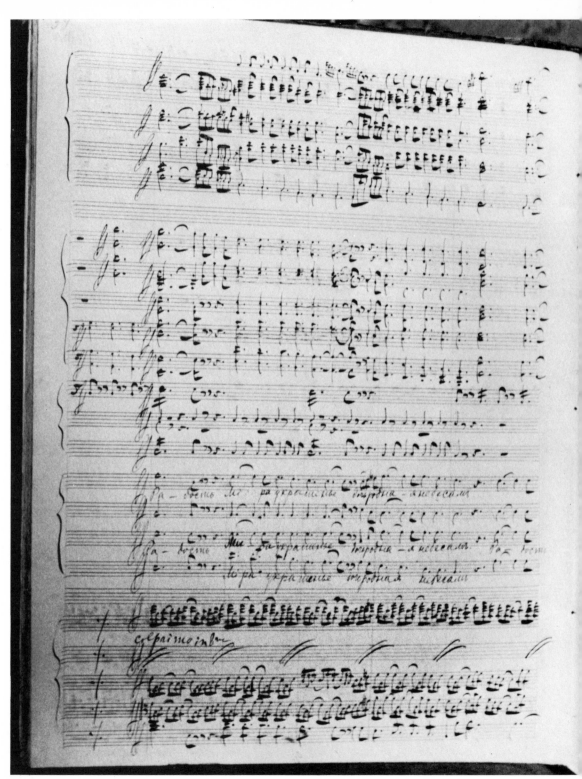

*MS. of a page of Tchaikovsky's setting of Schiller's* Ode to Joy

which included a folksong movement that alone survived the quartet's destruction and became the Scherzo à la Russe for piano, his Op. 1, No. 1. Another was a cantata in six parts, for solo quartet, chorus and orchestra, to Schiller's *Ode to Joy*, which Rubinstein, ignoring the daunting precedent of Beethoven's Ninth Symphony, pressed upon Tchaikovsky. On 12 January 1866 the work was performed at the distribution of prizes before the directors of the Russian Musical Society and a number of other eminences, though not before Tchaikovsky himself, whose nerve had failed him at the prospect of the viva voce exam which accompanied it. Annoyed, Rubinstein threatened to withhold Tchaikovsky's diploma, and refused to countenance public performance of the cantata unless it were revised. Two days later Tchaikovsky was awarded the diploma. His grades were given as theory and instrumentation – excellent; piano – very good; orchestration – good; conducting – satisfactory. The cantata fared less well. Rubinstein, Serov and Cui all disliked it, the last declaring that a couple of long-forgotten nonentities whom he cited must be rejoicing to feel their ranks now swelled by Tchaikovsky. Only Laroche was faithful. Reminding Tchaikovsky that he had dismissed even *The Storm* as 'a museum of anti-musical curiosities', he comforted the composer,

> I tell you frankly I consider you to possess the greatest talent in contemporary Russia . . . more powerful and original than Balakirev, nobler and more creative than Serov, infinitely more cultured than Rimsky-Korsakov. In you I see the greatest, indeed the only, hope for our musical future . . . Your real creations may not appear for five years or so. But those mature and classic works will surpass everything since Glinka.

Depressed at leaving behind him his family, Laroche and his other friends, and his powerful mentor Anton Rubinstein, Tchaikovsky set off for Moscow in mid-January. He was met at the station by Nikolay Rubinstein, who welcomed him to his own house, found him a tailor, lent him other clothes, including a frock-coat left behind by Wieniawski, and lavished every hospitality upon him. Since his divorce in 1857, Nikolay had plunged into a life of furiously hard work and equally furious relaxation; and he seems to have found in the shy Tchaikovsky a welcome companion for his long nights of drinking and gambling. He also introduced Tchaikovsky to a number of friends who were to remain close to him all his life. They included Nikolay Kashkin, already an influential critic and later the author of

*Pyotr Jürgenson (1836–1904), Tchaikovsky's most important publisher*

some valuable reminiscences of the composer, and his future publisher Pyotr Jürgenson. New literary acquaintances were Alexey Pisemsky, Alexey Pleshcheyev, Count Vladimir Sollogub, and especially Alexander Ostrovsky. He also became friendly with a family named Tarnovsky, and told Modest that he was much taken with a niece nicknamed Mufka. This led Rubinstein, who had also once been attracted to Mufka, to tease Tchaikovsky by ostentatiously leaving the pair of them alone whenever they came to the house; but any possibility there might have been of the friendship turning into a real romance was put to an end by Mufka herself, who shortly married an army officer.

Professionally, his life began its new course somewhat hesitantly. After a nervous start, he became a competent teacher who was able to face his class without stage fright. He reworked the C minor Overture written at Kamenka the previous summer; Nikolay Rubinstein refused it, however, and Anton likewise declined to play it in St Petersburg. Coming upon the manuscript years later, Tchaikovsky added to his identification of it, in brackets, the words, 'dreadful rubbish'. Much of it is admittedly mechanical, but there are one or two characteristic touches, especially the fondness for woodwind scales, and at the time he liked at any rate one passage enough to re-use it in his opera *The Voyevoda*. He also reworked the F major Overture, substantially revising the material and rescoring it for full orchestra; and this Nikolay Rubinstein conducted, with great success, on 16 March. It is certainly a more characteristic work than the C minor Overture, and though it includes a somewhat dutiful and not very effective fugue, it shows something of Tchaikovsky's mature gift for generating and sustaining orchestral excitement. He had already felt able to write to Alexandra that he was settling down in Moscow and acquiring suitably professorial airs. His nerves were better; he was reading *The Pickwick Papers* with amusement; he began contemplating librettos for an opera; and began work on sketches for his First Symphony.

This mood of cautious euphoria was shattered by Cui's withering review of his cantata; and the succeeding depression, coupled to the extra work of writing an overture suggested by Rubinstein to celebrate the coming marriage of the Tsarevich, caused a return of all his nervous symptoms. He was unable to sleep, he suffered from pains in the head which he declared to be strokes, he became convinced that he would surely die before he was able to complete his symphony. Moreover, the public mood was darker following the repressions in the wake of a disaffected St Petersburg student's attempt on the life of Alexander II. Despite the general relief at the attempt's failure, expressed in a performance of *A Life for the Tsar* which Tchaikovsky attended when there were massive demonstrations of loyalty, Alexander interpreted it as a sign of too much liberalism; and he ordered a revision of school and university curricula, designed to stifle thought and resulting in the mass emigration of many of the brightest young men to study abroad. For Tchaikovsky himself the only encouragement was the news of a successful performance of the F major Overture under Anton Rubinstein himself in St Petersburg on 13 May. He had hoped to spend the summer again at Kamenka, 'a promised land'; but the state of the roads prevented the journey, and he was forced to make the best substitute he could of Myatlev, near Peterhof, and a holiday with Vera and Elizaveta Davidova. Here he was at least able to spend his time at the piano. A few years previously Jürgenson had begun publication of the first standard edition of the German classics in Russia, and Tchaikovsky was able to play through some of Schumann's symphonies and Mendelssohn's *Italian Symphony*. Only when he resumed work on his own symphony did troubles return. He suffered hallucinations, an oppressive sense of dread and physical symptoms such as numbness in his hands and feet; a doctor found him 'on the verge of madness' through overwork, and ordered rest. Unable to complete the symphony without the nocturnal work he had to give up, he was compelled to return from holiday with it unfinished. He showed it to Anton Rubinstein and Zaremba, who condemned it and demanded revisions. Travelling on to Moscow, he was able to take part in the celebrations for

*Tchaikovsky celebrated the opening of the Moscow Conservatory in 1866
by playing Glinka's* Ruslan and Lyudmila *overture.*

the opening of the new Conservatory building by playing the overture to *Ruslan and Lyudmila* from memory, so that Glinka's music should be the first to be heard there. Shortly afterwards he managed to complete the commissioned Festival Overture, in which the Tsarevich's Danish bride is saluted by her National Anthem, and was rewarded by the Tsarevich with a set of cuff-links so grandiose that he promptly sold them to a colleague. The Scherzo of the symphony was given in Moscow in December, and the two middle movements were rather more warmly received in St Petersburg in February; but the complete work did not receive a performance until February 1868, under Nikolay Rubinstein. Tchaikovsky further revised and cut it in 1874, and this version was not performed until October 1886.

Tchaikovsky always remembered the symphony with affection. 'For all its glaring deficiencies, I have a soft spot for it,' he told a friend many years later, 'as it is a sin of my sweet youth'; and in drawing Nadezhda von Meck's attention to it he suggested that, 'although it is in many ways immature, it is fundamentally better and richer in content than many more mature works.' No more than any composer born into the Romantic movement did Tchaikovsky find symphonic form his natural mode of expression; and towards the end of his life he was still bewailing his inability to master it. Here, while he has not yet developed the extremely personal solution which marks his last three symphonies with greatness, he produces a work which is conventional in form but already strongly coloured by his own individuality. His example is not the classical symphony but the works which we know him to have been playing through at Myatlev; and the principal model is Mendelssohn. Though the Scherzo is an orchestral version of a movement from his own C sharp minor Piano Sonata, the delicacy and swiftness of the music in this handling show that Mendelssohn's scherzos had fallen fruitfully upon his ear; and the opening of the whole work, with its fluent melody over murmuring strings, is from Mendelssohn's world. But more particularly, the *Italian Symphony* and *Scottish Symphony* showed him how a skilled composer could distil into symphonic form a Romantically personal emotion at the contemplation of landscape. His own is subtitled 'Winter Daydreams'; and the landscape here described is of course his own Russia. The first movement is further subtitled, 'Daydreams of a Winter Journey'. Just as the hectic babble of excitement which opens the *Italian Symphony* records the explosive thrill which Mendelssohn expected of his crossing into Italy but did not actually find, so Tchaikovsky's first movement represents an imaginative distillation of the Russian landscape of his heart. Moreover, he has learned from Mendelssohn the virtues of generalizing the emotion in the opening movement, where it must be accommodated to sonata form, and only turning to more direct description with the slow movement. Hence it is from the vividly portrayed Pilgrims' March of the *Italian Symphony*, or still more the 'Holyrood' Adagio of the *Scottish*, that Tchaikovsky takes the example for his own Adagio. Subtitled 'Land of desolation, land of mists', it is a memorable picture of a bleak, deserted winter landscape through which presently sounds the voice of an oboe, inescapably suggesting some solitary marsh bird. But the theme shares with the two principal subjects of the first movement deeply Russian characteristics, especially the habit derived from Russian folk music of building a melody around certain prominent intervals which are obsessively reiterated, one phrase growing out of its predecessor by modified repetition, the whole creating an atmosphere of either ritual concentration or sometimes the fixed reverie that is here intended. The same melodic characteristic marks the Finale, in which Tchaikovsky once again introduces a fugue perhaps more out of a sense of duty and in order to help him survive a formal crisis rather than out of real musical conviction. He has by now abandoned subtitles; and it would be hard to see how an appropriate one could be found for a scherzo in which the Mendelssohnian elegance is interrupted for a trio section that is really the first, and by no means the least charming, of Tchaikovsky's waltzes. Other fingerprints of his mature style can already be seen in the work – the little woodwind scales decorating a theme, certain harmonic traits, the tendency to allow skilful orchestration to do duty for more basic musical variety, the reliance on melody and its felicitous repetition rather than on a musical cell which can generate real symphonic energy. The merits and defects are already present; and if Tchaikovsky ruefully acknowledged the latter, he was also right to take pleasure in the music's youthful freshness and charm.

*A tavern in the* 1860s

Writing to Anatoly in November 1866, Tchaikovsky reported that he was going to make Rubinstein's suggested alterations to the symphony; and he added, 'Then perhaps an opera. There's a chance that Ostrovsky himself will write a libretto for *The Voyevoda*.' By the middle of March Ostrovsky had indeed completed a draft text for Act 1 of an operatic version of his play, and within three days Tchaikovsky had begun work on it. He interrupted himself to write a piano caprice, later entitled *Russian Scherzo*, which subjects a folk theme to somewhat strenuous piano figuration; it was dedicated to Nikolay Rubinstein, who gave its first performance in April. Turning back to the opera, Tchaikovsky found to his dismay that he had lost the libretto. Ostrovsky rewrote what he had already done from memory; later, he seems to have wilted under the bombardment of requests for alterations, revisions and further rewritings, for the text after Act 1 is Tchaikovsky's own. In June, he set off with Anatoly for a holiday in Finland; running short of money, they were forced to return to St Petersburg and then to travel on to Hapsal (Haapsalu), a watering-place on the Estonian coast, on the assurance that Vera Davidova and her family were holidaying there.

Arriving with the last of their money gone on the cheapest steamer fare, they found the Davidovs, and Tchaikovsky settled down to a summer's work. Vera Davidova's timely hospitality was acknowledged in a little triptych of piano pieces dedicated to her, entitled *Souvenir of Hapsal*: the first, *The Castle Ruins*, is a sombre little tone-picture with a more lively middle section; the second, a revision of a student piece, is a nimble scherzo; and the third was to be the first of Tchaikovsky's pieces to attain wide popularity, the pretty *Song Without Words*. He also continued work on *The Voyevoda*, and in general the holiday seems to have been both happy and fruitful. We need not, perhaps, take too seriously the luxuriant melancholy of a letter to Alexandra in which he confesses his weariness of life and warns her that one day she will have to find some portion of her maternal care for her tired old brother, since he cannot find the energy to consider marriage. However, back in Moscow, having left Anatoly in St Petersburg, he managed to summon up enough energy to resume his riotous evenings with Nikolay Rubinstein; for whatever he may have lacked in social self-confidence, Tchaikovsky always enjoyed friendly company, and his capacity for alcohol impressed even Rubinstein. However, working hard on the opera (without, significantly, any of the neurotic symptoms that accompanied his symphony) he managed to complete the third act by December; and on the 14th Nikolay Rubinstein conducted the dances from the opera, with great success. He also nerved himself to make a graceful speech in French in honour of Berlioz, who, aged and exhausted, 'as tired as eighteen horses' but very respectful of the musical life of Moscow, was making his second visit to Russia at the instigation of the Grand Duchess Elena. It was a speech from the heart, for Tchaikovsky profoundly admired Berlioz and was moved by the sight of a man he regarded as a heroic fighter against artistic ignorance now evidently 'aged and broken, persecuted by fate and by his fellow men'. It was also the occasion of Tchaikovsky's first meeting with Stasov and with Balakirev, as a result of which he came to feel that the viewpoint of the consciously nationalistic *Kuchka* need not be so impossibly far from his own.

Encouraged by the friendly reception he and his music seemed now to be receiving, especially after the performance of the First Symphony in February,

*Berlioz posing for the camera on his 1867 Russian visit*

Tchaikovsky agreed to conduct his *Voyevoda* dances at a charity concert. It was his first public appearance as a conductor, and only as he came on to the platform did his friends in the audience see that he had panicked. Kashkin later described the occasion:

> I saw that he was distraught; he came on timidly, as though he would have liked to hide or run away, and on mounting the rostrum he looked like a man in anguish. He seemed to have completely forgotten his composition; he did not see the score before him, and gave all the leads wrong, or to the wrong instrument. Fortunately the players knew the music so well that they paid no attention to him and, smiling to themselves, got through the dances quite creditably in spite of him. Afterwards Pyotr Ilyich told me that in his panic he had had the illusion that his head would fall off his shoulders unless he held it firmly in place.

To prevent this, Laroche reports, he kept a tight grip on his beard throughout. It was ten years before he overcame his terror of conducting. However, the music was cordially praised in a review which also dismissed a piece by Rimsky-Korsakov; Tchaikovsky's angry defence of Rimsky, in an article that was his first venture into criticism, was naturally well received by the *Kuchka* and, in a letter acknowledging the score of the *Voyevoda* dances which had been sent him by the hopeful composer, Balakirev wrote respectfully and cordially. When Tchaikovsky visited St Petersburg in the spring, he also met the other members of the circle. Despite the hostility between the *Kuchka* and Rubinstein's Conservatory group of composers, Tchaikovsky was kindly received, and Rimsky records that they were all much taken with the first movement of his symphony when he played it to them. Another contact with the *Kuchka* was established through Vladimir Begichev, the Intendant of the Moscow Imperial Theatre. Begichev had recently married Maria Shilovskaya, a talented amateur singer and a popular society hostess who had been a pupil of Dargomizhsky and with whom Mussorgsky had been in love. One of her sons by her first marriage, Konstantin Shilovsky, later became the librettist of *Eugene Onegin*; Vladimir Shilovsky, a consumptive boy with musical leanings, became Tchaikovsky's pupil and close friend. When Begichev took Vladimir abroad, Tchaikovsky accompanied them and continued the lessons. In Paris, where they went in search of a specialist to attend Vladimir, Tchaikovsky spent his spare time at the opera, greatly admiring the polish of the performances, and in finishing the scoring of *The Voyevoda*. Back in Moscow in September, he learned that his salary at the Conservatory had been increased, and that plans had been made for a production of *The Voyevoda* in October. Both his personal and his professional life seemed calm and assured; and he settled down to his autumn work in the expectation of a fruitful new winter season.

*Désirée Artôt*

On 21 September 1868 Tchaikovsky went to the Bolshoy Theatre for the performance of Rossini's *Otello* which opened a season given by a visiting Italian opera company. Laroche dismisses the singers as fifth-rate, possessing neither voice nor talent, with one exception. Evidently he overlooked the gifted young Roberto Stagno, who had already begun an international career, for the artist he had in mind was Désirée Artôt. The daughter of a distinguished Brussels horn player, she had trained under Pauline Viardot and made her début in *Le Prophète* in 1858 at the age of twenty-three; subsequently she had turned to Italian roles, and had raised her voice from mezzo to soprano, conquering London in concerts and in opera during the early 1860s. By any standards the visiting company was fortunate to include her; and certainly she seems to have won them their success in Moscow almost single-handed. Tchaikovsky was bowled over by her. For a budding opera composer there was obviously the attraction of a striking artistic personality and a fine voice. Laroche speaks of her sensitivity and her charm, as well as of her talent, though he did not find her good-looking; his friend was infatuated perhaps largely as a romantic ideal, but on meeting her he discovered a 'nice, good, sensible woman' and by the end of the year the friendship had progressed to the point when marriage was being considered.

The opera chorus and orchestra had been so much occupied with the Italians that Tchaikovsky prudently asked for a postponement of *The Voyevoda* until they could rehearse concentratedly; but he himself put aside work on a tone-poem, *Fatum*, to give most of his attention to Artôt. Apart from a somewhat empty *Waltz Caprice* written for Anton Door, his music of that autumn consists of choruses and recitatives for Auber's *Le Domino Noir*, for Artôt's Benefit, and the suitably ardent and tender F minor *Romance* dedicated to her. The courtship flourished, though in writing to tell his father the news, Tchaikovsky reported that her formidable mother was opposing the match and that several of his friends, in particular Nikolay Rubinstein, were afraid that he would find himself in the role of prima donna's husband with little time for his own work. They may well have had other reasons for doubting Tchaikovsky's capacity for marriage; but he himself pressed ahead with plans, and was pleased when his father wrote an affectionate reply encouraging him to dismiss any doubts about marrying another artist provided he was really sure of his emotions.

With the departure of the Italian company, rehearsals of *The Voyevoda* were resumed; highly excited, Tchaikovsky wrote to Anatoly of secret ideas for another opera, and only later did he admit that things had begun to go wrong with his marriage plans. Rehearsals continued, and though they were to prove inadequate he appreciated the trouble that everyone was taking. Then, at one rehearsal, Nikolay Rubinstein came up to him with a piece of news he was no doubt only too delighted to give: Désirée Artôt had just married the Spanish baritone Mariano Padilla y Ramos in Warsaw. Possibly she had never taken Tchaikovsky's proposal as seriously as he had himself; possibly she, too, was attracted by an obviously gifted and intelligent musician, but, particularly under the influence of her mother, soon began to see that they would not make a successful match. As for Tchaikovsky, though the blow was a sharp one, it does not seem to have been wholly unexpected or as devastating as one would expect in someone of his temperament, for within a couple of days he was back at rehearsals, apparently unruffled. When Artôt returned in the following December to sing Marguérite in *Faust*, he watched her performance through his opera glasses with tears running down his face; but it seems that it was her stage personality that had always really captivated him. Like Berlioz with Harriet Smithson, he had failed to distinguish between the artist and the woman; but in his case, the impossibility of achieving any real emotional contact with a woman condemned him to situations in which a strong element of fiction was an essential ingredient. The reality of Désirée Artôt would probably have proved almost as disastrous as his later marriage did.

*The Voyevoda* was produced at the Bolshoy on 11 February, and an enthusiastic audience gave the composer fifteen curtain calls. However, the work was not a success. It was repeated only four times before being dropped from the repertory; and it was the occasion of Tchaikovsky's break with Laroche over a review deploring the prevalence of German and Italian influences and the lack of innate Russian qualities. Some years later, Tchaikovsky accepted the unfavourable verdict, admitting that his music was too symphonic for the theatre and too elaborately orchestrated. He destroyed the score, having salvaged some of the more usable portions for use, chiefly in *The Oprichnik*, but also in *Swan Lake* and *1812*. Thanks to the survival of some material – the Overture and Entr'acte, the orchestral and chorus parts, some sketches, a vocal score and the libretto – reconstruction and publication have been possible, and the opera was again performed in Leningrad in 1949. The plot may be briefly summarized:

> ACT 1: Praskovya, elder daughter of the wealthy Vlas Dyuzhoy, is betrothed to the Voyevoda Shaligin; her younger sister Maria is in love with a young noble, Bastryukov. But on seeing Maria, the Voyevoda falls in love with her and carries her off, despite Bastryukov's efforts.
>
> ACT 2, *Scene 1*: Bastryukov's servants are awaiting his return from hunting. He comes in with Roman Dubrovin, who describes how two years previously the Voyevoda had outlawed him and carried off his wife Olyena. The two men agree to try to rescue the girls in the Voyevoda's absence on a pilgrimage. *Scene 2*: Maria mourns her fate; Olyena arrives with news of the escape plan. Praskovya's nurse Nedwiga comes with the maids to comfort Maria with songs and dances.
>
> ACT 3: Bastryukov and Dubrovin break into the Voyevoda's garden by night, but having resuced Maria and Olyena they delay too long and are discovered by the Voyevoda. He tries to stab Maria, but in the nick of time the Tsar's emissary arrives to announce the arrest of the Voyevoda for his crimes.

Too much is simplified in this libretto, and there are sacrificed too many of the subtleties of character and milieu, typical of Ostrovsky's subtle realism, to which even the inexperienced Tchaikovsky might have responded well. The dramatic pace is, moreover, awkward and the situations exaggerated; since Tchaikovsky himself abandoned the work after preserving the best music, it is difficult to regard the subsequent salvaging of the work as much more than an honourable act of piety. He was happy to pass the subject on to Arensky, who set it as *A Dream on the Volga* (1891).

Tchaikovsky had meanwhile been able to finish his tone-poem *Fatum,* and, encouraged by his improved relations with the *Kuchka* and by the first performance by Nikolay Rubinstein on 9 March, he sent the score to Balakirev, asking him to accept the dedication if he liked the work. Balakirev at once replied that whatever his opinion he would arrange for a performance; and this duly took place on 29 March. He followed this up with a letter in which, in a manner familiar to Balakirev's friends and soon to Tchaikovsky himself, he launched into a detailed criticism of the music, correcting, objecting and recommending different procedures. Urging Tchaikovsky to abandon his adherence to the classics and to disciplines acquired under Zaremba, he concluded by renewing his high regard for Tchaikovsky's talent and hoping that, in spite of his own frankness, he would be allowed to retain the dedication. Tchaikovsky responded to this candour in kind, and while admitting that he had hoped for at any rate a crumb of comfort, he agreed (with some justice) that much was wrong with what he himself called a concoction. He had come to trust Balakirev, who was never happier than when writing his friends' compositions for them, and he accepted with remarkably good grace the barrage of detailed advice, extending to key-structures and even to habits of work, which was the price of being counted among Balakirev's colleagues. Later he destroyed the work, though it has been posthumously reconstructed, but he let the dedication stand; and when Balakirev came into sharp conflict with the Grand Duchess Elena, Tchaikovsky wrote a vigorous article in his defence.

In his letter to Balakirev, Tchaikovsky also mentions that he has finished one act of the 'secret' opera he mentioned to Anatoly; the other two he hoped to score in the summer. This was *Undine*: having toyed with a Graeco-Babylonian subject offered him by Ostrovsky, he had fastened with enthusiasm upon De la Motte Fouqué's tale, which had long been popular in Russia in the version by Vasily Zhukovsky. A libretto was ready to hand, for in 1848 Alexey Lvov had composed his *Undine* to a text by Count Vladimir Sollogub, a translation of a French version; and this Tchaikovsky took over. It is a simple treatment of a tale that won wide popularity among the Romantics for its dramatization of the split between man and nature, between reason and instinct, and of the forlorn attempt to bring about reconciliation in the attempted marriage of a human to a water spirit. Unfortunately the story's touching quality here sinks under the weight of the Romantic paraphernalia of knights and storms and fateful warnings; the characters have little substance, and less motivation for their capricious actions. But Tchaikovsky believed himself to have found a good subject in it, and settled down enthusiastically at Kamenka in the summer to finish it. Scoring the opera in his room one day, he overheard a carpenter singing the folksong that he was to make famous as the Andante Cantabile movement of his First String Quartet. The opera was dispatched to St Petersburg with Begichev; but two other operas were already scheduled, and after many delays *Undine* was finally rejected. Eventually Tchaikovsky recovered the score and burned it, saving from it only a few numbers – a wedding march that went into the Second Symphony, a love duet that became an Adagio in *Swan Lake*, and the Introduction and an aria that were used for the incidental music to Ostrovsky's *Snow Maiden*.

Returning to Moscow at the beginning of August, Tchaikovsky found Balakirev temporarily living there. They spent a good deal of time in each other's company, but Tchaikovsky, though continuing to like and admire the older man, never became close friends with him. 'He is a good fellow, and kindly disposed towards me,' he told Anatoly, 'but, I don't know why, I never feel quite at home with him. I particularly don't like the narrowness of his musical views and the sharpness of his tone.' Nevertheless in a fallow autumn he owed Balakirev much, not only in the way of companionship but for allowing him to use some of his own folksong collection

*Mily Balakirev*
(1837–1910)

for a new selection, and for the stimulus to begin original composition again. Balakirev had been working on an overture to *King Lear*, and now suggested that Tchaikovsky might try his hand at a similar concert piece on *Romeo and Juliet*. Finding him slow with ideas, Balakirev offered his usual help: he described in a long letter how he had begun his own *Lear* by planning the dramatic sequence of events, and suggested that Tchaikovsky might set about matters in the same way: 'then arm yourself with goloshes and a walking-stick and set out for a walk along the Boulevards, starting with the Nikitsky; let yourself be steeped in your plan, and I am sure that by the time you reach the Sretensky Boulevard some theme or episode will have come to you'. He adds a few bars of music representing the fighting Montagues and Capulets which had just come into his head and which he passes on helpfully. When Tchaikovsky sent – or perhaps submitted – the principal themes to Balakirev, the opening was rejected as resembling a Haydn quartet rather than the Liszt chorale Balakirev recommended, and the love theme was criticized for its lack of spirituality. However, Balakirev was basically full of admiration and encouragement, and gratefully acknowledging the dedication, he called the work the first of Tchaikovsky's complete successes.

This was sound judgment. Though he can hardly have realized how apt it was, Balakirev had hit upon a subject that exactly matched Tchaikovsky's talents and his whole approach to music. No longer bound by formal requirements, he was free to fashion his own design for the music; yet whereas in his previous orchestral tone-poems he had either attempted to follow the drama too slavishly, with disjointed musical results as in *The Storm*, or lacked a compelling formal idea at all to give expression to a general mood as in *Fatum*, here he has sensed how the basic ingredients of the drama imply a musical form. Though he disliked programme music, he always needed a subject; and he finds it here in the one that was to obsess him all his life and to form the substance of all his greatest work, the crushing of love by a hostile fate. It is not hard to see how bitterly acute the subject was to Tchaikovsky. Though the ingredients of the drama are perceptible – Friar Laurence's priestly motive, the clashing swords of the warring families – these are made into an abstract drama. Love, represented in one of Tchaikovsky's most ravishing melodies, is opposed by the violence of the feud, in some of his most thrilling orchestral clashes, and ends in death, not as Wagnerian transfiguration but in fruitless oblivion. The threefold exposition of the themes does not parallel the course of the play, and Tchaikovsky's intention is really to take it not as subject so much as analogy. The subjection of this emotional and musical material to a kind of sonata form has its own expressive force; for as well as conferring a coherent form upon the music, it can embody the notion of something inexorable guiding the music, a course of events imposed from outside the actual themes and thus seeming to rule them arbitrarily – in fact, representing the notion of a Fate which Tchaikovsky had already come to believe ruled his own life and would mercilessly crush his own emotional longings.

On 16 March 1870 Nikolay Rubinstein conducted the first performance of *Romeo and Juliet* in Moscow; it was a failure, but Rubinstein himself was sufficiently impressed with the work to arrange for its publication by Bote and Bock when he was in Berlin that May (Balakirev, on seeing the published version, regretted that this rush into print prevented there being time for more revisions). At the same time as he had been working on the Overture, Tchaikovsky had completed his first set of songs. Though not a great *Lieder* writer, he nevertheless produced among his 103 songs a larger number of masterpieces than neglect would suggest. Time and again he can concentrate into a few pages a musical image that ideally matches the substance of a poem, most successfully when he is treating the subject of love and its loss or frustration. To this first group (Op. 6) belong two or three of his finest songs, among them Lev Mey's Goethe translation 'Nur wer die Sehnsucht kennt', known in the English-speaking world as 'None but the lonely heart'.

But despite the failure with *Undine*, his thoughts were still never very far from opera. Late in 1869 he was offered a libretto by a professor of botany, Sergey Rachinsky, entitled *Mandragora* in which we again find a knight falling in love with a fairy being, a girl this time, transformed from a flower, and losing her back to her original element through his infidelity. He set first an Insect Chorus, a pretty, delicately scored piece in which Laroche not surprisingly found the influence of Berlioz; though behind the 'Chœur des Gnomes et de Sylphes' of *Faust*, which is its obvious inspiration, we may also hear the fairies of Weber's *Oberon*. Kashkin admired the piece, but after fierce argument managed to persuade Tchaikovsky that the libretto was hopeless. He turned instead to a play by the historical novelist Ivan Lazhechnikov, *The Oprichnik*, and by 17 February was able to tell Alexandra that work had begun on it. This news comes at the end of a letter in which he laments his loneliness in Moscow, and dreams wistfully of his happiness, if only, 'you, or someone like you, lived here. I long for the sound of children's voices and for a share in small domestic matters – in a word, for family life.' Like many homosexuals, he found women sympathetic, in any role but a physical one, and could also long for the stability of a household, for the presence of children and all the bustle and even the fret of domestic life that clearly seemed so desirable in the home Alexandra was successfully making at Kamenka. To other friends he mourned that he was gloomy, bored, poor, bad at teaching, neglected and fat. He leaped at the chance of a trip to Paris on hearing that Vladimir Shilovsky was seriously ill there.

After three weeks in Paris, during which Tchaikovsky found time for the theatre, Shilovsky had recovered sufficiently to be moved, and they set off for Soden, a resort for consumptives near Frankfurt. Gloom was only briefly dissipated by a Prussian military band which Tchaikovsky persuaded to play Glinka's *Kamarinskaya*, by a trip to Mannheim for the Beethoven Centenary Celebrations, where he was deeply moved by the *Missa Solemnis*, and by a visit to Wiesbaden, one of the German spas long beloved by itinerant Russians, where he came upon Nikolay Rubinstein, 'in the act of losing his last ruble at roulette . . . He is quite convinced that he'll break the bank before he leaves.' Then in July the Franco-Prussian War broke out; certain that the French would soon be sweeping eastwards, the Russians fled to Switzerland. Six weeks in Interlaken worked an improvement in Shilovsky's health, and they were able to press on to Vienna by way of Munich, and thence back to St Petersburg, reaching Moscow again by the middle of September. Tchaikovsky resumed work on *The Oprichnik*, though with so little success that he considered breaking off to write a four-act ballet on *Cinderella*. His own health had collapsed again, or so he complained; the creative work of the autumn, apart from the opera, consisted of work on *Romeo and Juliet*, a song and three minor salon pieces for piano.

Even shorter of money than usual, despite an increase in his Conservatory salary, and depressed at the slow progress his music was making in the public eye, he decided to follow Nikolay Rubinstein's advice and give a concert of his own work. He could not afford an orchestra, so he decided on a programme of chamber music. Rubinstein was naturally willing to take part; Elizaveta Lavrovskaya, then already one of the Maryinsky Theatre's most popular younger artists, agreed to sing 'None but the lonely heart'; and some Moscow singers were to sing other songs and an excerpt

from *The Voyevoda*. For the pupils of Berta Valzek, Moscow's leading singing-teacher, Tchaikovsky wrote a special piece, *Nature and Love*; and for the quartet of the Russian Musical Society, which included the Czech violinist Ferdinand Laub, the ballet composer Aloysius Minkus and the cellist Wilhelm Fitzenhagen, Tchaikovsky wrote a string quartet. On 28 March 1871, the new quartet opened the concert at the Russian Society of Nobles: a latecomer, impressing the audience by having turned up because of the composer's reputation in Europe, was Turgenev. The quartet which he missed is a fine work: though made famous, not to say notorious, by the Andante Cantabile movement (based on the tune Tchaikovsky overheard being sung at Kamenka, together with another of his own invention) it is the remaining movements which show a real mastery of string quartet style, and the ability to think musically in the medium. It shows little sign of the haste with which it was composed, none at all of Tchaikovsky's inexperience.

*Nikolay Hubert (1840–88), critic and student friend of Tchaikovsky's*

The composition of the quartet was, however, an interlude in work on *The Oprichnik*, to which he devoted himself for the remainder of the Conservatory term. In June he set off on a holiday trip. First he visited his elder brother Nikolay at Konotop; from there he travelled to Kiev to meet Anatoly and take him on to Kamenka, where his sister's children delighted him so much that he composed for them a little ballet: it was on the subject of *Swan Lake*, and Modest played the part of the Prince. Next he called on a wealthy friend, Nikolay Kondratyev, at Nizy, where he finished his *Guide to the Practical Study of Harmony*. Although the country was green and cool, he found the social round too like that of the town, and was glad to move on to Usovo to see Vladimir Shilovsky. Here he found the quiet he was increasingly needing for his work – so much so, that on returning to Moscow for the autumn term he left the kind but exhaustingly hospitable Nikolay Rubinstein's house and took a small three-roomed flat on his own. Modest tells us that the furniture consisted of a large sofa, a few cheap chairs, and two pictures – a portrait of Anton Rubinstein and another of Louis XVII in the care of the cobbler Simon. He engaged a servant, Mikhail Sofronov; it was Sofronov's brother Alexey who succeeded him as the devoted companion and servant of Tchaikovsky's later years.

To his Conservatory salary he now also added a small income as a music critic. On leaving Moscow for an appointment at the St Petersburg Conservatory, Laroche had been succeeded on the *Moscow Gazette* by Nikolay Rubinstein's new housemate, Nikolay Hubert; but with Hubert showing signs of neglecting his work, pressure was brought to bear upon the editor to allow Tchaikovsky and Kashkin to deputize for him. Like most composers set to the task, his opinions are interesting chiefly for the light they shed upon his own attitudes; and, with the new enthusiasm of the opera composer, he was able to reverse the unfavourable opinion he had formed of Patti in London when she delighted Moscow in *Il Barbiere di Siviglia* in November. He kept up his contacts with the *Kuchka*; Balakirev's plans for him included detailed recommendations for a cantata, *Night*, to be developed around the *Mandragora* chorus, with a chorus of sprites, an instrumental scherzo on the lines of Berlioz's *Queen Mab*, and a descriptive epilogue in which the orchestra would depict

*Staff of the Moscow Conservatory in 1872. Top row, left to right: Kashkin, Mme Valzek,
Hubert, N. Rubinstein, Tchaikovsky, Alexandrova-Kochetova, E. Langer; group on left:
Vilshlu, Shpekin, Klindworth, Barthold, Kashperov, Fitzenhagen; group on right: Dubuque,
Hřímalý, Zeiler, Laub, Galvani, Richter; bottom row: Gut, Razmadze, Albrecht, Razumovsky,
Zverev, L. Langer, Büchner*

dawn and sunrise. Tchaikovsky replied that he liked the idea, but, 'at the moment
I am spending all my few free hours on my opera *The Oprichnik*, which I am very
anxious to finish this winter. I dare say this unlucky opera will share the fate of my
*Undine*, but all the same I want to finish it, so I can't begin another work just yet.'

But life in Moscow was oppressive: the Conservatory was in the throes of a financial crisis and was even threatened with closure, which Tchaikovsky publicly declared he would angrily deplore while privately confessing his relief at being spared
so much exhausting work; and he began to realize that his self-imposed target of
finishing *The Oprichnik* by the end of the year was unrealistic. He needed little per-
suasion when Shilovsky proposed a foreign holiday. However, a trip in the middle
of the season with a young man needed some explanation, particularly since

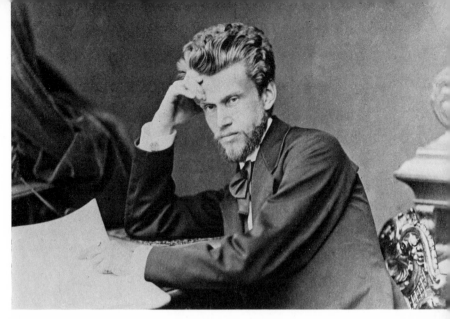

*Eduard Nápravnik (1839–1916), first conductor of many of Tchaikovsky's works*

Tchaikovsky had grown disturbed about the rumours concerning his private life which were inevitably circulating in Moscow. He was, moreover, commissioned to write a cantata for the celebrations of the 200th anniversary of the birth of Peter the Great that summer. He begged Anatoly to let it be known that he had gone to Kamenka, and quietly set off in mid-December. From Nice, in mid-January, he wrote to Anatoly describing the pleasure of leaving a Russian winter for the Riviera sun; and the world-weary thirty-one-year-old adds, 'I am old, and can enjoy nothing more. I live on my memories and my hopes. But what is there to hope for?' From Nice, the two moved on to Genoa and Venice, to Vienna and thence home; the musical outcome of the holiday was a couple of piano pieces dedicated to Shilovsky, an F major Nocturne and the sprightly G major Humoresque. He settled down to his neglected work: he was editing some children's songs and adding piano accompaniments for a volume which Jürgenson was bringing out; he was busy with the Festival Cantata, which was partly cobbled together from some of the First Symphony's music to a text that Laroche described as being 'as unmusical as possible'; he found time to write to Balakirev asking him to pass on thanks to Cui for a very sympathetic review of *Romeo and Juliet* after the St Petersburg performance on 17 February, though his usually voluminous correspondence thinned out in the spring under pressure of work; he finished *The Oprichnik* on 20 March, writing to tell Nápravník in St Petersburg on 4 May that he would be sending him the score the next day; and on 12 June, after the première of the Cantata, the exhausted composer set off for Kamenka.

Though *The Oprichnik* eventually had to wait until April 1874 for its first performance – at the Maryinsky Theatre in St Petersburg – it was Tchaikovsky's first real success in the form he had been cultivating so assiduously. Performances followed that year in Odessa and Kiev, and the following year in Moscow, though Tchaikovsky himself soon formed a dislike for the work and near the end of his life

[63]

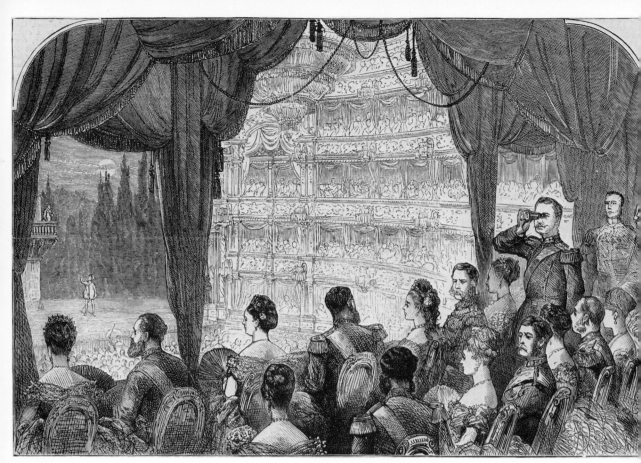

*View from the Imperial Box at the Bolshoy Theatre, St Petersburg*

was still contemplating a major revision. However uneven, *The Oprichnik* served to school him in opera of the kind he had set himself to write. And throughout his career, this was basically the traditional Italian opera which had formed the diet of his impressionable first encounters with opera as a boy. He disliked Wagner, when he came to know his music, with the vehemence and wilful incomprehension that were the backhanded compliments Wagner always met from those who recognized but feared his genius; and for all his good relations with the *Kuchka*, he resisted the search for realism that marked the work of Dargomizhsky and Mussorgsky. Their music, he thought, would end up by denying the very stuff of opera; and this, for him, was inseparably bound up with Verdi and with the Russian graft onto the Italian tradition that had been effected by Glinka. Like most Russian musicians, up to and including Stravinsky, it was the Italian tradition that meant the most to him in opera; and though he was to bring into his own operatic idiom the French influence that was part of his whole aesthetic outlook, he needed the clarity and sense of balance, not to mention the touch of an artificial convention, which Italian opera represented for him.

Throughout his entire composing life, there was hardly a moment when he was not contemplating a new opera, from the abortive *Hyperbole* when he was fourteen to a possible setting of George Eliot's *Amos Barton* he was considering at the time of his death. Opera had been his first introduction to the stage and to good music well played and sung; and he was practical enough to become quickly aware not only of its problems but simply of the fact that a composer could advance himself best in the opera house. He once confessed as much to Nadezhda von Meck in answer to her questions about *The Voyevoda*:

> I simply wrote music for the text provided, not in the least thinking of the endless distinctions between operatic and symphonic style. In composing an opera, the author must constantly bear the stage in mind, i.e. remember that the theatre needs not only melodies and harmonies but also *action* so as not to abuse the attention of the opera-goer, who has come not only *to hear but to look*, and, finally, that the style of music for the theatre must correspond to the style of decorative painting, hence be *simple, clear, colourful*. Just as a painting by Meissonier would lose all charm and fail to receive its due appreciation if it were to be put on the stage, as a result of which all the delightful details of that genre of painting are lost and become unnoticeable, so exactly music abounding in harmonic subtleties gets lost in the theatre, where the listener needs sharply drawn melodies and a lucid harmonic design. But in my *Voyevoda* I concerned myself precisely with this filigree elaboration of themes, and quite forgot the stage and all its conditions. These conditions to a significant extent paralyse the composer's purely musical inspiration, and that is why symphonic and chamber music stand far higher than operatic music. In a symphony or a sonata I am *free*; there are no limitations or constraints on me; but on the other hand opera has the advantage that it provides the possibility of speaking to the masses in the language of music. An opera might perhaps be performed at least forty times in a season, and this gives it an advantage over a symphony that will be performed once in ten years ! ! !

Writing to Nadezhda von Meck some six years later, he reiterated these views, adding significantly, 'It isn't just a question of pursuing external effects, but of choosing subjects of artistic value, interesting and touching the quick.' It was his failure to light upon subjects that did indeed 'touch the quick', that concerned themselves with warm human emotions in difficulties or under threat, which was responsible for the comparative failure of most of his operas. Having twice come to grief with a subject concerning the impact of the real and the magical worlds, he now tried to rescue *The Voyevoda* by adapting much of its music to another plot on a Russian historical subject. Lazhechnikov's play had been written in 1859, though its banning by the nervy authorities kept it off the stage until 1867; and Tchaikovsky was clearly impressed by its operatic potential in the mixture of an unhappy love story with a powerful episode from Russian history. The *oprichnina* was an invention of Ivan the Terrible, a huge area of power set apart (the word *oprichnina* derives from the term for the wife's or widow's portion), answerable only to the Tsar and administered by a grim body of *oprichniks* who travelled the country, dressed in black and riding on black horses. Part of the ritual of admission to their ranks involved an elaborate and fearful oath of loyalty to the Tsar; and though he is identified in the libretto by being addressed as *grozny*, the Russian word for 'dread' which we usually translate as 'terrible' when applied to Ivan IV, it was the intention to represent him on the stage which (inconsistently, in view of Rimsky-Korsakov's *The Maid of Pskov* and *The Tsar's Bride*) caused the censor to intervene and call for changes.

For his libretto, Tchaikovsky reduced Lazhechnikov's play to a simple, not to say crude, piece of melodrama.

ACT 1: Prince Zhemchuzhny (bass) has promised to Molchan Mitkov (bass) his daughter Natalya (sop.) in marriage. She bewails this fate to her old nurse Zakharenya (sop.) and her maids. Her true love Andrey Morozov (ten.) arrives with his friend Basmanov (alto), the Tsar's favourite, and a group of oprichniks. He has decided to join them so as to revenge himself on the Prince for having robbed and evicted him and his mother. When they have gone, Natalya returns and mourns his loss, unconsoled by the singing and dancing of her maids.

ACT 2: Andrey's mother, the Boyarinya Morozova (mezzo), is not lifted from her gloom over her fate by Andrey coming to tell her of his friendship with Basmanov; she refuses all help from the oprichniks, whom Andrey does not tell her he is going to join. He takes their solemn oath of total loyalty to the Tsar, though not without shedding tears that are noticed with pleasure by his father's old enemy, Prince Vyazminsky (bar.) (Vyazminsky is a replacement for the Tsar demanded by the censor).

ACT 3: In a Moscow square, the Boyarinya is mocked by some boys as a 'she-oprich-nik'. Natalya runs into her arms for protection from the pursuing Zhemchuzhny. Andrey appears in time to save her, but the two women are appalled to find that his companions are the oprichniks. Basmanov suggests that the Tsar might consent to release him from his oath.

ACT 4: Amid the wedding festivities in the Tsar's palace, it is revealed that Andrey is to be released from his oath at midnight and be allowed to marry Natalya. But Vyazminsky interrupts with the news that the Tsar has sent for Natalya. Despite Basmanov's insistence that this is only a test of Andrey's loyalty, he breaks his oath by refusing to let her go. The oprichniks take her to the Tsar, and Andrey to execution. Vyazminsky leads the Boyarinya to the window, where she sees Andrey being executed.

Tchaikovsky's act in transferring to *The Oprichnik* not only much of the music of *The Voyevoda* but also a good deal of the text seems less extraordinary when we remember that certain situations in such plots were similar to the point of being virtually interchangeable. After all, when the convention is that of a number opera proceeding from one powerful 'situation' to another, the difference between one lamenting heroine and another or one triumphant villain and another is not very great. However, the fact that such convenient switches were possible means that it is situation rather than character with which we are dealing; and this in turn suggests a composer not yet moving confidently beyond stock operatic gestures to a portrayal of individuals. Herein lies the weakness of *The Oprichnik*. It contains some excellent numbers: outstanding among them are Natalya's magnificent arioso (which looks forward to the passionately lyrical character of Tatyana), the Boyarinya's monologue, part of the love duet and some of the choruses of the oprichniks. But the choruses sound less powerful than Tchaikovsky evidently hoped, for though they sing with an unmistakably Russian accent in the cast of their melody and in the harmony that accompanies them, they lack the gritty realism we have grown to associate with Russian crowd choruses through Mussorgsky. Tchaikovsky can round off their numbers neatly, as with their opening chorus, but in resisting realism he commits himself to a somewhat dull generalizing. His own voice can show in unexpected places, somewhat intrusively when Andrey and Basmanov in the last act find themselves conversing over a waltz (which Tchaikovsky has the grace to abandon fairly quickly), effectively as the future ballet composer for the delightful wedding dance, and as an opera composer who has not yet found his subject in certain moments of lyrical intensity. The latter is most striking with Natalya, when the rather thin elegance of the musical language suddenly moves away from stereotype and becomes charged with a particular emotion. Tchaikovsky had not yet found his individual touch with *The Oprichnik*; but in the handling of his reminiscence motives (they are too simply employed to earn the description of Leitmotiv) and in the effective pacing of a few scenes, as well as the beauty and dramatic potency of certain moments, we can see the characteristics that were to flower in *Eugene Onegin*.

Happily settled in at Kamenka in mid-June 1872, Tchaikovsky began work on his Second Symphony. However, after the strain of the spring he was in need of relaxation, and he spent the first part of his holiday paying visits to various friends in the company of Modest. After staying with Kondratyev at Nizy, they set off at the end of July together, Tchaikovsky for Usovo and Modest for Kiev. Their paths were to separate at Vorozhba; and at a posting station on the way they treated themselves to a luxurious lunch washed down with plenty of wine and spirits. Carried away, Tchaikovsky reacted to the news that no horses were available by loftily demanding the complaints book and signing his entry, 'Prince Volkonsky, Page-in-Waiting'. Within a quarter of an hour the alarmed overseer had harnessed a pair of horses and vigorously abused the head ostler for not having reported that they had unexpectedly returned from a journey. Delighted at the success of their ruse, the brothers set off; at Vorozhba, Tchaikovsky reached for his wallet to buy his train ticket and found to his horror that he must have left it at the posting station. The train pulled in, and Modest was obliged to leave his miserable brother to spend the night in the local inn, having told the driver of the post-wagon to return next day with the wallet. But the overseer refused to part with the property of so distinguished a personage as Prince Volkonsky except to His Highness in person, and after a wretched night in the rat-infested inn Tchaikovsky was forced to return to the posting station.

*An old Ukrainian* bandurist

Here he nervously asked for his wallet, and found to his relief that the overseer's respect had evidently been too great for him to open it. Pulling himself together, he managed to commend the fellow grandly and asked him his name. 'Tchaikovsky', was the straight-faced reply. This was the last straw. The humiliated composer fled, and only much later did he learn from Kondratyev that the overseer's name really was Tchaikovsky.

A month at Usovo in Shilovsky's company served to restore him. He worked hard at the Second Symphony, and by the end of August, much refreshed and pleased with the work he had done, he was back in Moscow and settling into new rooms. He continued his musical journalism together with his other duties during the autumn; but it was the symphony which was absorbing his thoughts, so much so that even the pleasure of a visit to St Petersburg in November, during which he learned that *The Oprichnik* was accepted for production by the music committee, could not deter him from hurrying back to Moscow and further work. His continuing loneliness, however, is revealed in a letter to his father in which he speaks again of his wish to marry and mentions his poor eyesight ('I have been obliged to get myself some glasses, which I am told are very becoming to me'); and both here and in a letter to Modest he complains of nervous depression. Back in St Petersburg at Christmas time, he appeared before the final committee of the Imperial Theatre directors with his *Oprichnik* and was told that it was unanimously accepted. At the Rimsky-Korsakovs' he played through the Finale of the new symphony: 'The whole party nearly tore me to pieces, and Mme Korsakov implored me to arrange the finale for four hands.' Among the guests was Stasov, with whom Tchaikovsky discussed possible subjects for a symphonic fantasia; and a few days later Stasov wrote with detailed suggestions for a work based on *The Tempest*, since Tchaikovsky had expressed interest in a Shakespearean theme, with alternative suggestions of *Ivanhoe* and *Taras Bulba*. But it was *The Tempest* that attracted Tchaikovsky, and with a wealth of detail and advice that Balakirev himself would have envied, Stasov followed his first letter up with copious suggestions for the plan and structure of the projected work. In a letter of 8 February 1873 Tchaikovsky gratefully acknowledged this help, though he feared that it might be some time before he could make use of it; meanwhile, he was glad to be able to report that the Second Symphony had been enthusiastically received at its first performance by the orchestra of the Russian Musical Society under Nikolay Rubinstein the day before.

It is not surprising that the warmth which Tchaikovsky felt for Kamenka and the second home which his sister had encouraged him to make there should have found expression in his use of local songs for the symphony: it was the contemporary nickname for the Ukraine that led the critic Nikolay Kashkin to subtitle the work the 'Little Russian' Symphony. But for all the enthusiasm with which the symphony was greeted by the *Kuchka* and their friends (though Cui was not among them), it represents no reconciliation with their musical outlook. The true Nationalists saw folksong as part of the Russian collective unconscious; Tchaikovsky liked it because it reminded him of his mother and of the security of his country childhood, which perhaps he felt was in some way re-enacted in his happy summers spent with Alexandra on her estate. Moreover, unlike Mussorgsky, he regarded folksong as something to be drawn upon for what he felt was an inexplicable beauty, he later told Nadezhda von Meck, rather than as a generative force in his music. This carries with it a stylistic problem, through the tendency of Russian folk music to repeat phrases and intervals in a manner that creates a static and even ritual effect. Instead of a brief melodic cell, or a theme built of a few such cells, which can be made the matter of symphonic argument, we find a complete tune, one designed for a different function and tending to be formed by modification rather than development or contrast. The problem for the composer will be to accommodate this to a structure that is genuinely symphonic rather than merely episodic.

Tchaikovsky was fully aware of this problem. He was not trying to develop the atmosphere of his First Symphony into a more detailed impression of Russia; nor was he even trying to write a folksong symphony, for only three actual folk tunes are used. His concern was rather to extend and improve his symphonic style, which he believed to be inadequate, using the folk music which he felt to be valid material for a symphony. The opening horn melody is a variant of a local song, 'Down by Mother Volga', and also bears some relation to a city song, 'O you winter, little winter'; it was a student favourite, and was associated with the Cossack rebel Stenka Razin. But Tchaikovsky uses it for more than its atmospheric qualities.

Having set a mood in the slow Introduction in which the tune is sounded and repeated over the scale passages that were already a fingerprint of his style, he seems to abandon it for a sonata form movement based on the traditional exposition, development and recapitulation of two contrasted themes. However, the first of these themes derives from a figure Tchaikovsky has skilfully built into the Introduction, and the second is hardly more than a token theme whose function is more one of contrast than of matter for symphonic discussion. And indeed, Tchaikovsky reveals his hand when he reintroduces the apparently forgotten folk tune in the development; while the recapitulation moves ingeniously towards the moment when the natural, satisfying outcome is the reintroduction of the folk theme as conclusion. The essence of the movement lies less in the conventional relationship of the two symphonic themes than in the relationship of the first of them to the folk tune.

For his second movement, Tchaikovsky revived the Bridal March of *Undine*, using it as the basis of a simple rondo in the pattern A B A C A B A : A is the march, first played by clarinets over a steady drum beat with somewhat Mahlerian effect; B is a contrasting figure that includes an elegant string melody; and C is a variant of another Russian folksong, 'Spin, O my spinner', which Tchaikovsky had included in his *Fifty Russian Folksongs*. By replacing the normal slow movement with this simple, very attractive march, Tchaikovsky avoids an Adagio or a more lyrical Andante in which he would have found it hard to avoid the use of folk music for its own sake; it is substantial enough to fulfil the role of slow movement, however, and provides sufficient balance and contrast for the succeeding Scherzo. This has a distinct flavour of Mendelssohn, or still more of the *Queen Mab* Scherzo by which Tchaikovsky had no doubt been impressed when he heard *Romeo and Juliet* on Berlioz's visit to Russia; if the Trio is a folksong, as sounds at least possible, it has not been identified as such. But for his Finale, notoriously the most difficult movement for post-classical symphonists, he turns again to folksong, a version of the popular song 'The Crane' (which he heard from the Davidovs' butler). It is a clever device, for not only does the scheme of variations by instrumental colour alone suit his genius for orchestration, but the whole structure and handling of themes and the emotional lightness of the symphony have a natural outcome in a movement so simple, so bright and tuneful. After the mock-grandiose introduction, the only contrast to the 'Crane' theme is a charming little melody of Tchaikovsky's own, dancing across the bar-lines in what is actually rumba rhythm although the effect is of one of his waltzes with a beat missing. The two tunes draw increasingly close together, but the only development to which they are submitted is that of variation by key and by colour, before a Presto whisks the work home. It is a symphony that avoids large-scale engagement with the problems of the form, and for that reason among others has certain weaknesses of construction; sharply aware of these, as ever, Tchaikovsky revised the symphony in 1879, completely rewriting the first movement (for the worse, Taneyev felt). But it remains a delightful work, and it represents a stage in the development of the mature mastery Tchaikovsky was to find in turning symphonic processes to his own particular expressive needs.

The enthusiasm for the Second Symphony was led by Stasov, who found the Finale 'in terms of colour, *facture* and humour . . . one of the most important creations of the entire Russian school.' The public was behind him, and official recognition came with the repeat of the Symphony in the same season, the encouragement to enter for a competition for an opera to a libretto, *Vakula the Smith*, based on Gogol's *Christmas Eve*, and the commission, in March, to write incidental music for Ostrovsky's drama in blank verse, *Snegurochka* (The Snow Maiden). Needing a spectacle combining opera, drama and ballet as riposte to the abortive opera-ballet *Mlada* commissioned from Cui, Rimsky-Korsakov, Mussorgsky and Borodin by the Maryinsky Theatre the previous year, the Bolshoy Theatre pressed Tchaikovsky to supply music for Ostrovsky's 'spring tale'; and despite the need for revision when the playwright made changes, a score consisting of nineteen numbers was completed in three weeks. These, moreover, are substantial pieces of music, so complete and so thoroughly engaged with their subject that it would have been possible for Tchaikovsky to extend the work into an opera; according to his brother, he was annoyed at being subsequently forestalled by Rimsky-Korsakov. Once again Tchaikovsky had for his subject the love of a supernatural being for a mortal and her final return to her native element; and he responded with some delightful music in his fairy-tale vein that deserves to be better known.

For his holiday Tchaikovsky decided this year to travel abroad; and it is in this summer that he revived his habit of keeping a diary. He had done so as a child, but subsequently he came to find the tone of the entries embarrassing. His resolve now was to be more factual, though the purpose of the entries was still to enable him, with his lifelong sense of a lost, happy past and a future threatened by a hostile fate, to recapture in later times the feeling of events through which he had lived. 'Every day had its great value for him', writes Modest, 'and the thought that he must bid eternal farewell to it, and lose all trace of its experiences, depressed him exceedingly. It was a consolation to save something from the limbo of forgetfulness . . .' A later diary was entrusted to Modest for burning after his death; and in his concern to avoid any breath of scandal tainting his brother's reputation, Modest not only did this but suppressed passages in the other diaries, and in his biography went to some lengths to omit and distort facts. The diaries nevertheless remain a vivid and informative account of his life, of his emotional attitudes and his inner thoughts and feelings about his friends, his failings and his hopes; they include scraps of musical ideas that came to him, as in the first entry of all:

> Yesterday, on the road from Vorozhba to Kiev, music came singing and echoing through my head after a long interval of silence. A theme in embryo, in B flat major, took possession of my mind and almost led me on to attempt a symphony. Suddenly

the thought came over me to cast aside Stasov's not too successful *Tempest* and devote the summer to composing a symphony which should throw all my previous works into the shade.

He goes on to quote a striding theme over two alternating chords, and later scribbles in a waltz tune which is not in his best vein. But the entry confirms that composition was for him in the first place the *donnée* of the lyrical idea, more or less complete, and that with it, here, came the ambition to make of it a magnificent symphony. He was not taking as his starting-point the actual symphonic process and the consideration of themes effective and constructive to that purpose, the more natural approach for a composer with whom symphony was the instinctive method of musical thinking. His diary also records the petty irritations of travel and travelling companions, fussy details of hotels and their service, and his own reactions and his longing for solitude. This he was not to find on his journey through Germany and Switzerland, across the Alps to Lake Como and then by way of Milan and Turin to France. At Vevey he notes his homesickness for Russian scenery, and not until he was back at Usovo, alone, did he achieve what he described many years later to Nadezhda von Meck as the greatest happiness he knew, the chance to spend a few days quite alone in the heart of the Russian countryside:

> I was in a spirit of serene exaltation: by day I wandered in the woods, in the evenings I walked in the deep steppes, and at night, sitting at the open window, I listened to the solemn silence, broken now and again by some vague sound. During these two weeks, without the slightest effort, as if I'd been guided by some supernatural power, I sketched out a draft of my *Tempest*.

After the bliss of solitude in the country, even Shilovsky's return from a visit to Moscow was an intrusion; while Moscow itself and the autumn round of teaching and journalism, once he had settled into another flat, seemed more burdensome than ever. With the added struggle to get *The Oprichnik* past the censors and onto the stage, despite the help of his St Petersburg publisher Bessel, he had little time for composition, though he did bring out in November the *Six Piano Pieces* (Op. 19) and another set of *Six Pieces* (Op. 21) dedicated to Anton Rubinstein and based on a single theme: they include a highly respectable Fugue as well as a Funeral March, a lively Mazurka and finally a Scherzo in nimbly shifting rhythms. His letters are filled with anxieties and with frets about the difficulties over *The Oprichnik*; he moved his flat again; yet he was able to finish scoring the *Tempest* fantasia he had sketched so fluently in the summer, and at its first performance under Nikolay Rubinstein in Moscow on 19 December he was delighted to find it received with the same kind of enthusiasm that had greeted the Second Symphony. Nevertheless it has not won the same lasting popularity as either the symphony or the first of Tchaikovsky's Shakespeare fantasias, *Romeo and Juliet*. Stasov's programme is contracted in the score into a summary:

*A Moscow street tea-seller*

The sea. The magician Prospero sends his obedient spirit Ariel to raise a tempest. Wreck of the ship bearing Ferdinand. The magic island. First timid feelings of love between Miranda and Ferdinand. Ariel. Caliban. The lovers give themselves to the enchantments of passion. Prospero renounces his magic powers and leaves the island. The sea.

For all the graphic picture of the sea and of Ariel, there is not the same involvement with the events that had marked *Romeo and Juliet*, or the same capacity to make of them an abstract musical drama; while the comparative poverty of the love theme (let alone the crudity of the tempest itself) suggests that the touchingly innocent nature of Miranda's love for Ferdinand and its happy outcome did not find the emotional response Tchaikovsky gave to the star-crossed love of Romeo and Juliet. Where the new work is that of a highly talented composer applying himself to a set task, the earlier one has the stamp of genius. The other substantial work of the winter was his Second String Quartet, finished early in 1874 and after revisions following criticisms at a private performance by Anton Rubinstein, first performed on 22 March. Much of it is straightforward to the point of routine; but there is a characteristically lively Scherzo in flexible rhythm, and a melodious Andante that has genuine charm, even if it somewhat overplays its emotional hand by forcing the tension to the point at which orchestral rather than quartet textures have to be invoked in support of the general fervour.

In March, Hans von Bülow gave a piano recital at the Bolshoy Theatre in the course of his Russian tour. Tchaikovsky was deeply impressed: after the flamboyance of Rubinstein's school of piano-playing, what was time and again described as the 'passionate intellectuality' of Bülow's, with its powerful concentration on musical worth rather than on virtuosity, stirred him to some of his highest praise. Bülow in turn was much taken with Tchaikovsky's music, and was soon writing to a friend that he intended to play the Op. 19 pieces in one of his concerts. He was to follow this up on his return to Germany with articles drawing attention to this new talent, and the weight of his influence as well as the performances he himself gave did much to lay the foundation of Tchaikovsky's European reputation.

Meanwhile rehearsals of *The Oprichnik* had begun in St Petersburg. Having survived the censor, the opera was now subjected to further cuts from the conductor, Eduard Nápravník. Tchaikovsky was summoned to St Petersburg, and endured the altering and cutting of his score with increasing impatience and depression. Although he arranged tickets for his Moscow friends, he warned them all not to come to see a work in which he declared he had lost faith. He seems, in fact, to have been torn between the wish for them to share in his success and the fear that the opera would prove disappointing, and to have grown unnerved about the chances of his work when the performers seemed to lack the faith to accept it in its entirety. When Modest unwisely took him at his word in deploring *The Oprichnik* and made some teasing remarks about one of the scenes, Tchaikovsky flew into a rage with him. However, the première, on 24 April, was an undoubted success. Although the scenery was second-hand and the singers undistinguished, the performance seems to have been polished and enthusiastic. Tchaikovsky was called out after the second act; and Modest, sitting in a second-tier box with his father, saw the old man beaming with pride and ventured to suggest that such a triumph was worth more than the Order of St Anne which Tchaikovsky could have expected as the crown of his career as a government official. But Ilya Petrovich was not to be drawn. 'The order

*Hans von Bülow*

would certainly have been better,' he retorted. From a celebratory supper given him by the Russian Musical Society, at which it was announced in a speech filled with eulogy that he had been awarded the Kondratyev Prize of 300 rubles, the exhausted Tchaikovsky returned to his father's house for the night. Two days later he left for Italy, ostensibly to review the Milan première of *A Life for the Tsar* but really to avoid the public and private discussions of a work that had caused him so much nervous tension. In fact the reviews were mostly enthusiastic, and indeed the opera was fastened upon as a handy stick with which to belabour the *Kuchka* and their theories of dramatic realism. Cui, of course, attacked the work ferociously; and Tchaikovsky himself, on seeing this review, was honest enough to admit that in spite of its obvious partiality and the bitterness of its expression, this was the just evaluation of his work.

# The Growth of Talent
## 1874–7

Already depressed over *The Oprichnik*, Tchaikovsky was in no state to enjoy Italy, and he easily fell prey to the melancholy of Venice. With the Milan première of *A Life for the Tsar* postponed, he travelled on south to Rome and Naples, enjoying neither. Homesickness and loneliness pursued him, and when news came from Milan of a second postponement, he immediately packed his bags for home; for as he admitted, 'the chief source of my misery remains in Petersburg. *The Oprichnik* torments me.' Back at home he impatiently finished his term's teaching and by the middle of June was at Nizy, deep in work on a new opera that would expunge the memory of the old.

Some years previously the Grand Duchess Elena had commissioned the poet Yakov Polonsky to prepare for Serov a libretto based on Gogol's story *Christmas Eve*. When Serov died in 1871 with the work not begun, the Grand Duchess decided to offer in his memory two prizes for settings of the libretto. On her own death in 1873 the handling of the competition passed to the Russian Musical Society: the closing date was now 13 August 1875, and the prize-winning work would be produced at the Maryinsky. It was the latter consideration that weighed with Tchaikovsky; but at this stage of his career he was no longer interested in composing a long work unless he were virtually assured of winning. His first move was to ascertain that Balakirev, Anton Rubinstein and Rimsky-Korsakov were not competing. This may be accepted as a reasonable precaution; but unfortunately his anxiety over his operatic career led him into other machinations. Having finished his opera, now entitled *Vakula the Smith*, within a month under the impression that the closing date for entry was 13 August 1874, he now discovered that he must wait a year for a decision; he had already arranged for it to be publicly known that though neither Balakirev, Rubinstein nor Rimsky were competing, he himself was, and he now set about trying to persuade Nápravník and the Grand Duke Constantine to have his opera performed regardless of the other competitors. For this he was duly rebuked, and his letter of apology admits his foolishness and pleads over-eagerness to see his opera on the stage. But he was to have the Overture publicly performed under Nikolay Rubinstein, who was one of the judges. The score, submitted according to the rules in a copyist's hand, bore in several places Tchaikovsky's motto, *Ars longa, vita brevis*, in his own writing, which was known to most of the

*The Grand Duke Constantine*
(1827–92)

panel; and shortly before the contest he wrote Rimsky-Korsakov, another of the judges, a sycophantic letter in which he stressed his anxiety to win. Rimsky was later to console himself that no great damage was done since Tchaikovsky's opera was by some way the best of those submitted, and duly it won the prize; but the affair was not one upon which Tchaikovsky could congratulate himself.

So obsessed does Tchaikovsky seem to have been with opera that he refused even to acknowledge the success of other works during the winter season. The First String Quartet was well received in Moscow; and after performances of both his quartets in St Petersburg, even Cui was moved to praise the Second. Criticism was more divided over *The Tempest*, though again it was Cui who was enthusiastic. Tchaikovsky had little to say about the first performance of the *Vakula* Overture; only the triumphant first performance of *The Oprichnik* in Kiev moved him. To Modest and his friends he continued to lament his failure as a composer, the mis-understanding of the public, the disloyalty of those who should count themselves as his friends. Touchy, and by his own admission timid in his dealings with others, he found himself growing more and more misanthropic, while the growth of his reputation as a composer, both at home and – thanks largely to the continued championship of Bülow – abroad, did nothing to strengthen his precarious self-esteem.

This was to receive a new and serious jolt. Part of Tchaikovsky's abstractedness during the winter months had been caused by his absorption in the composition of a piano concerto. Not being a virtuoso, he felt in need of advice about the solo part; the obvious man to turn to was Nikolay Rubinstein, who would moreover have been offended, Tchaikovsky feared, if the opinion of anyone else had been sought. Accordingly arrangements were made for a private playthrough at the Conservatory to Rubinstein and Nikolay Hubert. Three years later Tchaikovsky was to write his account of the event to Nadezhda von Meck.

I played the first movement. Not a single word, not a single remark! If you knew how stupid and intolerable is the situation of a man who cooks and sets before a friend a meal, which he proceeds to eat in silence! Oh for one word, for friendly attack, but for God's sake one word of sympathy, even if not of praise. Rubinstein was amassing his storm, and Hubert was waiting to see what would happen, and that there should be a reason for joining one side or the other. Above all I did not want sentence on the artistic aspect. My need was for remarks about the virtuoso piano technique. R's eloquent silence was of the greatest significance. He seemed to be saying: 'My friend, how can I speak of detail when the whole thing is antipathetic?' I fortified myself with patience and played through to the end. Still silence. I stood up and asked, 'Well?' Then a torrent poured from Nikolay Grigoryevich's mouth, gentle at first, then more and more growing into the sound of a Jupiter Tonans. It turned out that my concerto was worthless and unplayable; passages were so fragmented, so clumsy, so badly written that they were beyond rescue; the work itself was bad, vulgar; in places I had stolen from other composers; only two or three pages were worth preserving; the rest must be thrown away or completely rewritten. 'Here, for instance, this – now what's all that?' (he caricatured my music on the piano) 'And this? How could anyone . . .' etc., etc. The chief thing I can't reproduce is the *tone* in which all this was uttered. In a word, a disinterested person in the room might have thought I was a maniac, a talentless, senseless hack who had come to submit his rubbish to an eminent musician. Having noted my obstinate silence, Hubert was astonished and shocked that such a ticking off was being given to a man who had already written a great deal and given a course in free composition at the Conservatory, that such a contemptuous judgment without appeal was pronounced over him, such a judgment as you would not pronounce over a pupil with the slightest talent who had neglected some of his tasks – then he began to explain N.G.'s judgment, not disputing it in the least but just softening that which His Excellency had expressed with too little ceremony.

I was not only astounded but outraged by the whole scene. I am no longer a boy trying his hand at composition, and I no longer need lessons from anyone, especially when they are delivered so harshly and unfriendlily. I need and shall always need friendly criticism, but this was nothing resembling friendly criticism. It was indiscriminate, determined censure, delivered in such a way as to wound me to the quick. I left the room without a word and went upstairs. In my agitation and rage I could not say a thing. Presently R.ein joined me, and seeing how upset I was he asked me into one of the distant rooms. There he repeated that my concerto was impossible, pointed out many places

*Tchaikovsky in* 1875

where it would have to be completely revised, and said that if within a limited time I reworked the concerto according to his demands, then he would do me the honour of playing my thing at his concert. *'I shall not alter a single note,'* I answered, *'I shall publish the work exactly as it is!'* This I did.

Even after three years, Tchaikovsky's anger and distress at the memory of this scene are immediately rearoused, as is obvious not only from the whole tone of mounting indignation but from the small but significant fact that he can hardly bring himself to refer to Rubinstein by either his surname or his Christian name and patronymic. Clearly it was, at the very least, tactless of Rubinstein not to see how much he would upset the notoriously touchy Tchaikovsky; but we should remember that we have no 'disinterested person' to give an account of the incident, which Tchaikovsky was no doubt human enough to colour somewhat to his own credit. It has, moreover, been a long-enduring habit for Russians, concerned about the role of their creative work, to introduce the concept of 'correctness' as a major aesthetic consideration, hence to submit to direction and criticism in a way unfamiliar in the West, from Balakirev and Stasov organizing Tchaikovsky's works according to plans of their own, to, in our own day, official intervention and the willingness of even major composers to pay attention to it. Further, Rubinstein was neither hostile to Tchaikovsky nor a fool. His criticisms really fall into three categories. He thought the piano-writing was bad; and certainly there are passages which even the greatest virtuoso is glad to survive unscathed, and others in which elaborate difficulties are almost inaudible beneath the orchestra. He pointed to outside influences and unevenness of invention: it is difficult to see whose influence he had in mind, but it must be conceded that the music is uneven, and that the concerto would, like all works, seem the more uneven on a first hearing before its style had been properly understood. Lastly he was baffled by the work as a whole. To a conservative musician such as Rubinstein it must indeed have seemed awkward. There is, for instance, the opening itself, the brazen tune delivered on violins and cellos over pounding piano chords: this is in a 'wrong' key, but it could still have a role to play either as one of Tchaikovsky's favourite slow introductions (the original marking was, indeed, Andante), to be brought back in the course of the succeeding movement, or as a motto theme such as he was to adopt in the later symphonies. But neither as motto nor in any other way does this music recur, not even as a triumphant finish to the entire concerto. It is simply attached to the front of a work which never returns to this manner, like some grandiose portal which one would hardly wish to see removed but which bears no relation to the structure behind it. Rubinstein is by no means the only musician to have been baffled by its presence, and the fact that for many music-lovers it is the most memorable feature of the concerto does not invalidate his judgment.

He was, however, precipitate in condemning the work on this account or for the formal structure of all that follows. Tchaikovsky is very effective with his foreshadowing of his second subject, one of his most touching melodies, while the toccata-like brilliance of the first, based on a song common among blind beggars, is still predominant; and by making the second subject's continuation a gently rocking string figure, similar in manner to the answer to the love theme in *Romeo and Juliet* but thematically close to the first subject, he can construct a splendid double exposition in which virtuoso and expressive elements are both worked out. It is, for all Rubinstein's reservations, a genuine example of concerto thinking; and the contrast is ingeniously maintained in the Andante Semplice, which combines the functions of slow movement and scherzo. The gentle flute melody of the open-ing has something of the mood of Tchaikovsky's love music: it is, however, calm and free from tension, and possibly refers to his brief engagement to Désirée Artôt since the Scherzo section quotes a fragment of one of her songs, 'Il faut s'amuser, danser et rire'. With the Finale, the contrast of reflective lyrical elements with virtuo-sity is sharper; but this kind of alternation, or confrontation, is dramatically apt to the Finale of a large-scale concerto. Tchaikovsky has, throughout, seen to it that the different elements are both clearly defined and effectively related to one another; and it is a pity that Rubinstein did not consider the work's virtues more steadily before pointing out its defects and distressing the over-sensitive composer. It was four years before the breach between the two men was healed: Tchaikovsky was all too inclined to magnify incidents out of all proportion, and Rubinstein was not forgiven until he had made handsome amends by apologizing, admitting his mistake and taking the work into his own repertory. Tchaikovsky had meanwhile dedicated the work to the highly flattered Bülow, who gave its first performance in Boston in the course of his 1875 American tour.

The episode served further to depress Tchaikovsky's already low spirits. Not even Modest, normally quick to defend his brother, was wholly sympathetic, and with some reason tended to regard the deepening melancholia as a disease. When in Moscow, Tchaikovsky would protest about his friends' behaviour, and when away would write them the most urgently affectionate and touching letters; he would long for the moment of escape into the country or abroad, and then fall prey to miserable homesickness; he craved the stability of a home or of some enduring relationship in his life, even marriage, yet found himself unable to sustain it; a natural solitary, he also desperately needed companionship; and a composer with strong, individual ideas about his art and the course it should take, he also depended upon the reassurance of friendly criticism. Yet when he played *Vakula* to his circle, so badly that their enthusiasm was somewhat cool, he was hurt by their attitude. The music of these months consists chiefly of the *Sérénade Mélancolique* for violin and orchestra (a charming, wistful piece written for Leopold Auer) and some songs; he took little pleasure in his teaching, and though consoled by his concert-going and opera-going he was vivid in his accounts to Anatoly and Modest of his despair and his wish to die. His attention was chiefly centred on *Vakula*, and having submitted the corrected score to the prize committee, he left for his summer holiday. His time was to be divided between Usovo, Nizy and Verbovka (another Davidov estate near Kamenka); he had in mind two projects, for a Third Symphony and, the fruit of a commission from the Imperial Theatres, for a ballet, *Swan Lake*.

The sense of gloom which had haunted Tchaikovsky throughout the winter is exorcized in the Third Symphony. Written very quickly, in less than a month between June and July, and scored by early in August, it opens with a powerful Funeral March and places at the centre of its five movements a beautiful Andante Elegiaco. Tchaikovsky seems alternately concerned with matching his gifts to comparatively orthodox symphonic processes and with writing music as a vehicle for his emotional life: the Funeral March serves as more or less token introduction to a movement (Allegro Brillante) that merely brushes aside the gloom and proceeds in somewhat doggedly regular sonata form; and similarly the Finale, an Allegro con fuoco 'in tempo di polacca' which led Sir August Manns to give the symphony its irrelevant English nickname 'Polish', is rather academic in its handling and even includes one of Tchaikovsky's studious fugues. On either side of the central Andante lie a brisk little Scherzo, Mendelssohnian in manner, and another charming genre movement marked 'alla tedesca', a *Ländler* by intention and, needless to say, a Tchaikovsky waltz in effect. In the Andante, freed from the obligations he seems to have felt in the outside movements for orthodoxy of form, he

*Sergey Taneyev (1856–1915),*
*composer, pianist and the*
*most trusted musician*
*among Tchaikovsky's friends*

turns to a mood picture; and it is here, when he discovers a form that is a product of the music's emotional demands rather than an abstract canon to be satisfied, that he is of course at his most successful. The halting horn and woodwind phrases that open the movement are followed by a consoling string melody; and the two then come together in true emotional contact, so that when the sombre theme of the opening achieves at the very end of the movement a bright major chord, there is a sense of peace truly won out of darkness and distress.

At the same time as he was completing the new symphony, Tchaikovsky was also at work on *Swan Lake*; by the time he was ready to return to Moscow, two acts (in which some of the music written for the Davidov children three years previously was included) had been sketched out. Meanwhile the judges in the opera competition had been conferring, and Rimsky-Korsakov at any rate was in no doubt as to the authorship of the best of the operas in front of him. The others were a sorry reflection on the state of Russian music, he wrote to Tchaikovsky, assuring him that there could be little doubt that a work so filled with originality would win the prize; and he even sent some fugues of his own with the request that Tchaikovsky would look them over and make some criticisms. November saw first the Russian première of the First Piano Concerto in St Petersburg, an occasion which Tchaikovsky assured Bülow was deliberately wrecked by the malevolent conducting of Nápravník, and then a few days later, while the composer was still in St Petersburg, the première of the new symphony in Moscow. Tchaikovsky himself seems to have been fairly cool about the work, though he was delighted to find the Piano Concerto enthusiastically received when Nikolay Rubinstein conducted the Moscow première with Taneyev as soloist. His new compositions of the autumn consist of a

Cantata (in reality, hardly more than an extended chorus with solo and orchestra) contributed to the splendid celebrations in honour of the great bass Osip Petrov's fiftieth year on the stage, and a single piano piece. The latter was part of a commission for an appropriate piece for each month of a year's issues of the magazine *Nuvellist*: June receives a pleasant Barcarolle and November a vigorous Troika, but Tchaikovsky's interest in the task was purely journalistic, and he composed each piece at a sitting just before press day.

Much encouraged by the successes of the closing months of 1875, Tchaikovsky began the new year in unusually high spirits. His music was making its way steadily at home, with *Vakula* having won the competition, performances of his works now regarded as major events, and criticism even from the *Kuchka* now turning in a friendly and constructive direction. Abroad his reputation was spreading through Europe, thanks largely to Bülow, and across the Channel with the English première of the First Piano Concerto in March; while America had already had interest awakened by the Boston performance of the same work and was eager to hear more. His income had increased; and though his private life remained unsatisfactory, his interests, both musical and general, were widening. He was delighted to take the opportunity of joining Modest on a foreign holiday. Having resigned the government service and taken a post as tutor to a deaf and dumb boy, Nikolay (Kolya) Konradi, Modest was planning to spend some months studying at a renowned school for deaf-mutes at Lyon. From Berlin and Geneva, where they spent ten days with the Davidovs, who were also there on a visit, the brothers travelled on to Paris; and here on 15 March Tchaikovsky for the first time saw *Carmen*. It was, as Modest recalled, one of the most powerful musical impressions

*Osip Petrov (1807–78),*
*the greatest Russian bass*
*of his day*

of his entire life. A year previously Shilovsky had been so moved by the work as to buy a vocal score and send it to Tchaikovsky, who was still studying it with excitement when the news reached him of Bizet's death that June. Now at the performance he was completely carried away by the music itself and also by the brilliant performance of Célestine Galli-Marié in the title role and by what Modest described as her 'unbridled passion and an element of mystical fatalism'. It was a combination calculated to appeal to Tchaikovsky, and it duly awoke in him what Modest felt was 'an almost unwholesome passion for this opera'. Possibly *Carmen* appealed to the French blood which he had inherited from his grandmother. Certainly his instinctive love of clarity and elegance, coupled to his belief in a Fate linked to erotic feeling which hung over his own life, drew from him an enthusiastic response. Just as Nietzsche found an antidote to Wagner in Bizet ('the last genius to perceive a new beauty and a new seduction'), so Tchaikovsky now saw *Carmen* as a refreshing contrast to what he felt was a deliberate seeking after novelty in the music of most of his Russian contemporaries:

> Here is a Frenchman with whom these savours and spices seem the result not of *fabrication* but pour out in a stream; they gratify the ear but at the same time they touch and trouble. He seems to say to us, 'You don't want something majestic, forceful and grandiose; you want something *pretty*, so here's a *pretty* opera.' And indeed, I know of no music which has a better title to the quality which I would call *pretty, le joli*. It is charming and delightful from beginning to end. Piquant harmonies, completely new combinations of many sounds, but this isn't their exclusive purpose. Bizet is an artist who pays tribute to modernity, but he is fired with true inspiration. And what a marvellous subject for an opera! I can't play the final scene without tears. On the one hand, the crowd enjoying itself and coarsely making merry as they watch the bullfight, on the other, a terrible tragedy and the death of the two principals who, through fate, *fatum*, ultimately reach the peak of their suffering and their inescapable end.

The chance of attending a far larger musical occasion, though one which was to have a very different effect upon Tchaikovsky, reached him soon after his return to Moscow; for his European reputation was by now sufficient to earn him one of the official invitations to the first Bayreuth Festival. With the greatest interest he accepted, and settled down to his spring work. He had brought back to Moscow with him sketches for a Third String Quartet, written in memory of his friend Ferdinand Laub, the Czech violinist who had led the ensemble at the première of his First String Quartet five years previously in 1871 at the first concert of his music. It is an uneven work, some of it rather mechanical, and despite the circumstances the first violin predominates unduly; but the slow Introduction with which it opens contains a beautiful elegiac melody, 'cantabile e molto espressivo', in the same vein as the Andante Cantabile of the Fifth Symphony, and the slow movement itself, Andante Funebre e Doloroso, is a sombre and eloquent gesture of mourning centred on a magnificent tune built on the falling phrases that Tchaikovsky was

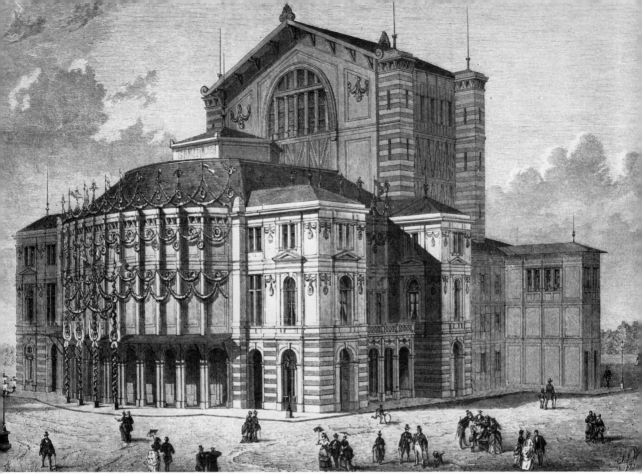

*The Festspielhaus, Bayreuth*

still more memorably to associate with death in his last symphony. After this movement the brisk Finale, even if seen as a summons from grief into action, falls somewhat emptily on the ear. The quartet was a success when first played at Nikolay
Rubinstein's house; but Tchaikovsky was dissatisfied and later revised it before its
first public performance.

Easter was spent with Shilovsky at Glebovo, where *Swan Lake* was finished;
but so far from being refreshed by the holiday and by the completion of a large
work, Tchaikovsky returned to Moscow irritable and unwell. By May his doctor
was suggesting a cure at Vichy. At Kamenka in June, Tchaikovsky complained of
fever and of a lack of any ideas in his head: as ever, mental cause and physical effect
seem to have been very closely linked in him, for on reaching Vienna early in July
the chief complaint he had to report was boredom. Travelling on to Lyon he met
Modest and Kolya Konradi (to whom he soon became greatly attached), and after a
cheerful week with them he moved on to Vichy. Here melancholy descended once
more, and it was with difficulty that the doctor persuaded him to stay for even a
'demi-cure'. New ideas for music were beginning to fill his head: Modest had

*Design for the Rhinemaidens in the first performance of Wagner's* Das Rheingold, 1876

proposed as subjects Hamlet, Othello and Francesca da Rimini, and parting from Modest and Kolya after a trip with them down the Rhône from Lyon to Avignon and Montpellier, he began reading Canto v of *The Inferno* and the story of Francesca as the train bore him towards Bayreuth.

Of all the accounts of that famous opening festival, Tchaikovsky's five reports constitute one of the most vivid.

I reached Bayreuth on 12 August, the day before the first performance of the tetralogy. The town presented an exceptionally animated spectacle. Both local people, and visitors who had thronged hither literally from all ends of the earth, were hurrying to the railway station to see the arrival of the Emperor Wilhelm. I witnessed the scene from the window of a neighbouring house. First to my view there flashed by some glittering uniforms; then a procession of the musicians of the Wagner Theatre with their conductor, Hans Richter, at their head; then came the handsome, tall figure of the Abbé Liszt, with the fine, characteristic grey head which has so often fascinated me in the pictures you can see everywhere; and lastly, sitting in a sumptuous carriage, the tiny, vigorous old man himself, with his aquiline nose and the thin ironic smile which lends such a characteristic expression to the creator of this cosmopolitan artistic festival, Richard Wagner. The orchestra crashed forth, an enthusiastic roar burst from the crowd, and the Imperial special train slowly pulled into the station. The old Emperor stepped into his carriage and quietly it moved off towards the castle, accompanied by shouts of welcome from the people. Almost as loud shouts greeted Wagner, driving off after the Emperor among the thick crowds of people. What an overwhelming pressure of proud feeling the little man must have experienced at finally seeing the festival surmounting all obstacles through his powerful will and through a talent that is the embodiment of his audacious beliefs! . . .

But Bayreuth was filled not only with the powerful and the famous; and Tchaikovsky was soon succumbing to the irritations which have remained a familiar part of Bayreuth festivals – the torrid climate, the crowds, the inadequacy of the hotels, the difficulty of finding a table at a restaurant, the poor service and worse food. 'On the very day of my arrival', he observes sardonically, 'I learned what "the struggle for existence" really means.' Although many prominent musicians had stayed away, those who had made the journey from Russia included Nikolay Rubinstein, Cui, Laroche, Alexander Famitsin and Berta Valzek; another member of the Russian contingent was Karl Klindworth, who had published his piano transcriptions of *The Ring* during his period from 1868 as Professor of Piano at the Moscow Conservatory. Though pleasantly surprised to find how well known he was, Tchaikovsky did not greatly enjoy himself. He was cordially received by Liszt, ever generous to his fellow composers, though Wagner seems to have been

*Richard Wagner*

unable to find time to receive him; and we have it on Laroche's word that the effort of coming to grips with the great cycle, unfamiliar in style and language alike, exhausted him so much that he seemed only to revive when seated before a large glass of beer afterwards. He was himself respectful but fundamentally unsympathetic:

> I carried away confused memories of many striking beauties, especially symphonic, which is very strange as Wagner has no intention at all of writing an opera in a symphonic manner; deeply respectful amazement at the composer's colossal talent and at the unprecedented richness of his technique; doubts about the truth of the Wagnerian view of opera; great fatigue but at the same time the wish to continue the study of this music, the most complex yet composed.
>
> Even if *The Ring of the Nibelung* seems at times boring; if much of it is at first confusing and incomprehensible; if Wagner's harmony occasionally suffers from over-complexity and over-subtlety; if Wagner's theory is false; if a large part of it is pointless quixotry; if the vast work is doomed and the Bayreuth theatre will sink into perpetual sleep, to be abandoned to its own fantastic memories of a gigantic labour, to have to concentrate on the contemporary world – still *The Ring of the Nibelung* constitutes one of the most significant events in the history of art . . . one of the most colossal artistic enterprises ever to be conceived in the mind of man.

Thoroughly exhausted by his travels, with neither the Vichy cure nor the exposure to new music and new ideas at Bayreuth having greatly refreshed him, Tchaikovsky retraced his steps thankfully to Kamenka. Gathering in him had been an increasing dissatisfaction with his way of life, exposing itself sometimes in his sudden nervous illnesses, hardly assuaged by the success as a composer which he had so deeply craved but which, now he was beginning to achieve it, was proving small consolation. His loneliness seemed impenetrable: he was quick to quarrel and slow to forgive, prickly even with his few warm friends and his well-loved brothers and his sister, easily prone to passing homosexual affairs but no less easily prone to self-disgust over them, devoted to a few close friends such as Shilovsky but, even had the climate of opinion made it possible, unable to achieve with one of them a stable, enduring relationship. Domesticity was for him associated not with homosexuality but with a normal household and children, in whom he delighted; and over the years he had become increasingly haunted by the nebulous spectre of a 'beloved' who would somehow embody all his longing to give and receive love, who would provide him with a home and children. What he had not faced up to in his roseate dream was the reality of a relationship with a woman; and so it was with considerable horror that Modest received a letter from his brother at the end of August informing him, 'I am now confronting the most critical period of my life. Presently I shall tell you about it in more detail; meanwhile I must tell you that *I have decided to get married*. This is irrevocable.' Alarmed, Modest and Alexandra (who also knew of his homosexuality) pleaded with him, perceiving as they did that his talk of finding the courage to take

the step or at any rate to discard his habits, of the 'beautiful, still undiscovered being who will make me alter my manner of living', of the delight of returning to a happy home and a book by the fire, even his assurance that he would not rush into anything, were so much wishful thinking. Nikolay Kashkin, in whom he also confided, put his finger on it when he observed that what Tchaikovsky really wanted was not a wife but some elderly spinster or widow who would understand him but not disturb him with feelings of passion.

They all underestimated – despite his assurances that what he frankly regarded as his vice was the greatest obstacle to his happiness and that he found the shame well-nigh unbearable – the determination in his mind to overcome the Fate which he saw as having wished this unhappy sexual disposition upon him. Admitting that he had sunk so deeply into the quagmire of his tastes 'that to discard them at once like an old glove is impossible', he told Modest that even more than the misery which these

*Three old photographs of Kamenka,*
*showing the river and*
*the Davidovs' house*

tastes brought him it was the feeling that his friends were pitying him or were ashamed for him that agonized him. Marriage, he declared, would at least silence the tongues of those for whose contemptible opinions he might not care but which had the effect of causing pain to his friends; and he would only promise that the marriage would at least be delayed until next year.

Meanwhile, catching the general mood of Pan-Slavism which accompanied the outbreak of the Russo-Turkish War in support of the Serbs, he composed for a concert in aid of wounded soldiers the well-known *Slavonic March*. As well as quoting 'God preserve the Tsar', it bases its five sections on Serbian national tunes and performs its rousing task with the greatest exuberance. Rehearsals for *Vakula* were moving slowly; he was tinkering further with the Third String Quartet; but the main preoccupation of the autumn was his new orchestral piece, and by the end of October he was able to write to Modest to say, 'I have only just finished the composition of a new work, the symphonic fantasia *Francesca da Rimini*. I have worked on it *con amore*, and believe my love has been successful.'

Tchaikovsky had originally intended to write an opera on the subject of Paolo and Francesca; and there was even the chance of making use of a libretto by Konstantin Zvantsyev (who had had a hand in Serov's *Judith*). But Zvantsyev was also a critic with an enthusiasm for Wagner, and when he tried to insist that the opera should be constructed on Wagnerian lines, Tchaikovsky promptly abandoned the project. However, the subject had taken hold of his imagination. The tenderness of the episode, the most famous of the entire *Divina Commedia*, and the presentation of love as associated with sin yet infinitely attractive must have awoken a response in him. His lifelong sense of present unhappiness bitterly contrasted with past felicity would have found an echo in Francesca's much-quoted lines:

> Nessun maggior dolore,
> Che ricordarsi del tempo felice
> Nella miseria.

At the head of his score, Tchaikovsky set a brief summary of the lovers' story, of how Francesca, wedded through a deception to a hunchback, fell in love with his handsome younger brother Paolo and how it was their reading of the romance of Lancelot and Guinevere that drew them together; and he quotes twenty-two lines of the poem. He manages to construct quite a successful and personal form out of the events of the canto: we may assume that the opening Andante Lugubre section, with its gloomy harmony and orchestration, stands for the Gate of Hell and the inscription on its lintel, 'Lasciate ogni speranza, voi ch'entrate', and that the ensuing Allegro Vivo represents the ceaseless buffeting of the winds of the Second Circle that torment the souls of the lustful, 'la bufera infernal che mai non resta'. However, it is not until the love music of the Andante Cantabile, a graceful melody tinged with melancholy, that Tchaikovsky strikes his best vein of invention. The whirling away

*The Maryinsky Theatre in St Petersburg, where many of Tchaikovsky's operas and ballets were first given*

of the lovers into their renewed torment with the return of the Allegro is both musically and dramatically apt, if somewhat stiff when the music lacks imaginative impetus. Tchaikovsky himself felt that it had not turned out quite as he had wanted. Yet for all its weaknesses, *Francesca da Rimini* has distinct power of its own, absorbing both ideas and atmosphere from Dante but also proving its composer's capacity to construct musically satisfactory forms on the basis of a poetic idea.

Despite Tchaikovsky's request to Nápravník to include *Francesca* in a forthcoming concert, the dances from *Vakula the Smith* were substituted; and it was not until 1877 that *Francesca* received its first performance. But with its appetite thus whetted, the public that gathered in the Maryinsky Theatre for the première of *Vakula* was full of expectation: Tchaikovsky's name was by now well enough known to cause a stir of interest, and even Cui had encouraged the composer to hope for a great success. Nápravník conducted, and the cast included Petrov, now nearly seventy, and Fyodor Stravinsky, the father of the composer. All seemed set fair; yet after the enthusiastic reception of the Overture, interest declined, and by the final curtain Tchaikovsky knew that he had once again failed in his efforts to conquer the public with an opera. His letter to Taneyev praises the care and thought that had gone into the preparation of the work, and lays the blame entirely at his own door: only a few days after his hopes were at their highest, he is declaring that the work is crowded with unnecessary detail, over-scored and badly written for voices, wholly unoperatic in every way. Cui's review supported some of this in the light of experience of the work in the theatre, but held to a high opinion of the actual music.

ACT I, *Scene* 1: On a moonlit night in the village of Dikanka, the witch Solokha (mezzo) is approached by the amorous Devil (bar.). As he flies off, he raises a snowstorm and steals the moon so as to revenge himself upon Solokha's son Vakula (ten.) for making an ugly painting of him in the church; this storm, he hopes, will wreck Vakula's courtship of Oxana (sop.), daughter of the Cossack Chub (bass) who is now seen stumbling drunkenly through the murk with his friend Panas (ten.). *Scene* 2: In Chub's hut, Oxana is admiring herself in her mirror and has little time for Vakula's wooing when he arrives. When Chub lurches in covered with snow, Vakula fails to recognize him and throws him out; Oxana in turn drives Vakula away, pretending that she loves someone else. But alone, while the village girls sing Christmas carols, she admits her love for him.

ACT 2, *Scene* 1: In Solokha's hut, her flirtations with the Devil are interrupted by knocking. He hides in a sack while she admits the mayor (bass), the schoolmaster (ten.) and Chub, each of whom in turn hides in a sack as the next one appears. The final knock announces Vakula; unhappy love must have made him weak, he feels, as he staggers out carrying the mysteriously heavy sacks to make room for the Christmas festivities. *Scene* 2: Among the crowd of carollers is Oxana, who admires a pair of *cherevichki* (slippers) a friend is wearing. When Vakula, who arrives with the sacks, offers to get her a better pair, she demands the Tsaritsa's own and promises in return to marry him. Mocked by them all, Vakula leaves, still carrying the sack containing the Devil and miserably resolved to kill himself. Out of the remaining sacks crawl the others, with Chub trying to pass it off as a seasonal joke.

ACT 3, *Scene* 1: By the icy river, Vakula is tempted by the *rusalki* (water-sprites) to throw himself in. But when the Devil creeps out of the sack and tries to bargain for his soul, Vakula seizes him by the tail and makes the sign of the Cross; with the Devil in his power, he leaps on his back and flies off to St Petersburg to find the Tsaritsa. *Scene* 2: They arrive at the Royal Palace of Catherine the Great at the same time as a band of Cossacks. *Scene* 3: A ball is in progress: Vakula and the Cossacks are received in the throne-room by His Royal Highness (bass) (an alteration from Catherine herself, demanded by the censor). His request for the slippers is granted, and amid the festivities he slips away again on the Devil's back.

ACT 4: On a clear winter morning in front of the church in Dikanka, only Solokha and Oxana of all the rejoicing villagers are silent, anxious at Vakula's disappearance. When he appears with the slippers Oxana admits that it has always really been him that she wanted; and all ends in jubilation.

Cui was right to hold to his praise of the music while reserving doubts about the total effect of the opera. *Vakula*, or *Cherevichki*, shows Tchaikovsky moving into a much stronger operatic position than he had hitherto occupied, not yet in full mastery of the stage and making some miscalculations (even in the revised version), but developing a vein that is both personal and effective. It is the characterization that is, fatally, the weakest part of the work. The three figures of the mayor, the schoolmaster and Chub arrive in Solokha's hut to music that is agreeable and certainly different in manner for each of them, but that offers neither succinct comment with

a dash of caricature nor a real piece of character study. For all that this opera reflects his love of Glinka and even comes at times quite close to the ideals of the *Kuchka*, Tchaikovsky lacks the earthy comic realism to bring rustic and fantastic elements successfully together; and when a sharp, witty or even coarse point is demanded, he tends to take refuge in a kind of generalized, bland lyricism. The quintet begins promisingly, but cannot be effectively sustained without the feeling for characterization to give its separate lines meaning and life. Oxana herself emerges as pretty but cold, a fair account of her nature though one seen with insufficient depth by a composer whose emotions could hardly have been aroused by her; craving warmth in human relationships and a remote ideal of love as he did, it is not surprising that we find the best and most characteristic music given to Vakula, the rejected, lovelorn, suffering suitor whose two ariosos achieve a heartfelt lyricism worthy of Lensky in Tchaikovsky's next opera. There are further anticipations in the surging, exuberant Polonaise in the palace, in the delicate Minuet with which he evokes the manners of another and more graceful age, in the *couplets* sung to announce a victory, in the contrast of the aristocratic dances with the vehement Cossack stamping: these, more than the rather conventional village scenes or the somewhat meagrely illustrated snowstorm and riverside scenes, are the passages which strike from him his most memorable music, and in which he is already feeling his way into an operatic style that was to assume genius when engaged with the ideal subject in *Eugene Onegin*.

One of the most effective lessons Tchaikovsky learned from *Vakula* was almost incidental. The rococo minuet is scarcely more than a passing idea, a touch of period colour in the ball scene; but it has a particular vividness, representing as it does for Tchaikovsky a world of order and balance that seemed hopelessly lost. He is by no means the only Romantic composer to feel an ache for the rejected classicism – it is, indeed, one of the typically contradictory ingredients of Romanticism. But in him the reaction was as usual acutely personal, a dramatization of his sense of being cut off from a once-familiar security and delight. Thereafter he was often in his music to find occasion for what he frankly regarded as escape. Yet the recognition that it was indeed escape involved acceptance of his real situation as one of unhappiness to which the world had no answer; and at this stage he was only at the beginning of his cultivation of escape as capable of producing substantial artistic rewards. In the aftermath of *Vakula*, with depressing news coming from Germany and France of the reception given even to *Romeo and Juliet* and the collapse through insufficient funds of a plan to mount a concert at his own expense in Paris, he turned again to the rococo for consolation. Written for his friend the cellist Wilhelm Fitzenhagen, the Variations on a Rococo Theme are his most concentrated and effective homage to the spirit of Mozart. His sympathy with the rococo is shown in his ability to construct for his theme a melody that is impeccably classical yet unmistakably marked with his own personality; and the artistic device releases some of his most charming, fresh and relaxed music. It is not parody, any more than Prokofiev's Classical Symphony of forty years later was to be parody: each is in its way a suggestion that this is how the composer would have written a symphony or a set of variations were he able to enter the classical world with his own sensibilities, and with Tchaikovsky it is a demonstration of the truth that the conscious assumption of a mask may often serve to release a genuine part of the creative personality.

In the middle of December 1876 Tolstoy paid a visit to Moscow, and in the course of it was taken by Nikolay Rubinstein to a concert of Tchaikovsky's music. The First String Quartet was on the programme, and many years later Tchaikovsky was to describe his feelings in his diary: 'Probably never in my life have I been so moved by the pride of authorship as when Lev Tolstoy, sitting by me and listening to the Andante of my quartet, burst into tears.' Tolstoy followed this up with a letter of profuse gratitude: 'Never have I received such acute pleasure in the rewards of my literary works as on that wonderful evening', and went on to offer a copy of one of his books to each of the players and of course to Tchaikovsky himself. The composer's choice was *The Cossacks*. As a profound admirer of *War and Peace* he was greatly flattered by this attention, though at their actual meeting he had feared that 'this great searcher of hearts' would immediately see far more of his true nature and all its defects than he cared to have revealed. When he found that Tolstoy merely wanted to chat about music, he was relieved. However, he was depressed to find Tolstoy attacking Beethoven, an attitude which he felt was better left to smaller spirits. Further disillusionment followed when Tolstoy sent him some folksongs to arrange, and it became clear that the great prophet of folk life and of the residual wisdom of peasant simplicity had been taken in by someone who had completely falsified them, altering their individual modal flavour and trimming their rhythmic asymmetries into regular bar-lengths. Any question of finding a subject for music in Tolstoy was ruled out since he 'often advised me to give up the search for theatrical success; in

*A contemporary drawing of the first performance of* Swan Lake

*War and Peace* he made his heroine baffled and dismayed by false conventions of operatic effect' – the scene when Natasha attends an opera which Tolstoy ridicules as unworthily as he was to ridicule the Orthodox Liturgy in *Resurrection*. Yet Tchaikovsky's respect for Tolstoy's genius never left him; though shocked at first by *Anna Karenina* (then appearing in instalments) he subsequently came to recognize it as a masterpiece, and he several times read through the collected works which (in French as well as Russian) form part·of his surviving library. If latterly he shared the distress of Turgenev and many others at the apparent abandoning of Tolstoy's genius in favour of polemics, he retained all his admiration for the work up to and including *A Confession*, which deeply moved him; and there is a strong likelihood that Tolstoy's personal gift of *The Cossacks* exercised an immediate influence on the symphony, his Fourth, which he was to begin in May.

The early months of 1877 were also occupied with rehearsals for *Swan Lake*. The completed score consisted of an introduction and twenty-nine numbers divided into four acts, based on a scenario drawn up by the director of the Bolshoy who had commissioned the work, Vladimir Begichev, the stepfather of Konstantin and Vladimir Shilovsky; it was in their salon that more than one successful Romantic ballet had been born. From the notes in the score and for the first production, this can be seen to fall into a very effective four-act pattern.

*A photograph of a group from an early performance of* Swan Lake

ACT I: 1 *Scène* – On a summer evening in the park before his castle, Prince Siegfried, son of the Princess of the District, is celebrating the eve of his coming-of-age. At the ball tomorrow he must choose one of six Princesses coming to seek his hand in marriage. Wolfgang, his aged tutor, introduces a group of peasants come to join the merry-making. 2 *Valse*. 3 *Scène* – The Princess, Siegfried's mother, reproaches her son for frivolity; but encouraged by his friend Benno he resumes the revelry when she has gone. 4 *Pas de trois* – Dances for the peasants. 5 *Pas de deux* – Dances for the merry-makers. 6 *Pas d'action* – Wolfgang attempts to show his skill, but collapses drunk. 7 *Sujet* – With the sun setting, Siegfried suggests a final ensemble. 8 *Danses des coupes* – A polonaise for the entire gathering. 9 *Finale* – A flock of swans is seen flying across the sky, home to their lake in the forest. The Prince agrees to Benno's suggestion of a hunt for them, and they leave Wolfgang in a state of total stupor.

ACT 2: 10 *Scène* – A vast lake is shimmering in the moonlight; across its surface pass the swans before the wondering gaze first of Siegfried alone and then of his friends.

11 *Scène* – As the hunting party takes aim, the swans are transformed into beautiful maidens. Their leader asks Siegfried, 'Why do you persecute me?', and tells him that she is the Princess Odette and that all of them are bewitched by her wicked stepmother and watched over by her companion Rotbart. Only a marriage vow can break the spell which holds them bound as swans by day and humans by night. Rotbart appears in the guise of an owl and threatens Siegfried. 12 *Scène* – Siegfried confesses the love he has begun to feel for Odette, and she promises him she will attend the ball tomorrow though she warns him of the danger from her stepmother. 13 *Danses des cygnes.* 14 *Scène* – To the same music as that of No. 10, Odette and her companions return to swan form as dawn breaks.

ACT 3: 15 – In the castle, Wolfgang orders the valets to admit the guests to the ceremonial ball. 16 *Danse du corps de ballet et des nains* – The Master of Ceremonies signals the revels to commence; among the dancers is a group of dwarfs. 17 *Scène* – La sortie des invités et la Valse. The six Princesses enter. 18 *Scène* – Siegfried refuses to name his bride to his mother. Rotbart appears with his daughter Odile disguised as Odette; Siegfried delightedly welcomes her. 19 *Pas de six* – Dances for the Princesses. (*Pas de deux*: Tchaikovsky later supplied an extra number here for Siegfried and Odile.) 20 *Danse hongroise.* 21 *Danse espagnole.* 22 *Danse napolitaine.* (At the request of the choreographer, Julius Reisinger, Tchaikovsky satisfied the wish of the prima ballerina Karpakova and of the management to have an additional *Danse russe* here.) 23 *Mazurka.* 24 *Scène* – Siegfried announces Odile as his bride; Rotbart and his mother join the couple's hands, at which Rotbart turns into an owl and flies screeching from the hall

*Anna Sobeshchanskaya
as Odette in* Swan Lake, *1877*

while the Prince rushes into the night in pursuit of a vision he has glimpsed of the true Odette.

ACT 4: 25 *Entr'acte.* 26 *Scène* – Odette's friends await her return by the lake. 27 *Danse des petits cygnes.* 28 *Scène* – Odette rushes into her companions' arms and tells them of what has happened. A storm breaks out, and through it Siegfried manages to reach her. 29 *Scène finale* – He begs her forgiveness, but she dies of grief in his arms. He casts her coronet upon the waters, whose waves rise to engulf the lovers; when they subside, the swans are seen gliding silently away across the lake.

Nothing is known, and no sketches remain, of Tchaikovsky's first attempt at ballet, a projected four-act work based on *Cinderella* which he began in 1870 but which seems to have been abandoned at an early stage. But with *Swan Lake* he conquered the genre of Russian ballet with a masterpiece, raising it to new heights and setting standards that influenced composers of succeeding generations and were to colour the work of even Prokofiev and Britten. Before *Swan Lake* ballet in Russia stood at a high pitch of interpretative artistry, but was largely confined to trifling scenarios and to music that aimed at little more than the craftsmanlike and the pretty, in support of what were often hardly more than extended *divertissements*; though traditionally it was in Moscow that more was demanded in the way of plot and action than in St Petersburg. As Tolstoy pointed out, it was substance that prevailed in Moscow life, form in Petersburg life. Tchaikovsky's inspiration was Delibes, whom regrettably he preferred to Wagner as a composer. In later years he was to tell Nadezhda von Meck that *Swan Lake* was 'poor stuff compared to *Sylvia*'; and it was from Delibes, particularly from the brilliant example of *Coppélia*, that he took his model for a full-length ballet that could make the art of the decorative organic to a plot of some substance. *Swan Lake* is, of course, based entirely on the sophistication of a child's fairy-tale to meet the demands of an elaborate artistic technique. But Tchaikovsky has seen how a virtue can be made of the necessity for the regular introduction of dances and *divertissements*, and the score as he constructed it, before it was subjected to its various mutilations, was well and strongly designed.

He has, for instance, based the work on an effectively expounded key-structure. This is more than a matter of private technique appreciable only by musicians; for it is on the expressive force of the relationship of keys, expected or startling, brightening or darkening the harmonic colour, that a skilled composer depends for some of his effect, and it is unnecessary to be aware of the technical process at work for it to have expressive meaning. Thus Tchaikovsky sets his third act in the key of C. From this bright opening, he darkens his effect by moving down through progressively flatter keys as Siegfried is lured into accepting the false Odette; and each of these new keys is approached in exactly the same way. The Variations of No. 19 for the Princesses are within this flat key-structure, because the presentation of their charms is part of the plot and part of the attempt to draw Siegfried away from his true love. But when the guests from distant lands, from Hungary, Spain and Naples, go through their paces, as pure *divertissement* that has no connection to the main plot, they do so in sharp keys that have the effect of sounding outside the main musical progression (by an ingenious stroke Tchaikovsky makes the Russian dance he was forced to add later in the minor of one of these sharp keys, A, which is related technically to his main key, C: Russia is thus made to seem less distant than the other lands without confusing the key 'plot'). The return is through the Mazurka (No. 23) in the key with only one degree of sharpness, G, which is the natural way back to the central key, neither sharp nor flat, of C, as Siegfried rushes out after the vision of the true Odette.

Tchaikovsky is, moreover, careful to differentiate between the emotional weight of the numbers which are incidental to the plot, and of those which are organic. The Finale itself is quite a substantial piece of symphonic music, developing the wistful, graceful little oboe theme that has been associated with Odette and her swan manifestation (part of the original children's diversion) into an impassioned number that, as the lovers find their union in the waters of the lake, turns from B minor to a triumphant B major (though the last bars are on an enigmatic open B, neither major nor minor). Throughout, Tchaikovsky reserves for the *scènes* the numbers in which action and character are developed, music of some complexity and subtlety. In so doing he was taking ballet forward to the point at which a new expressive gesture was demanded: not until Stravinsky was the art of movement wholly absorbed with music of unprecedented power into a new expressive entity, and Stravinsky himself never forgot his Russian origins or his allegiance to Tchaikovsky. But this was not Tchaikovsky's intention. Ballet was for him associated with the decorative, and therefore with a grace added to life that could delight and afford relief from life rather than, as with opera and symphony, be an expression of life. The rococo had provided one piece of emotional décor; the dance was to release his most delightful, relaxed and charming flow of melody, the 'lyrical idea' which he always claimed as the first inspiration of his music and which is here found at its freshest. Turning away from a life that had grown increasingly tense and miserable, he was able to compose, for his ballet, music that was involved with nothing more disturbing than a pretty story totally divorced from the pain of reality.

It was this detachment that enabled him to view the vicissitudes of *Swan Lake* with composure. No sooner had the work gone into rehearsal than the orchestra were complaining about the difficulty and complexity of ballet music that was certainly more elaborate than anything they could previously have encountered. Confronted with a score that demanded more of them than the usual series of numbers designed to flatter their technique and their appearance, the dancers also rebelled. The décor, parcelled out act by act between three designers, Shangin, Waltz and Gropius, was lamentable; the choreography of Julius Reisinger (whom a contemporary magazine asserted was completely unable to produce ballets) failed to respond to the demands of the subject; the conductor, Stepan Ryabov, was described by

Modest as a 'semi-amateur who had never before been faced with so complicated a score'; Pelageia Karpakova, the Odette, was a poor mime; and to cap it all, Tchaikovsky was required to abbreviate and alter his music and to supply new numbers. Small wonder that at the first performance on 4 March 1877 *Swan Lake* was only moderately well received: Laroche was alone among the critics when he found Tchaikovsky's score, 'the best ballet ever heard by this author'. As time went by, more of Tchaikovsky's music was quietly replaced by inferior pieces of French ballet music, so that three years later Nadezhda von Meck was able to write to the composer that the performance she saw represented a complete muddle of the original intentions. After his death the mutilations increased, and for many years there was no opportunity of seeing one of the masterpieces in the history of the dance in its true form.

What Tchaikovsky superstitiously continued to regard as his personal *Fatum* seemed to be little concerned in the composition of *Swan Lake* until the Finale, when the passion which overcomes the music reflects his bitter belief that love was to be found only against the direst opposition and might even then be cruelly denied realization. He had meanwhile become involved with the two women who were to prove his tragic inability to achieve the fulfilled love in his own life which he so deeply craved. One was a young Conservatory student whom he had hitherto barely noticed, Antonina Milyukova. The other was the wealthy widow whom he was never to meet but whose influence was to rule the remainder of his life, Nadezhda von Meck.

*Nadezhda von Meck*

Nadezhda Filaretovna Frolovskaya was born in 1831. Her father, Filaret Vasilyevich Frolovsky, was a Smolensk landowner and a capable violinist with a keen interest in music; her mother, Anastasia Dimitryevna Potemkin, was the daughter of a retired lieutenant-colonel, Dmitry Demyanovich Potemkin, who was related to Catherine the Great's most famous lover, Grigory Potemkin. From her father Nadezhda inherited her love of music; but from her mother, evidently a capable, businesslike woman, came her own energy, determination and especially her business acumen. When in 1847, not yet seventeen, she was married to the engineer son of a German Balt family from Riga, Karl von Meck, she wasted little time in setting about reorganizing his life for him. As a government official, his life was uneventful and his work poorly paid; but with several children soon added to his responsibilities, he was reluctant to make a break with a steady post. However, his young wife (as she later told Tchaikovsky) found the demanding life of acting as mother, nurse, governess, dressmaker, housekeeper and valet far easier to bear than the humiliation of seeing her husband as a puppet in the hands of a government organization. When he finally gave in to her and resigned, they had only twenty kopeks a day to live on. But she was right to trust in his talent as an engineer: Russia

*The Von Meck family. Nadezhda is holding Milochka, with Alexander Yolshin seated on the left; Karl von Meck is seated at the back, behind the teapot.*

was desperately short of railways in an age in which communications were expanding rapidly, and Nadezhda was far-sighted enough to see that a future for her husband lay here. In her childhood, railways had hardly existed in Russia; by 1860 there were still only 1000 miles of track; but by the early 1880s there were over 15,000 miles. The rapid development of the railways was an excitement in Russia which can be sensed in the novels of the period. It was in part the work of Karl von Meck, and it made his fortune. Lines for which he and his partners were responsible included Kursk to Kiev and the highly profitable Moscow to Ryazan link, with its monopoly of the transport of grain from the black earth area. His map of the project to cover much of Russia with a railway network was a testament to a vision that was ultimately fulfilled. When he died in 1876 he left his wife large estates and several million rubles.

Nadezhda von Meck's efficiency as a wife extended over all areas of her household. She managed the business side of her husband's career; and she ran his house like a business, with teams of servants acting under exact supervision and the children kept in their place with a precision extreme even by the standards of large establishments of the day. She bore twelve children, six boys and six girls, and continued to organize their lives even after they were grown up and married. Yet the obsessive activity of her life was clearly a compensation for its lack of an emotional centre. She once told Tchaikovsky that she wished children could be produced artificially so as to avoid the need for marriage; and it is difficult not to feel that here was the case of a woman with very strong emotions upon whom sexual experience had never made a full and satisfying emotional mark. With her autocratic temperament and rigidly disciplined nature, as well as her confessed shyness, this might well have served to turn her away from sex, to relegate unsatisfactory experiences to the position of another item on the busy agenda of domestic duties. But a woman with so vivid an imagination and so strong a personality must nevertheless have been acquiring a vast store of pent-up frustration. Subsequently it became known in the family that she had had an affair with Karl von Meck's secretary, a young engineer named Alexander Yolshin, and borne him a daughter, Lyudmila (Milochka). Karl, deeply dependent upon his wife as the rock upon which his life was founded, did not suspect that Milochka was not his own child and grew very fond of her; but on a business trip to St Petersburg in 1876 his second daughter Alexandra, bitterly jealous, told him the truth, and it was the shock of this discovery that caused his fatal heart attack, at the age of fifty-seven. Alexandra, who later married Count Ben-

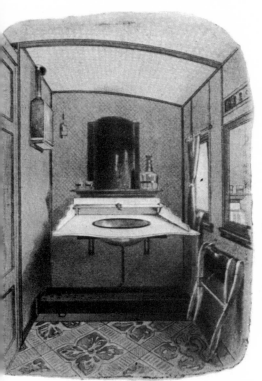

*The interior of a train on the Imperial Russian Railways in* 1864: left *a second-class* cabinet de toilette; right *the* wagon-restaurant

*Four graduates of the Moscow Conservatory. Left to right: Anatoly Brandukov, Yosif Kotek,
Stanislav Bartsevich and Andrey Arends*

Right *The Moscow Conservatory*

nigsen, was also responsible for telling her mother of Tchaikovsky's homosexuality,
of which Nadezhda is always supposed to have been ignorant; it can, however,
have come as little or no surprise to a woman so intelligent, and so diligent in
discovering all she could about her composer. In any case (according to Von Meck
family tradition) the revelation was if anything a reassurance that there could be no
other woman in his emotional life.

Travelling continually, partly because of the threatened tuberculosis that contributed to her alternating fits of excitement and depression, and partly as a release for
her energies, restless and autocratic, like Tchaikovsky himself a martyr to migraines,

she found her real emotional outlet in music. On her husband's death she began using her wealth to patronize young musicians: later she was to include Debussy in the household as a pianist, but at first she supplemented her keen but somewhat secretive concert-going with help for young musicians at the Conservatory who were recommended to her by Nikolay Rubinstein. Her fortune and position gave her access to his friendship; he in turn seems to have understood her nature well and to have behaved with tact and kindness. When soon after Karl's death she decided to employ a violinist who could play to her own piano accompaniment, Rubinstein suggested the most brilliant student of the spring graduation exercises of 1876, Yosif Yosifovich Kotek.

Modest describes Kotek as 'a good-looking young man, warm-hearted, enthusiastic and a gifted virtuoso'. He was a member of the composition class taken by Tchaikovsky, whom he passionately admired and who in turn was much taken with the personality of his lively young pupil. By the time Kotek had graduated, a close friendship had developed between them; and it was natural that Kotek should discuss, no doubt with some pride, his distinguished friend with his new employer. Nadezhda von Meck was much interested: she knew and liked Tchaikovsky's music, in which she found something personally very sympathetic, and she was curious to hear more about his character and his life. When she learned that he was chronically short of money, she leaped at the chance of extending her help. Accordingly some time in December 1876 Tchaikovsky received a commission for a violin and piano arrangement which Mme von Meck could play with Kotek. He performed the task with professional speed, and on 30 December he received a letter of thanks:

> Gracious Sir, Pyotr Ilyich,
>     Allow me to express my gratitude for the swift execution of my commission. To tell you into what ecstasy your work sent me I would consider out of place, since you are accustomed to praise and admiration such as a creature so musically insignificant as I cannot offer; it would seem to you funny, and my delight is so dear to me that I do not want it laughed at; so I shall only say, and I ask you to accept it as the literal truth, that your music makes life easier and more pleasant.

Probably on the following day Tchaikovsky replied in a similarly courteous and formal vein:

> Gracious Lady, Nadezhda Filaretovna,
>     Thank you most sincerely for the kind and flattering things which you have been good enough to write to me. For my part, I assure you that for a musician, among failures and obstacles of all kinds, it is a consolation to think that there is indeed a small minority of people, to which you belong, who sincerely and warmly love our art.

Some weeks later Tchaikovsky received another commission, and in acknowledging it at the end of February, Nadezhda von Meck cautiously opened the door to a closer relationship.

Truly I do not know how to thank you for your kind indulgence of my impatience. If it were not for my deep sympathy for you, I should be afraid that you would spoil me, and I value your kindness too much to allow that to happen.

I should very much like to tell you at length of my imagined attitude to you, but I am afraid of taking up your time, of which you have so little free. Let me only say that this imagined attitude is dear to me, the best and highest of all feelings possible for human nature. So, if you like, Pyotr Ilyich, call me fanciful, perhaps even extravagant, but do not laugh, for it would indeed be funny if it were not so sincere and so true.

To this Tchaikovsky replied cordially:

Allow me to thank you for the generous reward for so small a work. You are wrong not to want to tell me what is in your thoughts. I make so bold as to assure you that I should be extremely interested and pleased, as I in turn have deeply sympathetic feelings for you. This is not in the least merely a manner of speech. I know not quite so little about you as perhaps you think.

If you do me the honour one happy day of favouring me with a written account of all you want to tell me, I shall be extremely grateful. In any case, I thank you from my heart for your remarkable sympathy, which I very much appreciate.

Thus encouraged, Nadezhda von Meck replied with a letter running to several pages in which she poured out her enthusiasm for his music, for his character, for a chance opinion of his which she had heard and which convinced her of the similarity of their natures, for the good fortune that had brought her into contact with someone in whom character and talent seemed ideally matched. It was the beginning of a correspondence, running to just over 1100 letters in all, that is the entire substance of one of the most extraordinary and celebrated friendships in the history of music. Apart from a couple of chance encounters, immediately broken off, Tchaikovsky and Nadezhda von Meck never met, and only accidentally did they ever even set eyes on each other. The more enchanted she was with this relationship, she wrote in this letter, the more she feared a meeting; and when Tchaikovsky indicated that he quite understood her reluctance to meet someone in whom he well knew man and musician were neither ideal nor ideally blended, she hastened to assure him that in her eyes they most certainly were and that quite another reason lay behind her hesitation. Clever and self-aware, she seems to have divined from the start that the only hope of this affinity forming itself into a true relationship between them lay in a certain element of fiction which could only be maintained at a distance. She needed someone upon whom she could lavish a romantic affection without being required to associate it with domestic burdens or a physical relationship. Her wealth gave her the means of this; her sharp intuition told her that she had found the ideal object of her feelings in Tchaikovsky; his own emotional make-up gave the improbable relationship the chance of working. For his part, he had long stood in need of some kind of feminine protection to fill something of the aching gap left in his life by the death of his mother. The financial security produced by the pension which she soon allowed him, so far from being an embarrassment to their pure relationship, afforded it a practical basis: she could feel that she was setting her wealth to work in a way that gave her the satisfaction of involving her in music, while he was given a prompt to composition and enabled to avoid the feeling that he was merely a rich woman's emotional plaything. His need for a woman to whom he could stand in some kind of relationship was answered by the arrangement, and her stipulation that they should not meet naturally avoided the need for carrying the relationship onto any kind of physical level. For two lonely, unusual and unhappy people it was a solution that provided each with great contentment; and though the tone of the letters is emotional, not to say gushing, and the protestations of devotion hysterical on her part, with sometimes a rather touching girlishness hinting at her emotional inexperience, and on his strained and (he privately admitted) at times cynically insincere, it should be remembered that each was thereby provided with the deepest emotional relationship that their lives were to produce.

As far as the financial side of their relationship was concerned Nadezhda von Meck found that matters were far from simple. Though willing to accept reasonable, even generous, payment for arrangements or original works which she wanted for her own pleasure, Tchaikovsky was unwilling to compromise his artistic conscience by turning out music which was demanded in detail by her (he was reluctant to fulfil her request for a piece for violin and piano to be entitled 'The Reproach') and too proud to accept for his work a ludicrously exaggerated fee that was thinly disguised charity. Yet when she decided openly to make him regular allowances, he was happy to accept; and in the same letter, only the fifth which he wrote her, in which he delicately refuses her commission for 'The Reproach' for fear that without inspiration he would be returning false metal for true, he asks her for a loan of 3000 rubles – the equivalent of a year's salary. He was in debt to this extent, partly due to his inability to manage his affairs, partly through a natural generosity which led to his giving away money almost casually when he did find himself briefly solvent. Late in life, when his income from music was healthy but his funds as chronically low as ever, a friend asked him how he invested his money. He burst out laughing at the ludicrous idea of doing anything with money except buying what one wanted for oneself and one's friends. As to capital investments, his last was at the Kokorev Hotel in Moscow and his next he would not know until he had decided where he was going. It has been suggested that throughout his life he probably gave away about half the money he ever possessed, in sums ranging from substantial help to friends in difficulties and presents to current favourite young men to daily tips to the peasants and children who came to know exactly where to find him on his daily walks around Klin. Improvident but proud, he would naturally find a regular arrangement with Nadezhda von Meck which was open and which, he sensed, gave her pleasure, or even a direct loan whose repayment he conscientiously planned by various methods, preferable to ill-concealed charity by over-subsidizing works for

Но въ темномъ зеркалѣ одна
Дрожитъ печальная луна.

*Tatyana fortune-telling: an illustration from the first edition of Pushkin's poem,* Eugene Onegin

which he had no enthusiasm. He once told Jürgenson that he would write music to advertise corn-plasters if the price was high enough, but for her he would only write his best music. He was right: she was delighted to be asked for the loan, for she took the request as evidence of the closeness with which they stood to each other in this fictive friendship they were constructing; and she was deeply honoured by the other offer he contained in his letter: the dedication of his new symphony.

Work on this Fourth Symphony, which had been occupying him since the winter, could not wholly prevent his thoughts turning once more to opera. His friends were full of suggestions: Stasov offered Alfred de Vigny's *Cinq-Mars*, and at a party at the singer Elizaveta Lavrovskaya's house, other equally unsuitable ideas were produced. At first Tchaikovsky thought Lavrovskaya's own suggestion, Pushkin's *Eugene Onegin*, to be as bad as any; but lunching alone in a restaurant later, he told Modest, he began to change his mind. He hurried off to find a copy of the poem, spent a sleepless night working on a sketch of a libretto, and the next day sought out Konstantin Shilovsky and set him to work. 'You have no idea how mad I am about this subject', he went on.

> How pleasant to avoid all the routine pharaohs, Ethiopian princesses, poisoned cups and all the rest of these tales about automata. What poetry there is in *Onegin*! I am not blind to its faults. I fully realize that it gives little scope for treatment, and will be poor in stage effect; but the richness of the poetry, the humanity and simplicity of the subject, embodied in Pushkin's inspired verse, will make up for whatever it lacks in other ways.

When Modest nevertheless expressed his doubts, Tchaikovsky swept them aside: never mind the lack of stage effect, he repeated, or of action, he was fascinated by the image of Tatyana and the tragedy that resulted from the heartless Onegin's rejection of her touching declaration of love. Totally under the spell of Pushkin's poetry, he was irresistibly drawn to compose music for it.

Meanwhile, at about the same time that Nadezhda von Meck was attempting to persuade Tchaikovsky to compose her a piece about reproach, he had received another letter. It came from one of his pupils at the Conservatory, a girl named Antonina Ivanovna Milyukova, and it was a declaration of love. Instead of tactfully discouraging her, Tchaikovsky replied that he could only offer in return gratitude and sympathy; but at the same time he did not reject her. Longing to be married, and with no experience whatever of the realities of a relationship with a woman, he could only interpret the situation in terms of fiction; and the fiction closest to hand was Pushkin's. Was he to play the cruel Onegin to this touching little Tatyana? Would he, too, spend the rest of his life in regret if he spurned her love? The situation must have framed itself all too easily in dramatic terms. He retained enough of his reason to have discreet inquiries made about Antonina from a friend; but his feeling for drama and for Fate proved stronger than his common sense when his friend returned with a highly unfavourable account of her. Whatever it contained, the facts about her were that she was adequately good-looking and of sound moral reputation although (unusually for the day) she lived alone, was twenty-eight years old, was profoundly stupid and nursed weird notions about being the object of every man's passion. The latter delusion was eventually to lead into total mental and moral collapse; but lost in his own imaginary emotional world, Tchaikovsky had no reason to see anything unusual in the nature and persistence of her approach, indeed would tend to find the drama of the whole situation an atmosphere natural to him. When she invited him to call upon her, he accepted, but repeated that he had nothing to offer her but gratitude and sympathy. Continuing to cherish the possibility that she might fill the role of his long-desired Beloved, he began dropping dark hints to his friends about his plans for marriage. Her letters waved aside his doubts about his suitability for her, insisted that, despite the urgent attentions of another man who

*Tchaikovsky and his bride,
Antonina Milyukova*

had been in love with her for years, she was true to Tchaikovsky and that her first kiss would be his, and protested her undying passion to and beyond the grave. She even threatened suicide if he rejected her; and his repeated assurances that he would make a bad husband failed to deflect her. It seems likely that on one of his many visits to her, Tchaikovsky nerved himself to try to explain the real reason why he was so unsuited to marriage. Possibly she failed, or refused, to understand, possibly she nursed the far from uncommon feeling that she was capable with her love of rescuing her errant, suffering lover; at all events, Tchaikovsky found himself so totally enmeshed in a web partly of his own weaving that early in June he proposed marriage and was accepted.

His first reaction was one of calm. To Anatoly he wrote a level letter emphasizing the suitability of his bride, so level that his account of her acceptability as marriage material and of his own relaxed progress with some two-thirds of the opera must have aroused the alarm of anyone who knew his usual nervous reactions to an emotional situation. He describes Antonina as no longer young but in every way appropriate as his wife, and goes on almost casually to discuss wedding plans and to enclose a letter about the matter for his father. Ilya Petrovich, who was presumably ignorant of his sons' homosexuality, professed himself willing to jump for joy and sent back a touchingly formal old man's blessing; but Modest and Alexandra, told the news the day before the wedding when any protest would be too late, were as disturbed as

Anatoly. Only when, three days before the wedding, he felt obliged to write to Nadezhda von Meck did some sense of what he was really doing begin to overcome Tchaikovsky: his long letter is one of somewhat panicky self-justification, admitting that he does not love the girl and confessing his stupidity in having allowed himself to become embroiled with her in the first place, but protesting that he cannot now do otherwise, despite his anxiety about it all, and begging that, in the unhappiness which he was only now for the first time admitting would lie ahead, she will continue to remain his Best Friend. This was to be the form of dedication of the new symphony; and in replying to accept, Nadezhda von Meck managed to restrict herself to courteous good wishes for the step Tchaikovsky was taking.

On 18 July 1877, at the Church of St George on the Malaya Nikitskaya, Tchaikovsky and Antonina were married. Anatoly and Kotek stood witness; and that evening the newly married couple left for St Petersburg to visit Ilya Petrovich and then, after a call on Antonina's mother in the country, to settle in Moscow. Scarcely had the train started when the nightmare began, Tchaikovsky wrote to Anatoly.

> I was on the point of screaming, choked with sobs. Nevertheless, I had to amuse my wife with conversation as far as Klin so as to earn the right to remain in my own chair in the dark, alone with myself. My only consolation was that my wife did not understand or realize my ill-conceived misery. She has looked quite happy and content all along. *Elle n'est pas difficile . . .*

He goes on to speak quite sympathetically about her, clearly feeling that the situation was his responsibility, and hopefully describes the arrangement they have made whereby she will confine herself to looking after him, leaving him free to lead his own life and concentrate on his work. The fact that she is so stupid, he adds, is a positive advantage, for a clever woman would only dominate him and with Antonina he feels completely in control. He reiterates the substance of this to Modest, adding that he could envisage love growing between them when they had become used to one another.

Needless to say, he was deceiving himself. He seems to have genuinely believed that something might be constructed out of the disaster of having married at all; and his efforts to be fair to Antonina, both to her face and behind her back, are in someone of his temperament full of courage. His natural kindness made him concerned for a girl to whom he felt the responsibility of an older and more intelligent man; but it seems clear that the greater his care for her welfare, the more she was led to expect a full emotional and even physical contact with him. Her constant presence, no doubt her continual, if unexpressed, expectation that he, too, would capitulate before her famous charms, especially the sense of being trapped in a situation far beyond his capacity to manage, drove him rapidly into despair. By the time they returned to Moscow, on 26 July, he was in a state of near-collapse. But relief was once more at hand in the form of Nadezhda von Meck's letter in reply to the news

Москва. 15 Iюле 1877 г.

№ 26

Вчера пріѣхалъ я въ Москву и отправившись въ Консерваторію получилъ письмо Ваше, дорогая Надежда Филаретовна. Въ томъ состояніи нервной возбуждённости, въ которомъ я теперь нахожусь, Ваши дружескія строки, Ваше тёплое участіе ко мнѣ, — подѣйствовала на меня самымъ благотворнымъ образомъ.

Надежда Филаретовна! Какъ это ни странно, какъ это ни смѣло, но я долженъ, я принужденъ опять обратиться къ Вамъ за матеріальной помощью. Вотъ въ чемъ дѣло. Изъ извѣстной Вамъ суммы у меня оставалось совершенно достаточное количество денегъ для путешествія на Кавказъ и вообще для того, чтобы не стѣсняясь въ расходахъ провести лѣто совершенно покойно. На сцену явилась женитьба. Всѣ эти деньги ушли на свадьбу и на сопряженныя съ нею расходы. Между тѣмъ я былъ совер-

of his marriage. Encouraged by her friendly reaction, he wrote to her at once. His purpose was to ask for an increase of the loan by 1000 rubles.

By normal standards, his behaviour must seem insensitive in the extreme. At the last minute he had confessed the fact of his marriage to Antonina to a woman who, whatever the distance she preferred to maintain, obviously had very strong emotional feelings for him; his first act on receiving from her a letter that was obviously written out of a real effort to overcome shock at the news, was to ask for money. Yet his instinct in trusting himself to her was sound. His explanation that Antonina's plans for the sale of some land near Klin had fallen through must have counted for less with Nadezhda von Meck than the fact that his marriage was a catastrophe and that in his anguish his natural inclination was to turn to her. She showed no surprise at the immediate failure of the marriage – which tends to support the fact that she knew of Tchaikovsky's homosexuality – and she would have been superhuman not to feel some satisfaction that it was to her that the distressed composer should appeal, especially since the purpose for which he needed money was to get away from the intolerable situation with Antonina and find time and solitude in which to pull himself together. He concluded by begging her to allow him to postpone a full explanation of all that had happened to him. She immediately replied with the money and with a note that asked no questions and simply recommended him to go as soon as he could to the Caucasus (she had herself warm memories of Odessa) and to let her know how he got on and how he was when he felt better. Before leaving, not for the Caucasus but for Kamenka, he sent her a brief fervent note of thanks and the renewed promise to explain all soon.

Two days later, from Kiev, he kept his word, and his own account of his marriage and his subsequent behaviour deserves quoting in full.

Nadezhda Filaretovna!

Here is the brief story of all I have lived through since 18 July, i.e. the day of my marriage.

I wrote to you that I married not through the urgings of the heart but through a set of circumstances I could not understand, and which forced upon me an embarrassing set of alternatives. I had either to desert an honest girl whose love I had thoughtlessly encouraged, or marry her. I chose the latter. In the first place, it honestly seemed to me that I would fall in love with a girl who was so sincerely devoted to me; in the second place, I knew that my marriage was realizing the dreams of my old father and of friends close and dear to me.

The moment the ceremony was over, and I found myself alone with my wife, and realized that our fate was to live inseparably with each other, I suddenly discovered that I did not have even ordinary feelings of friendship for her, but that she was *abhorrent* to me in the fullest sense of that word. I grew certain that I, or rather the best and perhaps the only good part of what is *me*, i.e. musical talent, had perished for ever. My future existence appeared to me wretched vegetating and an intolerable, ponderous comedy. My wife is in no way guilty: she did not ask for the bond of marriage. So to make her realize that I do not love her, that I regard her as an intolerable nuisance would be both cruel and shabby. All that is left is to pretend. But to pretend to the end of one's life is the highest torment. I was in the depths of despair, the more appallingly so as there was no one to support and encourage me. I longed ardently, greedily for death. Death seemed to me the only way out – but to kill myself was unthinkable. I assure you, I have deep ties with some of my family, i.e. my sister, my two younger brothers and my father. I know that if I decided on suicide and carried it through, I should be dealing a mortal blow to my family. There are many other people, some of them dear friends, whose love and friendship bind me indissolubly to life. Besides I have the weakness (if weakness it can be called) of loving life, loving my profession, loving my future success. Finally, I have *not yet said* everything I have to say, everything I want to say before the time comes to migrate to eternity. So, death does not come to me, I shall not and cannot go to him – what then remains? I have told my wife that I shall travel during August for my health, which really is disturbed and needs radical treatment. No sooner was that said than my journey began to seem to me like an escape from prison, however temporary, and the thought that the day of departure was not far off gave me strength to endure. We stayed a week in Petersburg, then returned to Moscow. There we found ourselves without money, as my wife had been tricked by one Kudryavtsyev when he made her believe he would sell her forest land. Then began a new series of anguishes and tortures: uncomfortable lodgings, the necessity of arranging a new home and the impossibility of doing so without money, the possibility of getting away removed by the same lack, finally, gloom and an idiotic life in Moscow without any work (I had no enthusiasm, and no energy for work, and our living quarters were uncomfortable), without friends, without a moment's respite. I don't understand why my mind didn't give way. Then I had to visit my wife's mother. There my torments increased tenfold. The mother and the whole *entourage* which I have entered are antipathetic to me. Their ideas are narrow, their opinions wild, they are all daggers drawn with each other the whole time; my wife (perhaps this is unfair) became every hour more abhorrent to me. I can hardly describe to you, Nadezhda Filaretovna, the dreadful degree to which I was rent by moral torment. Before leaving for the country, in a desperate effort to escape from the terrible situation and longing to get away on my journey, I turned to someone you know well, a sweet, dear friend now living at Brailov. The thought that she would help me, the certainty that she would free me from these dreadful bonds of anguish and madness, sustained me. But would my letter reach her? The supposition that the letter might not reach her tormented me.

We returned to Moscow. For several days that dreadful life dragged on. I had two consolations: first, I drank a good deal of wine, and it numbed me and gave me several moments of forgetfulness; secondly, talks with Kotek cheered me. I cannot tell you how much brotherly sympathy he showed me! Apart from you, he is the only person who knows all that I am writing to you now. He is a good man in the true sense of the word. It is a fact that sorrows do not come singly. I received news of the sudden death of one of my closest friends, Adamov. He and I were at school together, we started our service together; in spite of our ways having parted, we remained to the end on terms of intimate friendship. He had every good fortune in life: he enjoyed perfect health, he had an excellent official position, money in his wife's name, he was completely happy in his family life, and suddenly death! It completely overwhelmed me. At last, one happy evening I received a letter from Brailov . . . At that I suddenly cheered up, I spent three days in preparations for departure and in arrangements for future lodgings, and then, on *Tuesday*, at one o'clock, I left. I don't know what will happen next, but now I feel as though I had woken from a terrible, excruciating nightmare or, rather, from a terrible, lengthy illness. Like a man recovering from a fever, I am very weak, consecutive thought is hard for me, it was very hard for me even to write this letter, but what a sensation of sweet rest, what an intoxicating sensation of freedom and solitude! . . .

If my understanding of my constitution does not deceive me, it may very well be that, having rested and calmed my nerves, returning to Moscow and to the normal round of activities, I shall be able to regard my wife completely differently. Really and truly, she has many qualities which might contribute to my future happiness. She genuinely likes me and wants nothing more than for me to be peaceful and happy. Really I pity her.

I shall stay in Kiev for a day. Tomorrow I go to my sister, and from there to the Caucasus. Forgive, Nadezhda Filaretovna, the fact that this letter is incoherent, confused and vague. But I know that you follow me.

I have told you that my nerves, my entire soul are so tired that I can hardly put two thoughts together. However exhausted my spirit may be, it is not so broken that it cannot glow with profound gratitude to the hundred times dear friend beyond price who is saving me. Nadezhda Filaretovna, if God gives me the strength to survive the terrible present, I shall prove to you that this friend has not helped me in vain. I have not said a tenth of what I want to say. My heart is full. It wants to pour itself out in music. Who knows, perhaps I shall leave behind something truly worthy of the reputation of a first class artist. I have the boldness to hope so.

Nadezhda Filaretovna, I bless you for all you have done for me. Farewell, my best, my inestimable, dear friend.

P. Tchaikovsky

The admitted emotional confusion of this extraordinary letter – the genuine concern for Antonina struggling with revulsion, the jumble of ambition, self-pity, longing for death, fussiness and a degree of ruthlessness – was received by Nadezhda von Meck with calm, and there is even a faint note of complacency in her reply. She comforts him with somewhat conventional words, reiterates the pleasure she has had from his music, and concludes with some news of her holiday plans and of daily tasks with the regiments passing through Brailov on the way to the front. At Kamenka, where he received this letter, Tchaikovsky was more relaxed, and distinctly sheepish about his behaviour and his description of it. Work was resumed on the Fourth Symphony, and he wrote that he was looking forward to scoring the last three movements, in particular the Scherzo with its alternations of *pizzicato* strings, woodwind and brass. He had also resumed *Eugene Onegin*, steeping himself in the poem again in the house where Pushkin had often stayed and (according to family legend) written his verses sprawled across their billiard table; and to Nadezhda von Meck he wrote that it would be likely to disappoint a public hoping for theatrical effect, but perhaps would appeal to, 'those capable of seeking in an opera musical reproduction far removed from tragedy or theatricality – everyday, simple feelings common to all humanity; they (I hope) will be content with my opera.'

As the time drew near when he had to return to face up to his life in Moscow, his nervousness returned. Assuring Anatoly of his brotherly love, he lamented his indifference to Antonina; and there is a distinct note of trying to convince himself when he adds, 'She does not frighten me – she is simply an annoyance.' Pausing in Kiev for a performance of *La Traviata*, he reached Moscow on 23 September. Antonina was at the station to meet him, and they returned to the rooms she had been furnishing. By the next morning all his nervous symptoms had returned: to Anatoly he now wrote that he was indeed frightened, to Nadezhda von Meck that he was desperate for escape and longing once more for death. He attempted to work, but found it almost impossible in the conditions of the tiny flat with Antonina solicitously at hand. He put in appearances at the Conservatory, where the shrewd Kashkin saw through the exaggerated casualness of his manner and detected serious trouble. At last, at a supper given by Jürgenson, Tchaikovsky introduced to his friends the wife about whom they must have been speculating and certainly about whom gossip had been flying. First impressions were on the whole favourable; but when Kashkin tried to get her into conversation, he found Tchaikovsky always at her side, finding words when she hesitated and finishing sentences for her. Even though the conversation was on trivial subjects, Tchaikovsky seemed unable to let Antonina alone for an instant; it is small wonder that she left upon the much puzzled company 'a somewhat colourless impression'.

To his friends the strain in his appearance was obvious as the days passed; but they cannot have realized how near disaster he was. About a fortnight later, on a bitterly cold night, he set out and waded up to his waist with all his clothes on into the ice-strewn River Moscow. There he stood until he could bear the cold no longer, and emerged certain that now he would die of pneumonia. To Antonina he lamely explained that he had fallen in while fishing. When it became clear that his robust constitution had defeated his plan, his state became still worse. On 5 October he wired Anatoly in St Petersburg telling him to wire him back in Nápravník's name demanding his immediate presence; and the next day, having turned up at the Conservatory in a state of agitation and given this story to his colleagues, he set out for the northern capital. Anatoly was at the station to meet him, but did not at first recognize his brother's changed face. Hurrying him to a hotel, he put him to bed; and there, after a violent outburst, Tchaikovsky lapsed into a coma for two days. Anatoly never told anyone what had transpired during that time; but he must have explained some, if not all, of the truth to the mental specialist who was the only person apart from his brothers and his father to see him, for what was prescribed was a complete change of life and the recommendation that Tchaikovsky should make no attempt to renew his marriage and should not try to see his wife again.

*Anatoly Tchaikovsky*

Leaving his brother in St Petersburg, Anatoly hurried to Moscow to explain matters to Nikolay Rubinstein and to tell Antonina that she must consent to a divorce. So concerned was Rubinstein, and so worried that the gentle Anatoly might falter in his resolve to be firm with Antonina, that he insisted on accompanying him on this mission. They need not have been so apprehensive: Antonina received them cordially, ordered tea, and when Rubinstein went straight to the point and reported the doctor's recommendation of a divorce, merely replied that for Pyotr Ilyich's sake she would consent to everything, going on in the same breath to offer them their tea. Feeling that he had done all that was required of him, Rubinstein swallowed his and was seen out by Antonina, who returned to tell the confused Anatoly that she had hardly expected the honour of entertaining Rubinstein himself to tea that day. Anatoly could scarcely have been expected, in his own flustered condition, to have deduced from this unnatural calm the mental disorder that was eventually to overcome her. At first Alexandra Davidova kindly took her in and tried to console her; but Antonina's tantrums, her nerviness, her compulsive nail-biting soon taxed even Alexandra's patience, and eventually Lev Davidov was forced to write to Anatoly in Venice insisting that he should come and remove her. When the divorce finally came up, Antonina proceeded to bombard members of the family with alternately abusive and wheedling letters, protesting as ever that half Moscow was in love with her and none more so than Tchaikovsky. The arrangements fell through; and for long after he sought unsuccessfully to persuade her to allow him a divorce. But she would never consent to the legally necessary fiction that he had committed adultery, a humiliation to a woman of her delusions. He lived for years in the fear that either she would blurt out publicly the real reason why he could not have committed adultery or she would carry out the hints in some of her incoherent letters and set about blackmailing him. Eventually in the summer of 1880 Jürgenson, who had kept his eye on the whole matter and tried his best to intercede with her for Tchaikovsky, discovered that she really had in the previous winter taken a lover and had a child by him. She continued to have children at regular intervals and to deposit them all in a foundlings' home. By 1896 she was herself in a home, certified insane; and there, continuing to nurse delusions that of all the famous men who were in love with her the most ardent was Tchaikovsky, she died in 1917.

Tchaikovsky himself never laid any blame upon Antonina. His ill luck in falling in with her, at a time when he had grown desperate to be married for the sake of being married, was but part of what he regarded as his Fate. Certainly Fate at its most malevolent could hardly have found a wife less suited to him. Whether or not it would ever have been possible for a more tactful and intelligent woman to have come to terms with his homosexuality and provided him with the affection and care he longed both to receive and to give, he himself never lost his ideal of marriage. When Anatoly became engaged, Tchaikovsky wrote him a warm letter in which he confessed, 'Sometimes I am overcome by an insane craving for the caress of a woman's touch. Sometimes I see a sympathetic woman in whose lap I could lay my head, whose hands I would gladly kiss . . .'; and he goes on to remind Anatoly, wistfully, of the description of Levin's marriage in *Anna Karenina*. Yet the terms of this letter show that he was still a long way from a true relationship with a wife; for what he is describing is the vision of his lost mother.

*Karl Davidov (sitting),
with Vasily Safonov, an
outstanding conductor of
Tchaikovsky's works*

Once somewhat recovered – in his own phrase, 'returning to life' – Tchaikovsky set out with Anatoly on a prolonged foreign holiday. By mid-October he was in Berlin, with funds voted him by the Russian Musical Society at Nikolay Rubinstein's prompting in recognition of his services. From here he wrote to Jürgenson requesting commissions for small pieces, to keep him active until he felt able to resume work on the Fourth Symphony and *Eugene Onegin*. In Clarens, on Lake Geneva, he received an offer from Karl Davidov, the head of the St Petersburg Conservatory (and no relation to Tchaikovsky's brother-in-law), to act as delegate to the 1878 Paris Exhibition; but unable to face the social and diplomatic side of the task, he ignored it and turned instead for money to Nadezhda von Meck. She had meanwhile returned to Moscow, and alarmed at Tchaikovsky's disappearance had cautiously questioned Nikolay Rubinstein. Her immediate reaction to what she learned was to make him the first instalment of what was from now on to be a regular allowance of 6000 rubles.

She accompanied this with a letter in which she reproves him for worrying about asking her for money again, arguing that the ties of feeling and spiritual kinship which bind them give him a greater claim to material help than those of blood, and telling him with mock severity to stop interfering with her wish to take care of his affairs. And to his fear that she may despise his behaviour over his marriage, she replies, with an enthusiasm wholly absent from her polite congratulations on his engagement, that she knows he is right to have abandoned the 'lies and deception' of life with Antonina, that she is relieved now to be able to speak frankly her opinion of the whole business, that she admires his attempt to make it work and then his step in escaping from the suffering, that so far from despising him she sympathizes with his misery and would herself have managed to endure for far shorter a time. To her request for a description of Antonina, Tchaikovsky returned one that is pitched on the hard side but that makes some effort to be fair, and once more lays the blame entirely upon himself for allowing the whole incident to take place. Nadezhda von Meck's reply hardly troubles to conceal her triumphant scorn for Antonina; and having berated her for being materialistic and without imagination, she goes on assert that she herself is no dreamer – as Antonina had by now become in her mind – but a realist with a poetic nature.

With this renewal, indeed consolidation, of their relationship, their correspondence turned towards the things of the mind which, she insisted, were the essence of their affinity for one another. To his question about her beliefs, she returned a long, rambling, muddled letter disclaiming membership of any established faith but setting forth the philosophy she declared she had formed for herself and upon which she rested contentedly. Tchaikovsky, now sufficiently recovered to take the initiative in the correspondence, was not slow to see through this. With the rueful respect of the man who admires a faith he cannot share, he gently disarms her of the illusion that what she has formed for herself must be stronger than traditional faith by being of her own building. 'The intelligent man', he writes, 'who is at the same time a believer (and, you know, there are *very* many) possesses armour against which all the blows of fate are utterly useless.' It is not spiritual contentment but a yearning such as his own for some spiritual ideal, he goes on to suggest, which has attracted her to his music. Nor will he accept that someone of her mental cast and her aspirations can properly be called a realist. That she is a sceptic he does not doubt; but he suggests that 'A clever man is perhaps never not a sceptic. At least, his life must contain a period of painful scepticism.' Trying to find a way out of the doubt of her scepticism she has found some help in her pantheistic notions, but not peace.

He is, moreover, concerned to recall her to a more respectful view of established religion.

> I feel quite differently from you about the Church. For me it has kept a great deal of its poetic appeal. I often go to mass; the liturgy of St John Chrysostom is, I think, one of the greatest of artistic creations. If one follows the service attentively, examining the

*Nikolay Rimsky-Korsakov, by Valentin Ser*

meaning of every symbol, it is impossible not to be spiritually moved in the presence of our Orthodox services. I dearly love the night service, too. To go on a Saturday to some ancient little church, to stand in the half-darkness laden with the smoke of the incense, meditating by oneself and searching for an answer to the eternal questions: *why, when, where, what for,* to be aroused from reverie when the choir begins to sing, 'Many passions contend with me from my youth up' and to abandon oneself to the influence of the enchanting poetry of that psalm, to steep oneself in silent bliss when the Royal Doors open and there rings out, *'Praise the Lord in the heavens!'* – Oh! I love it all tremendously, it's one of my greatest delights.

Clearly, however, it is not the substance of established religion which appealed to Tchaikovsky so much as the very powerful atmosphere which the intense, ornate ritual of Orthodox services creates; and he goes on to admit that only part of him is bound to the Church, that he is himself a mass of inconsistencies, convinced, for instance, that there is no personal immortality yet unable to believe that he will not one day again see his mother. Probably he was stating nothing but the sober truth when he added, 'Truly, there would be reason to go mad if it were not for *music*.'

About music he is both lucid and quite sharp with her. When she rhapsodizes about the intoxicating effect music has on her, sending her into roseate ecstasies and a vague sense of misty longing, he pounces upon her for her unfortunate comparison of his art with a glass of sherry:

> I particularly dislike your comparison of music with intoxication. This seems to me sham. A man takes wine to delude himself, to give himself an *illusion* of contentment and pleasure. And a heavy price he pays for that fraud! The reaction is terrible. It is true that wine gives forgetfulness of bitterness and anguish for a moment – only. Is this the same with music? It is not illusion, it is revelation. And the reason for its victorious strength is that it reveals to us different spheres of elements of *beauty*, to experience which is not transitory but is for ever a reconciliation to life.

Tchaikovsky himself, who habitually drank too much, was fully aware of the pleasures of temporary escape from an oppressive world; and there is in his musical make-up a similar awareness of the human desire to escape from the pressures of reality, a sharp feeling for the consciously artificial and pretty and for the distancing conventions of fairy-story or of rococo elegance. But in his insistence that essentially music was an art not of illusion but of revelation there is the conscience of a composer prepared to use his art for the highest expressive purposes.

About his colleagues, however, Tchaikovsky was as unreliable and as full of unspoken special pleading as most composers. Eager to know his views, Nadezhda von Meck bombarded him throughout the autumn with questions, and was delighted to find how closely her opinions matched his. Wagner he found, for all his grudging respect, fundamentally incomprehensible, and his account of Wagner as a symphonist who had mistakenly allowed himself to become entangled in the fustian of the theatre is a classic of one composer's misunderstanding of another. Brahms

he found dark, cold, pretentious, and at once obscure and shallow; far preferable to either of these Germans, who belonged to a nation in serious musical decline, was Delibes. His opinions of his Russian contemporaries are scarcely more respectful: Cui is a gifted amateur with taste and instinct but no originality, Mussorgsky possesses great talent but is narrow-minded and devoted to coarseness and untidiness for their own sake, Balakirev is brilliant but destructive, Borodin lacks Cui's taste and is unable to write a line without help. Finally he mounts a sustained attack on Rimsky-Korsakov as a dilettante turned pedant, at present in the throes of a crisis from which he will emerge either as a master or a mere pedagogue. It is important to remember that Tchaikovsky was not writing in public when he declared these views, and that he was honest enough to amend them in the light of changing events and new works from these composers' pens; but the real interest of his opinions is for the light they shed on his own music. Like almost all composers who are primarily composers and not critics, he makes his judgments by reference to his own creative necessities. Wagner represented a path along which he could not possibly travel; the *Kuchka* were the Slavophiles to his Westernizer, concerned with issues that neither interested him nor could engage his particular talent; yet Brahms, for all their common interest in reconciling the classical form of the symphony with Romanticism, must indeed have seemed heavy going to the composer whose sympathies were with the French. We may also sense, in his praise of Delibes, the not infrequent composer's habit of fastening with articulate enthusiasm upon the *petit maître* while arguing against those who are substantial enough to represent serious rivalry or superiority.

Whatever the vagueness of the musical and philosophical ideas with which Nadezhda von Meck pursued Tchaikovsky during these autumn and winter months of 1877, she was firmly practical in encouraging him to get on with his actual work. The restlessness of his condition after the disaster kept him on the move, unable to settle in one place. A visit to Paris to see a doctor whom he admired ended badly when the locum treated him with an offhandedness bordering on contempt. From here he and Anatoly went to Florence and Rome, finding each depressing, and only when he came to Venice on his way to Vienna did he begin to recover his spirits: here the chief cause for complaint was the habit of the newsboys of crying Turkish victories in the war with enthusiasm, but when Tchaikovsky tried to

reprove one of them he was merely mocked next morning with straightfaced shouts of fictitious Russian victories. Back in Venice, having picked up his servant Alexey Sofronov in Vienna, he settled contentedly into new rooms; and he was further cheered both by the belated arrival of funds from Nadezhda von Meck and especially by a warm letter from his sister Alexandra. Her womanly instincts had at first led her to sympathize with Antonina, but it needed only a few weeks at close quarters with her at Kamenka for family loyalties to reassert themselves.

In mid-December Tchaikovsky set out from Venice, by way of Milan, to meet Modest and Kolya Konradi in San Remo. On arriving there he was shaken to find that in the absence of his refusal to act as delegate in Paris, his acceptance had been taken for granted. When Nikolay Rubinstein learned the truth, he wrote angrily accusing Tchaikovsky of malingering. Replying mildly, Tchaikovsky admitted that probably his temperament did incline him to exaggerate his troubles and paid the fullest respect to Rubinstein's own qualities and kindnesses to him; but he firmly maintained his refusal to go to Paris. Through all these travels, he continued his hard work on the Fourth Symphony. The scoring was completed on 7 January, and on the 11th the work was dispatched to Nikolay Rubinstein. 'Today *our symphony* has winged its way to Moscow, to Rubinstein,' he told Nadezhda von Meck.

> With the heading I have written the dedication: '*To my best friend*'. What is in store for this symphony? Will it remain alive long after its author has vanished from the face of the earth, or will it immediately fall into the abyss of oblivion? I don't know, but I do know that at the moment I have perhaps some kind of parental blindness, and am incapable of seeing the faults of my youngest child. Still, I am sure that as far as style and form are concerned, it represents a forward step in my development, which proceeds very slowly. In spite of my mature years, I am still far from reaching that point beyond which my talent will not allow me to go.

*The sitting room in the Pension Joly, San Remo, shared by Modest, Kolya and Tchaikovsky.*
Below *San Remo in the* 1870s

Whether or not she expected what Tchaikovsky always described in his letters as 'our symphony' to concern itself with their relationship, Nadezhda von Meck was certainly impressed by the new mastery and the new expansion of his talent in the work; and soon after its première she was writing to ask if it had a programme. His reply began with an articulate account of his methods of work:

You ask if this symphony has a definite programme. Usually when asked this question about a symphonic piece, I reply: *none*. And indeed it is difficult to answer such a question. How can one express those inexpressible sensations which pass through one when writing an instrumental work without a definite subject? It is a purely lyrical process. It is a musical confession of the soul, which is full to the brim and which, true to its essential

nature, pours itself out in sound, just as the lyric poet expresses himself in verse. The difference is that music possesses incomparably more powerful means and is a subtler language for the articulation of the thousand different moments of the soul's moods. In general it is suddenly and in an unexpected shape that the *seed* of a future work appears. If the soil is receptive, i.e. if it is disposed to work, this seed takes root with astonishing force and swiftness, shows itself above the ground, puts out a little stalk, leaves, twigs and finally flowers. I can most precisely describe the creative process by means of this metaphor. The great problem is that the seed must appear in favourable conditions. The rest looks after itself. It is useless trying to find words to describe to you the unbounded sense of bliss that overcomes me when a new main idea appears and begins to take definite form. I forget everything, I behave like a madman, trembling and shaking in every limb, with scarcely time to jot down the sketches, so quickly do thoughts pursue one another. In the middle of this magic process it sometimes happens that an outside shock wakes me from this state of somnambulism. Someone rings the bell, the servant enters, the clock strikes and reminds me that I must be about my business. The interruptions are hard, inexpressibly hard. Sometimes inspiration flies away for quite some time; one must seek it again, often in vain. Very often a completely cold, rational technical process must be employed. Perhaps it is for this reason that in the great masters themselves it is possible to detect where there is a lack of organic coherence, where one notices the seams, bits of completely artificial coherence. But it's impossible otherwise. If that state of the artist's soul which we call *inspiration*, and which I have tried to describe to you, should continue uninterrupted, it would be impossible to survive a single day. The strings would snap and the instrument shatter to pieces! Only one thing is essential: that the main idea and the general outline of all the separate parts appear not by means of *searching*, but of their own accord, as the result of that supernatural, inscrutable and wholly inexplicable force which we call *inspiration* . . .

Possibly Tchaikovsky was, as in other places in his correspondence with Nadezhda von Meck, pitching his description in the most colourful terms possible so as to flatter the popular view, which she certainly shared, of the nature of artistic inspiration. Certainly his own craftsmanship was of a much higher order than he implies, and the sheer hard work, even drudgery, of forcing ideas into their most effective shape was well known to him as part of the process of inspiration. But there is also a ring of truth about his description, which points to some of his strengths and defects. For him, the essence of music was what he called 'the lyrical idea', the invention that occurred to him in a manner which, like all composers, he found he could not account for; and later in the year he was to return to an account of his working methods in reply to her eager questioning. This time he included what is perhaps the most authoritative account by any composer of the phenomenon which has puzzled many music-lovers and even a few musicologists – the discrepancy between an artist's mood or outward circumstances and his inner life. He begins by dividing works into two categories; firstly those composed on his own initiative and from inner creative necessity, and secondly those whose prompting comes from without, commissioned or requested works.

During the time when he is working, the artist must be completely calm. In this sense artistic creativity is always *objective*, even when it is musical. Those who think that a creative artist can, at the instant he is *moved*, by means of his talent use his art to express what he feels, are mistaken. The sad or happy feelings which he expresses are always, so to speak, *retrospective*. Without any special reason for rejoicing, I can be moved by a cheerful creative mood and, on the other hand, in the middle of happy circumstances a piece may be filled with dark and despairing feeling. In a word, the artist lives a double life: everyday human, and artistic; and moreover these two lives sometimes do not coincide. In any case, I repeat that for composition the main thing is to shake off for a while the cares of the first of these lives and devote oneself completely to the second . . .

For compositions belonging to the first category, not the least effort of will is demanded. It is enough to obey one's inner voice, and if the former of the two lives does not suppress with its depressing incidents the second, artistic one, then work progresses with absolutely unbelievable speed. Everything is forgotten, the spirit throbs with an absolutely unbelievably and inexpressibly sweet excitement, so that before one has time to follow this impulse *somewhere*, time has passed literally unnoticed. There is about this state something *somnambulistic*. *On ne s'entend pas vivre.* It is impossible to explain these moments to you. Everything that flows from the pen or merely remains in the head (for very often such moments occur at a time when there is nothing to write or think about) in these circumstances is always *good*, and if nothing, no outside interruption comes to arouse that other, normal life, it should turn out as the most complete achievement of which the artist is capable. Unfortunately, these outside interruptions are completely unavoidable. One has to do some job or other, one's called to dinner, a letter is delivered, etc. This is why there are so few compositions which are of equal musical quality throughout. From this comes the *seams, patches, unevennesses, discrepancies.*

For compositions in the second category one *sometimes* has to get oneself *attuned*. Here one must very often flee idleness, disinclination. Then there may be other chance circumstances. Sometimes victory is easily won. Sometimes inspiration vanishes, and is not recaptured. But I consider it an artist's *duty* never to give in, for laziness is a very powerful human trait. There is nothing worse than for an artist to give in to it. One must not wait about. Inspiration is a guest who does not like visiting the lazy. She comes to those who invite her . . .

I hope that you, my friend, will not suspect me of boasting if I tell you that my appeal to inspiration is almost never in vain. I can only tell you that that power, which I have called a capricious guest, has long become so familiar to me that we live our lives inseparably, and that she deserts me only when owing to circumstances oppressing my everyday life she feels herself superfluous. But scarcely has the cloud dispersed – there she is. Thus I can say that in a normal state of mind I am always composing, every minute of the day and in any circumstances. Sometimes I observe with curiosity this continuous work which, all on its own, apart from any conversation I may be having, apart from the people I am with at the time, goes on in that part of my head devoted to music. Sometimes this is the preparatory work, i.e. the polishing of details of some previously planned little piece, another time a completely new, independent musical idea appears, and I try to retain it in my memory. Where it comes from is an impenetrable mystery . . .

I write my sketches on the first piece of paper to hand, sometimes a scrap of notepaper. I write in an abbreviated form. A melody can never appear except with its attendant harmony. On the whole both these elements of music, together with the rhythm, are never separate from one another, i.e. every melodic idea brings with it its implied harmony and certainly its rhythmic structure. If the harmony is very complex, sometimes I note down a bass line, sometimes I mark figured bass signs, and in other cases I don't need a bass at all. It stays in my mind. As to instrumentation, if it is for orchestra, the musical idea appears already coloured by a certain scoring. Sometimes, though, the orchestration is changed from the original intentions. Words can *never* be written after the music, because if the music is written to a text, the text suggests the suitable musical expression. Of course it is possible to attach or adjust words to a little tune, but in a serious composition this kind of procedure is inconceivable . . .

Nor can one write a symphonic work and afterwards attach a programme to it, because here again every episode of the chosen programme evokes a corresponding musical illustration. This preliminary work, i.e. the sketch, is extremely pleasant, interesting, at times it provides quite indescribable delight, but at the same time it is accompanied by anxiety, a kind of nervous excitement. Sleep at this time is bad, sometimes one completely forgets to eat. But then the development of the project is done very peacefully and calmly. The scoring of a completely ripe work, one which has been worked out in the head to the last detail, is great fun. One cannot say as much about writing out works for piano, for a solo voice or for small pieces in general. This is sometimes boring . . .

You ask if I keep to established forms. Yes and no. There are certain kinds of composition which imply the use of familiar forms, for example *symphony*. Here I keep in general outline to the usual traditional forms, but only in general outline, i.e. the sequence of the work's movements. The details can be treated very freely, if this is demanded by the development of the ideas. For instance, in *our* symphony the first movement is written with very marked digressions. The second subject, which should be in the relative major, is minor and remote. In the recapitulation of the main part of the movement the second subject does not appear at all, etc. The finale, too, is made up of a whole row of deviations from individual forms . . .

Talking with you yesterday about the process of composition, I did not express myself clearly about that phase of work which follows the working out of the sketch. This phase is of prime importance. All that has been written in the heat of the moment must now be critically examined, corrected, augmented and especially contracted, as the form demands. Sometimes one must do oneself violence, be ruthless and brutal, i.e. completely chop up passages conceived with love and inspiration. Although I cannot complain of poverty of imagination or invention, I have nevertheless always suffered from lack of skill in manipulating form. Only with persistent hard work have I now achieved in my works form which more or less corresponds with content. In the past I was too careless, I was insufficiently aware of how important the critical scrutiny of sketches was. For this reason, the *seams* were always noticeable, there was a lack of organizing power in the sequence of separate episodes. This lack was crucial, and only with the years did I bit by bit remedy it, but *exemplary forms* my works will never be; I can only improve, not fully eradicate the essential characteristics of my musical make-up.

His talent, as he candidly describes it, is not therefore that of the born symphonist. The composers with the greatest ability to handle large abstract forms have always been gifted with the ability to invent themes whose full implications they may at first only sense. For Mozart the working out of the complete process of a movement was the act of composition, and the writing down of it so mechanical that he liked diversion while so doing. For Beethoven the process was, as is well known, one of strenuous mental wrestling with themes that needed much modification before they could be set to symphonic work, or might even turn out to be the creative substance of quite another work to that at first envisaged. Tchaikovsky's difficulties with form derive from the nature of the inspiration he describes in which the melody is paramount, and the working out something colder, more 'rational' and technical. For symphonic purposes the difficulty with a long and beautiful melody, completely expressive in itself, is that it will not be capable of much further development; whereas the short, vital themes which are generally the initial matter of a symphony by Beethoven or Mozart live in the creative process to which they are then subjected. What this forced upon Tchaikovsky was the need to repeat, modify and re-present his melodies in different guises and in contrasting situations, and the success with which he achieves this is the measure of his mastery of a process which he confessed did not come naturally to him; but it is a different matter from the instinct for active musical thought of the natural symphonist.

Yet with the last three of his six symphonies, Tchaikovsky wins his place in the history of music as one of the few composers who were able to impose their personality upon the symphony in the latter part of the nineteenth century and give the form new life. The reconciliation of the more personal, more dramatic and empirical forms and the heightened emotional statements that developed in Romanticism, with the classical structure of the symphony was a key crisis of the age, and was the fundamental cause of Brahms's hesitations over tackling symphony at all. For Tchaikovsky, already the author of three excellent but comparatively minor symphonies in which the concern for good form troubles his expression, there was a challenge which he may not specifically have recognized but which he was equipped to meet. For only when he was able to discover a method of putting his emotional life to work in large-scale abstract structures was he able to match his temperament fully to his talent; and in successfully doing so, he triumphantly enlarged the scope of his talent to its fullest potential. Out of the crisis that nearly wrecked his life in 1877 came the strengthened belief in himself as a composer, and with it came the still more powerful need for expression of what he had seriously come to believe was a personal Fate that dogged his life and would always wish upon him the most profound unhappiness.

Previously, in his Second Symphony, Tchaikovsky had tried making use of an introduction which would return in the course of the succeeding sonata movement.

But here, instead of a purely formal attempt at unity, he discovers the idea of giving his opening theme a specific, dramatic association, as he confided to Nadezhda von Meck.

> There *is* a programme to *our* symphony, i.e. there is the possibility of putting into words what it is trying to express, and to you, to you alone, I want to tell and can tell the meaning both of the whole and the separate sections. Be it understood, I am attempting this only in general terms.
>
> The introduction is the *seed* of the whole symphony, beyond question the main idea. This is *Fate*, the fatal force which prevents our hopes of happiness from being realized, which watches jealously to see that our bliss and peace are not complete and unclouded, which, like the Sword of Damocles, is suspended over the head and perpetually poisons the soul. It is inescapable and it can never be overcome. One must submit to it and to futile yearnings. The gloomy, despairing feeling grows stronger and more burning. Would it not be better to turn away from reality and plunge into dreams? O, joy! at last a sweet and tender vision appears. Some bright, gracious human form passes and beckons somewhere. How delightful! how remote now sounds the obsessive first theme of the Allegro. Little by little, dreams have completely enveloped the soul. All that was gloomy, joyless is forgotten. It is here, it is here, happiness!
>
> No! These were dreams, and *Fate* awakens us harshly. Thus, life is a perpetual alternation between grim reality and transient dreams and reveries of happiness. There is no haven. Drift upon that sea until it engulfs and submerges you in its depths. That, approximately, is the programme of the first movement.

For his Fate theme, Tchaikovsky sets down a battering figure on horns and bassoons that mercilessly emphasizes and re-emphasizes a single note before striding down a scale; and the notion that sonata form could be made the vehicle of his emotional life gives him the chance not only of some of his most vivid invention but of setting music in his most personal manner to work in a strong formal structure. The waltz, beloved by him as a graceful musical idea, can now assume a dramatic point as a *valse triste* for his first subject, hesitant, yielding ('futile yearnings'), falling and then rising up strongly as if to meet the challenge. It is a beautiful melody in its own right, and moreover a true embodiment of the character submitted to the attack of Fate, matching the vision of the glimpsed loved one in the song of this same period, 'In the clamour of the ballroom'. The 'dreams' or 'reveries' are, as one would expect, from the world of the ballet, represented by a delicate, dancing theme that introduces the vision of a beautiful human form, remote from the first theme in nature and not properly able to interact with it symphonically. But it is here that Tchaikovsky turns the deficiencies of his symphonic style to creative advantage; for in the essential separation of the two themes, each in turn subject to the constant intervention of Fate's battering, there is an expressive point about his own inability either to find comfort in escape or to avoid the sense of Fate besetting his life.

*The Von Meck estate at Brailov :* above *the entrance gates ;* below *the house*

The middle two movements pursue this subject with images of the sense of isolation that can be created by unhappiness in an extreme form.

> The second movement of the symphony expresses another phase of depression. This is that melancholy feeling which comes in the evening when one sits alone, tired from work, having picked up a book but let it fall from one's hands. A whole host of memories appears. And one is sad because so much is *gone*, *past*, and it is pleasant to remember one's youth. And one regrets the past, yet has no wish to begin to live all over again. Life wearies one. It is pleasant to rest and to reflect. One remembers much. There were happy moments when young blood pulsed and life was good. There were gloomy moments, too, irreplaceable losses. All that is indeed somewhere far off. And it is sad and somehow sweet to bury oneself in the past.

However much Tchaikovsky claimed that he relied on the *donnée* of a melody from some supernatural source, his symphonic melodies are beautifully matched to a larger expressive need. Here the mood is immediately set with a gentle oboe tune of no fewer than twenty bars of even, flowing notes, an apt musical image of the tired mind wandering without intent; the middle section, describing memories of the past, is a curious, remote little dance begun by clarinets and bassoons, and the return of the opening theme is accompanied by the little woodwind scales with which Tchaikovsky always liked to decorate his themes. The wandering of the mind in the next movement is brisker and more fanciful.

> The third movement does not express any definite sensations. It consists of capricious arabesques, elusive apparitions that pass through the imagination when one has drunk a little wine and feels the first stage of intoxication. The soul is neither merry nor gloomy. One is thinking of nothing; the imagination is liberated, and for some reason sets off painting strange pictures. Among them one remembers the picture of a roistering peasant and a street song. Then somewhere in the distance a military parade passes. These are completely disconnected images, like those which flit through one's head as one is falling asleep. They have nothing to do with reality; they are strange, wild and incoherent.

Here the first theme is, suitably, a brilliant flying tune, played by *pizzicato* strings, in which every nerve seems alert and pricking; the peasant has a wild, lurching little oboe theme which interferes with the formal strut of the military parade, and the outcome is a colourful jumble of all three elements. It seems as if there will here be sufficient encouragement to life:

> Fourth movement. If you find no cause for joy within yourself, look for it in others. Go to the people. Look, they know how to enjoy themselves, giving themselves up to undivided feelings of pleasure. A picture of festive popular rejoicing. Scarcely has one forgotten oneself and been carried away at the sight of someone else's pleasure than indefatigable *Fate* returns again and reminds you of yourself. But others pay no heed to you. They do not even turn round, they do not glance at you and do not notice how lonely and gloomy you are. Oh, how gay they are! how lucky they are that all their feelings are simple and spontaneous. Reproach yourself and do not say that all the world is sad. Simple but strong joys do exist. Rejoice in others' rejoicing. To live is still bearable.

So this Finale is whirled in on a note of hectic high spirits, introducing one of Tchaikovsky's beloved folksongs, 'In the fields there stood a birch', as witness of the power than could be contained in a simple melody of the people. As the festivities reach their climax, Fate thunders in, and seems to have silenced the music as the strings sink before it; but the village jollity returns and the symphony drives to a conclusion in the highest spirits.

For the first time in his output, then, Tchaikovsky has managed to absorb many elements of his style into a single symphonic experience – the love of dance, the folk music, the feeling for the atmosphere of the Russian people and countryside, the sense of Fate. To Taneyev's reproach that ballet music was out of place in a symphony, he merely replied that he could not see why; he refrained from pointing out to Taneyev the notion of escape which it represented, as he had explained to Nadezhda von Meck. In one sense, the entire symphony concerns escape, though it is a treatment of escape and not a demonstration of music as a refuge from reality, in the manner for which he had previously reproved Mme von Meck. Where the dance theme in the first movement deliberately represents a turning away from life into a world of illusion, and the impossibility of this as a solution, the two middle movements depict a different kind of musing with the back turned to reality; and the Finale is little else but a substantial effort at wishful thinking, an exteriorization of the personality described in the earlier movements so as to be capable of living to the full in the contented lives of the peasants. It would be truer for such a personality to find a cause of melancholy in the contrast between the happiness of simple people and the struggles of the sensitive observer; but Tchaikovsky was, as we have seen, absorbed at the time by *The Cossacks*, a copy of which he had chosen as a present from Tolstoy, and it is here that he may well have found an idea that contributed to his symphony. For though Olenin's attempt to escape from his troubles into the vigorous natural life of the Cossacks of the Caucasus proves a failure, he does return home with his own life set in a truer perspective; and the point would not have been lost on Tchaikovsky. The whole tone of his programme for the Finale suggests as much. Yet the authentic note is sounded in this Finale when Fate strikes the music down, and the feeling of manufacture which Tchaikovsky so despised is evident in the resuscitation of the peasant theme and its final jubilation. Fate, in fact, is not absorbed into the music but brushed aside, and the personality outlined in the first three movements has actually played no part whatever in this Finale. Yet however empty the triumph, there is an attempt to follow the consciously taken example of Beethoven's Fifth Symphony and to overthrow Fate; and if, as Tchaikovsky himself was the first to insist, he was no Beethoven, he achieved another kind of creative triumph in managing to rally his gifts and give them new power in what was the first of three magnificent subjective symphonies.

Continuing to fret about the future of his new symphony, Tchaikovsky turned nevertheless to the other major task that had been absorbing him during the months

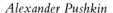

of his marriage and its crisis, and his subsequent return to creative activity – *Eugene Onegin*. A few days after dispatching the score of the symphony he had begun scoring the third act; and in a letter to Taneyev asking him to make a piano version of the symphony he also rejects suggestions that the opera seems to lack theatrical effect. Citing *Aida* again with some scorn, he dismisses the emotions of Egyptian princesses and pharaohs as lying so far outside his understanding that if he were to try to set them to music they would be as remote from human reality as a speech by Racine is remote from the real Orestes or Andromache. 'I do not want kings and queens, popular uprisings, battles, marches, in a word anything that belongs to grand opera. I am looking for an intimate but powerful drama on the conflict of circumstances which I have seen or experienced, and which can move me inwardly. I do not reject the element of fantasy . . .' Working at full stretch, he completed the scoring of *Onegin* on 1 February 1878.

   To his friends Tchaikovsky insisted as usual that the new opera was the finest he had yet written – he told Taneyev that the music came 'in the most literal sense from my innermost being' – but this time he was right. The starting point was his sympathy for Tatyana, compounded by the cruel coincidence of Antonina's approach to him, but soon his affection for the poem spread across its entire length and breadth. Tatyana herself, an enchanting creation whom Pushkin seems almost to take by the hand to introduce to us, had for him a particular poignancy in her appeal for love to the lofty Onegin; and Onegin, over-intelligent and under-emotional, one of the first 'superfluous men', proves to be a soul at war with himself, to understand with his mind less than Tatyana with her heart, to possess a nature potentially nobler than the behaviour which fate forces upon him. There was much here to fascinate Tchaikovsky. Like all his generation, he must have been delighted by the vivid picture of Russian life at all its levels, from the glittering St Petersburg ball to the homely images of the country people working in the fields or picking cherries, in the centre the life which Pushkin knew so well and which he had encountered at what he described in the fragmentary Chapter 10 as 'Kamenka's deep valleys', that of the civilized landowning class, remote from Moscow and prone to ennui but in touch both with the intelligentsia, whose visits would have been a welcome diversion to the menfolk and a pleasurable disturbance to the girls of the house, and with the ancient country life of Russia stretching far about them.

Russians have long regarded Pushkin as a national treasure, one which can never be fully shared with foreigners. There is, certainly, a subtlety of involvement with Russian life and history which the non-Russian can only watch from outside, and moreover a quality in the poetry which is found only in writers who have the command of a language in an ideal state of equilibrium, fully formed yet with the bloom of freshness still on it. More is lost in translation, one is assured, than with any other Russian writer; yet the merest beginner can at any rate sense his gift, comparable to that of Goethe and Shakespeare, for simple words, his delicate, elaborate use of alliteration and the actual sounds of Russian, the virtuoso command of alternating masculine and feminine rhymes that helps to make the intricate structure of *Onegin*'s stanzas at once tautly sprung and capable of a brilliant flexibility. Tchaikovsky was by no means alone in finding such poetry profoundly refreshing. There is no posturing, no gesticulating; and if Onegin himself has an obviously Byronic flavour as Romantic outsider, there is an un-Byronic economy in the poetry. The apparently casual framework, deriving from *Don Juan*, can include passages of acute observation, of intense lyrical beauty, of witty satire, of personal involvement on Pushkin's part alternating with ironic detachment, of charming and shrewd characterization – all at the service of a strong and moving narrative. The poem was the companion of Pushkin's finest creative years, and gave to the modern Russian language its crucial masterpiece, opening the way to the great tradition of imaginative literature. Tolstoy, Turgenev, Dostoyevsky, Gogol and all their generation acknowledged their allegiance to this 'novel in verse'; and of all Pushkin's creations *Onegin* remains the most cherished. Glinka himself, Dargomizhsky, Mussorgsky, Cui, Rakhmaninov, Nápravník, Rimsky-Korsakov and Stravinsky all wrote operas on works by Pushkin; but we may be grateful that *Eugene Onegin* was left to the composer whose talents were most true to it. For if the poem is as little

*Scenes from an early St Petersburg production of* Eugene Onegin

susceptible of an operatic treatment of all its riches as is, in a very different way, *Faust*, Tchaikovsky's 'lyrical scenes' admit us to its essential moments in a manner that might elude a more ambitious composer.

At the back of the libretto lies a feeling for the whole poem which makes a reading of one of the translations of Pushkin an illuminating preliminary to seeing the opera; but for all it is obliged to leave out, the libretto which Konstantin Shilovsky and Tchaikovsky drew up from the composer's original scenario is an intelligent compression of the poem into these 'lyrical scenes'.

ACT I, *Scene* I: In the garden of Mme Larina's country house, she and the old nurse Filipyevna are making jam, while inside her daughters Tatyana and Olga are singing a duet (taken from an early lyric of Pushkin's). When the peasants come with a decorated harvest sheaf, Tatyana reflects that their singing makes her thoughts fly far away, while Olga retorts that it simply makes her want to dance. Tatyana settles down with one of her romantic novels, attributing her sad looks to the story when her mother gently chides her and warns her that there are no real-life heroes. Olga's betrothed, Lensky, arrives, together with a friend from St Petersburg, Onegin. Onegin is surprised that Lensky should have chosen the lively but vapid Olga, while

Tatyana at once sees Onegin as the hero of whom she dreams and Olga observes her emotion with concern. Moving away together, Olga and Lensky are soon deep in each other's company; Onegin does not conceal his boredom with the country, but the deep impression he has made upon Tatyana is observed by Filipyevna. *Scene 2*: In Tatyana's bedroom Filipyevna is preparing her for the night; but Tatyana is restless, demands stories of Filipyevna's youth, and finally confesses to the confused old nurse that she is in love. Alone, she pours out her feeling in a long, passionate declaration of love in a letter to Onegin, assuring him that he is her ideal romantic hero and that she can never love anyone but him. By the time the letter is finished, dawn is breaking; to Filipyevna, astonished to find Tatyana awake and dressed, she gives the letter for Onegin. *Scene 3*: Peasants are gathering fruit in the garden, when Tatyana rushes in much confused at the prospect of the meeting arranged with Onegin. When he arrives, he explains kindly but firmly and somewhat loftily that though he was genuinely touched by her letter and its frankness, he must reply with equal frankness that he is not destined for marriage and can only think of her with the affection of a brother.

ACT 2, *Scene 1*: At Tatyana's birthday dance, Onegin waltzes with her but, bored with the occasion and irritated by some gossips speculating on their relationship, decides to stir matters up by insisting on dancing with Olga. Lensky is duly upset by this 'punishment' for having brought Onegin here, and when, after the old French tutor M. Triquet has sung some *couplets* in Tatyana's honour, he claims another dance, he and Lensky are soon quarrelling in earnest. Only when the enraged Lensky challenges him to a duel does Onegin realize that he has gone too far. *Scene 2*: By the banks of a stream early next morning, Lensky sadly awaits his opponent and muses on the love he had for Olga. He and Onegin regret their quarrel, but the conventions of the duel force them to go through with it and Lensky is killed.

ACT 3, *Scene 1*: At a ball in a fashionable house in St Petersburg, the guests are dancing a polonaise. Onegin, recently returned from lengthy travels abroad, is bored by the scene and unhappy at the lack of a wife and the death at his hand of his best friend; his whole life seems without meaning or purpose. When Prince Gremin arrives, he recognizes the Princess as Tatyana and is bewildered by her poise and grace; she in turn, on having it confirmed that he is indeed Onegin, is disturbed by old memories. The Prince, a relation of Onegin's, explains to him that he married Tatyana some two years ago, and that into his empty, simple life this beautiful girl has brought not only love but the reassurance that virtue and goodness can shine into the life of even a plain man such as himself. Tatyana and Onegin greet each other formally; but when she pleads tiredness and is taken home, Onegin realizes that he is deeply in love with her. *Scene 2*: Tatyana, much disturbed by Onegin's reappearance in her life, is awaiting him in her house. When he arrives and falls at her feet, she reminds him of how he once rejected her love: now she is married, and though she is compelled to admit that she does indeed still love him, she refuses to try to recall the past and to yield to Onegin's entreaties. It is her duty to leave him at once and forever. Onegin collapses in despair.

It was clearly by the character not of Onegin himself but of Tatyana that Tchaikovsky's affection was kindled. Though she lights the poem with her charm, it is

*Tatyana finishing her letter to Onegin*

Onegin who most engages Pushkin's interest; for Tchaikovsky, Onegin was merely unsympathetic and remote, a chilly intellectual whose complexity did not really absorb him and whose repudiation of love he found despicable. Long before the coincidence of Antonina's approach, he was haunted by the idea of Tatyana pouring out her love in a letter, risking herself in an impetuous action and meeting with a rebuff from calculation and coldness; and it was the famous Letter Scene which he set first (and may have contemplated some time previously as a song). Describing her as sad, silent and timid as a deer, Pushkin also uses of her the word *diki*, whose first meaning is 'wild' but can also mean shy, natural rather than acclimatized to society, and in this context suggests her detachment from the routine of life going on around her. She has little contact with her family or with other children, and is beautifully drawn as a girl whose real life is in her emotions and imagination, which are formed by the fashionable 'sensibility' of the English novels over which she pores. Tchaikovsky begins by suggesting this romantic isolation from the exuberant Olga and the bustle of family life, and it is only when she is left alone with Filipyevna that the impression of a gentle, somewhat raw yet mysterious charm begins to be filled out. To the old nurse, she is at first hesitant, and the music of the opening part of the scene brilliantly sketches the repressed excitement and warmth as she questions Filipyevna about her own marriage, before venturing that she herself is in love: the music here beautifully responds to the implications in the gradually increased weight which Pushkin places on the repeated words, 'in love'. Filipyevna had merely been given as a village girl to a suitable man whom she accepted as her lot, and Mme Larina, another devoted reader of Richardson, has never quite forgotten her own equivalent of Sir Charles Grandison, the dashing young ensign whom she renounced for the husband her father selected. Both the old women have grown contented; but the times are different, and Tatyana is less placid.

As the Letter Scene proper begins, Tatyana's warmth burgeons into the excitement of actually committing herself to telling her love to Onegin; but it is, after several false starts, when she comes to ask, 'Who are you – my guardian angel or an evil tempter?', that Tchaikovsky unfolds the ravishing theme, a soft, almost shy falling scale on the oboe with a warm answering phrase on horns, which is the heart of the opera and which returns whenever the vision of this ideal love is held up. Not as deliberate reference, nor even as a Leitmotiv set subtly to work, but more as the essential musical gesture to which a composer will only half-consciously refer, it suffuses the invention of the opera with its warmth. When Tatyana becomes the dignified Princess Gremin, Tchaikovsky's touch with her is less sure – until she is alone and able to reveal her fundamentally unchanged character in the poignant scene when she cannot prevent herself from disclosing her love to Onegin. Tatyana, so Tchaikovsky told his friends, was for him a real person; she possessed the centre of his imaginative life; she is the projection of his longing to be able to experience a woman's love, and so she has the warmest and most intimate of his lyrical invention.

Beside Tatyana, Onegin is remote and aloof, somewhat blank as in Pushkin, a character who in the opera lives more by contrast with the warmth of Tatyana and Lensky, the liveliness of Olga, the simple good nature of the Larins and their provincial friends, and the gruff humility of Gremin than by any very marked characteristics of his own. Musically he is painted as reserved, only in the last scene passionate and despairing; and so far from being a failure of portraiture, this approach serves Tchaikovsky's purpose of indicating his lack of any true emotional centre until he comes too late to recognize where it should lie. It is with Lensky that Tchaikovsky

really sympathizes: simple by comparison with Onegin, he is direct, kindly, more of a romantic and a poet than in Pushkin but affectionate and patient until he is provoked by Onegin and, like all weak men trying to act with strength, goes fatally too far. Possibly, had he survived the duel, his romantic ardour would have cooled before Olga's charming but superficial and too realistic nature; certainly in Pushkin she is not slow to marry another. Lensky's own character is not yet fully developed, which is one reason for his admiration of Onegin. Of the other characters it is certainly Gremin who most stirred Tchaikovsky's heart: his aria has no equivalent in Pushkin, but there is the authentic note in this picture of a sturdy old veteran, with no illusions about his own charms, amazed and humbled that it should be him whom the enchanting Tatyana has taken as husband.

Yet much of Tchaikovsky's success with these characters lies not only in his understanding of them in Pushkin's poem, but in his recognition of them as figures in a Russia to which he himself belonged. It is their milieu that has formed them and coloured their nature and actions. They are neither figures in an historical pageant with emotions remote from his, nor (as even in *Vakula*) Russian peasants and nobles vividly illustrated and contrasted but seen essentially as types: they are real human beings in a real landscape, familiar and well understood. The folksongs which Tchaikovsky loved can be used in Act I not merely as local colour but to suggest the rural life of the Larins into which Onegin comes, and the simple device of a shepherd piping to suggest the dawn acquires a peculiarly Pushkinesque freshness and bite after the heady outpourings that have occupied Tatyana's night. His beloved dance rhythms play a still more crucial part, for there is a powerful and indeed ironic contrast between the two ball scenes, between the courtly grace of the St Petersburg ball with its cosmopolitan Polonaise and Ecossaise, and the country-house birthday dance for Tatyana where the old men and women fuss and gossip on the crowded fringes while the young people leap and turn and stamp, to a captivating waltz whose earthy bounce is homely and comfortable. Tchaikovsky can even make a brief gesture to his beloved rococo with a charming little vignette, shrewdly placed between Onegin's two provocations of Lensky at the dance, when the old Frenchman living in the neighbourhood, M. Triquet, advances to sing his trim *couplets* in Tatyana's honour.

For all his belief in the work, Tchaikovsky was doubtful whether his 'lyrical scenes' would ever make their way on the stage. To Taneyev and Albrecht he wrote asserting that as far as success was concerned, 'I spit, spit, spit on the whole business.' But to Nadezhda von Meck he confided his fears that the emotions which had moved him would pass by all but a few choice spirits, and the work fail for its lack of the conventional scenic effect and action. He even seems to have feared seeing characters in whom he had vested so much emotion being subjected to the usual wear and tear of the opera house.

> Where shall I find the Tatyana whom Pushkin imagined and whom I have tried to illustrate musically? Where is the artist who can even faintly approach the ideal Onegin, this cold dandy penetrated to the marrow with worldly *bon ton?* Where on earth is there a Lensky, an eighteen-year-old youth with the thick curls, the impetuous and individual manner of a young poet à la Schiller? How Pushkin's captivating picture will be vulgarized when it is transferred to the stage with its routine, its senseless traditions, its veterans of both sexes who, without any shame, take on, like Alexandrova, Kommisarzhevsky and *tutti quanti*, the roles of sixteen-year-old girls and beardless youths!

Perhaps he also feared the reaction to his treatment, to any treatment, of so well loved a classic. When Turgenev, who once said that he would give both his little fingers for a single line of *Eugene Onegin*, wrote to Tolstoy praising the music, especially the lyrical passages, he added, 'But what a libretto!' Not for some years was there full appreciation of the nature of Tchaikovsky's achievement in capturing for the musical stage a subtle and many-sided masterpiece of literature. If the year of his marriage and the ensuing disaster brought Tchaikovsky to his lowest physical and mental ebb, nearly destroying him, it was at the same time the period in his imaginative life in which with the Fourth Symphony and *Eugene Onegin* he rose to full stature as a creative artist.

Certainly now that both works were safely on their way from Italy to Moscow, his spirits rose with the feeling of solid achievement. He went to the local opera, finding little to impress him, but took great pleasure in country walks, in rides on donkey-back to remote hill churches, in the Italian spring countryside. He declared to his friends that he had been on the verge of madness, and that he owed his sanity

*Modest Tchaikovsky*

to his brothers Modest and Anatoly and to Nadezhda von Meck. She, profiting by the return of this equanimity, embarked upon discussions about philosophy and love, even boldly asking him about his own love life. Whether or not she was inviting a real confession, he replied guardedly yet emphatically and without lying to her.

> You ask, my friend, if I have experienced *non-platonic love. Yes and no*. If this question were put slightly differently, i.e. asking if I have known complete happiness in love, the answer would be: *No, no and no!!!* However, I think that it is in my music that the answer to your question lies. If you asked me if I have understood the whole power, the whole immeasurable strength of this feeling, the answer would be: *Yes, yes and yes*, reiterating that I have passionately tried more than once to express in music the agony and at the same time ecstasy of love. Whether I have succeeded in this, I do not know or, rather, I leave to others to judge. I completely disagree with you that music *cannot fully communicate one's feelings of love*. I hold the complete contrary, that *only music alone can* achieve this. You say that *words* are necessary. Oh, no! Words alone are not enough, and where they are powerless there appears fully armed a more eloquent language, i.e. music. That verse form to which poets resort to express love is a usurpation of that territory belonging wholly to music. *Words* confined to the form of poetry cease to be simply *words*: they become music . . . Your observation that words often merely harm music, dragging it down from unscalable heights, is absolutely true. I have always felt it deeply, and that is perhaps why I have succeeded better with instrumental works than with vocal.

News of the Fourth Symphony's tepid reception was tactfully relayed to Tchaikovsky: a telegram from Rubinstein and others laconically reported its performance, without comment, and another from Nadezhda von Meck was more cordial, but it was some time before he discovered that a poor performance had hindered appreciation of what was in any case a more substantial and problematic work than the Moscow public was used to. It was Nadezhda von Meck's own puzzled curiosity that led to the exchange already quoted in which he gave full details of his intentions. Back in Florence early in March, he sought out a boy street singer who had previously captivated him with songs whose tragic nature sounded especially poignant on the lips of a ten-year-old; a new tune, which he sent to Mme von Meck, became his song 'Pimpinella'. From Florence he, Modest, Kolya Konradi and Alexey Sofronov travelled by way of Geneva to Clarens, where he found Kotek with news of the Fourth Symphony. They played through much new music; but the real task in hand was composition – a piano sonata, plans for some songs and, since Kotek was at hand to give advice, work on a violin concerto. At the beginning of April they played through the first movement, and within two days Kotek had mastered the work so well that he could, Tchaikovsky said, have given a performance of it. However, they were all, the composer included, dissatisfied with the Andante; and this was duly replaced with the present movement.

As with the First Piano Concerto, Tchaikovsky opens with a melody that he subsequently abandons: his fondness for atmospheric introductions was becoming an organic part of the symphonies with his Fate motives, but here the intention seems to be simply to present the violin, before the main musical action, with the lyrical character it retains throughout all that follows. Both the principal themes of his first movement are tender and eloquent in nature, and the virtuoso elements of the concerto are on the whole left to connecting passages and to the decoration of these themes; even the cadenza is designed as further enhancement of the two themes rather than as a piece of pure display. This design naturally imposes the most demonstrative role upon the orchestra, and leads to some rather strenuous scoring in the attempt to provide sufficient dramatic contrast; but it is seldom that Tchaikovsky's hand fails him in keeping the violin at the front of the musical action without demanding of it a more extrovert nature than is suggested by the substance of the music.

With the Canzonetta that replaced the original Andante he can turn towards the pure song which the title implies; and with his usual sense of key-structure, he improves his effect by flattening the tonality instead of maintaining that of the first movement. The link to the Finale is ingeniously devised; and with its arrival he at last allows the violin to exteriorize its character into a cheerful little folk-like theme. The Russian element is strong here, both with the almost Cossack abandon of the opening tune and the village bagpipe effect of a second tune. For all the exuberance of the dance, it is not display but the varied, entertaining and colourful presentation of the original lyrical idea which is the essence of the movement, sustaining to the end this aspect of the violin's character.

Doubtless it was the feeling that a good deal else had been left out of account in the writing of a complete virtuoso concerto which led to Leopold Auer, to whom it was dedicated when Kotek withdrew, declaring it impossible to play. It was not until 1888 that Adolf Brodsky introduced the work, in Vienna, where it caused an uproar in the hall. Hanslick, who was by no means wholly unsympathetic to Tchaikovsky, went so far as to declare that the work proved that music could actually give off a bad smell. Auer, following Rubinstein's example with the First Piano Concerto, later repented of his judgment and became one of its greatest interpreters.

As the time approached for the return to Russia, so Tchaikovsky's apprehensions increased. Restored in health and in spirits, he nevertheless disliked the idea of renewing the drudgery of teaching, and especially he feared the necessity of facing up to the whole question of Antonina and the divorce. He was also much cast down by the progress of the Russo-Turkish War, finding himself and his country the objects of suspicion or open dislike wherever he went. Despite his refusal to identify himself with the conscious Russianizing of the *Kuchka*, he shared to the full his countrymen's intense patriotism and their long-enduring sensitivity towards the West, with its longer artistic traditions and its tendency, real or imagined, to regard Russians as barbarians off the steppes. Too subtle and complete an artist to approve of achieving a national art by massive injections of folksong, he none the less retained all his life a strong feeling for his origins, as he told Nadezhda von Meck that March.

> As regards the Russian *elements* in my works, I assure you that I often set about matters with the full intention of somehow or other working into a composition a folksong that I like. Sometimes (as for instance in the finale of our symphony) this comes of its own accord, completely unexpectedly. On the whole, as far as the Russian element in my music is concerned, i.e. the relationship between the national songs and my melodies and harmonies, this is because I grew up in the backwoods, from earliest childhood saturated with the indescribable beauty of the characteristic traits of Russian folk music, because I passionately love their Russian element in all its manifestations, because, in a word, I am *Russian* in the fullest sense of the word.

This is volunteered in the course of a letter in which he attempts to satisfy her continuing curiosity about his methods of work; and here he amplifies his original remarks about the necessity of inspiration.

> Don't believe those who tell you that musical composition is a cold and rational pursuit. The only music which can touch, disturb and move us is that which flows from the depths of an artistic soul when it is stirred by inspiration. There is no doubt that even the greatest musical geniuses have sometimes worked when not fired by inspiration. It is like a guest who does not always respond to the first invitation. Meanwhile, it is necessary always to *work*, and a really genuine artist must not sit with arms folded on the pretext that he is not in the mood. If we wait for the *mood* and do not try to go to meet it, we easily sink into *idleness and apathy*. It is necessary to have patience and faith, and inspiration will inevitably appear to him who can overcome his *disinclination*. This happened to me only

*The Battle of Karahassankoi*
*the Russo-Turkish W*

today. I told you a few days ago that I was working every day without enthusiasm. It cost me an effort not to give in to the reluctance to work, when I should probably have done nothing for a long time. But faith and patience have never failed me, and this morning I was struck by that inexplicable and unfathomable glow of inspiration of which I told you and thanks to which I know in advance that all I write today will have the quality of touching the heart and leaving an impression there. I hope you will not suspect me of boastfulness if I say that this *disinclination* I mentioned to you very seldom happens to me. I put this down to the fact that I am gifted with patience and have trained myself never to give in to *reluctance*. I have learned to master myself.

If Tchaikovsky is here perhaps painting his working methods in bold colours for Nadezhda von Meck's benefit, encouraging her to feel that even as he wrote to her the fire of inspiration had descended but must wait until he had finished his letter, it is still a consistent account of his patience. He became increasingly a man of habit as he grew older, not merely with the fussiness about routine of the middle-aged bachelor, but as a discipline designed best to encourage the working of his invention. Even though he was flattered by her passionate interest in the processes of his mind, and felt obliged by the terms of their relationship to answer her questionings as fully as he could, he was careful not to let her be misled by sentimental notions about the composer's art. Much of what he wrote to her over the years is, as he well knew, exaggerated and over-emotional; but about his own craft he was always sincere, and did much to lead her gently away from her more extreme illusions. When she sent him a panegyric comparing him favourably to Mozart, he did not snub her but replied with a warm appreciation of the chamber music and especially of his first musical love, *Don Giovanni*. Nurtured on the nineteenth-century view of Mozart as a piece of Dresden china, she could not understand his enthusiasm, not least since temperamentally the two composers seemed so far apart.

You say that my worship of him is contrary to my musical nature, but perhaps it is just because as a child of my time I am broken, morally sick, that I search Mozart's music, which for the most part reveals that exceptional joy in life which was part of a nature

sound, unified and *not disrupted by introspection*, for calm and consolation. On the whole it seems to me that in an artist's soul his creative ability is completely independent of his sympathy with this or that master. It is possible to love Beethoven, for instance, and by nature be closer to Mendelssohn.

To depress him further as he returned to take up his real life, the news from home was bad. The Russian spring, that violent annual miracle which has set up such powerful reverberations in Russian art, had turned the roads into swamps; typhus had closed the schools in St Petersburg, and diphtheria and smallpox were rife in Moscow, wrote Nadezhda von Meck, so that the streets were littered with uncollected refuse and her house stank of carbolic; and the collapse of the war with Turkey into an undignified peace served to create a mood of disillusionment in which the briefly silenced revolutionary movement broke out with renewed strength. Tchaikovsky, a monarchist more by temperament than from serious political conviction, was distressed at the state of affairs, but continued to hope that the Tsar might grant liberal measures. A letter from Anatoly described the student riots, and sympathetic as he could not help being to the incident when Vera Zasulich fired at the brutal General Trepov, to be acquitted by the jury and then rescued from re-arrest by the mob, Tchaikovsky feared for what would happen if the young intelligentsia really captured the leadership of the people. It was a new 'Time of Troubles', with public riots, disturbances in prisons and a wave of violence and assassination attempts from organized student groups who now had terrorism preached by their leaders as the only means of achieving their ends.

Tchaikovsky had nevertheless expected to feel what he described as 'strong and sweet sensations' on his return to Russia. But trouble at the frontier with tiresome customs men and a drunken passport official, together with the discomfort of the crowded train, spoiled any pleasure he might have had. He was, moreover, nervous at how Alexandra would now receive him. He need not have worried: he was immediately calmed by the warmth of her welcome, and, her house being full, he settled contentedly into a room she had taken for him nearby complete with a piano, a pretty garden and a pleasant view of the river. By the end of April he was able to write to Nadezhda von Meck with the news that his Piano Sonata was finished. It is not one of his successes: the large gestures come to seem merely grandiose gesticulating, the form somewhat manufactured, the nature of the ideas derived from something less than real conviction. The piano was never for him so natural an instrument as the orchestra, with its array of colours and effects in which his thought naturally moved. Faced with an extended work for the single instrument, he was bereft of the opportunity for the drama and effect that encouraged his most vivid and personal ideas, while the necessity to construct a strong piece of abstract formal thought was for him a positive discouragement to inspiration. He was more successful with the genre pieces of two other piano works upon which he was engaged at the time, the charming and sometimes touching trifles of the *Children's Album*,

*Tchaikovsky's nieces,*
*Natalya and Vera Davidova*

and the *Twelve Pieces of Moderate Difficulty*, which include the well-known 'Chanson Triste'. The last, 'Interrupted Reverie', is a souvenir of Venice, where he would overhear from his hotel room a street singer with his daughter; the effect pleased him so much that he included an abbreviated version in the *Children's Album*. With these deft little sketches, colouring a brief idea or evoking some fugitive mood, he is more in his element than with the large-scale construction of the sonata.

From Kamenka, Anatoly returned to Moscow largely with the intention of pushing forward his brother's divorce proceedings. Antonina had meanwhile recovered herself sufficiently to make herself a nuisance to the family with her importunate or abusive letters. Nadezhda von Meck, worried by the situation and by the gossip that was circulating, urged a speedy financial settlement, with Rubinstein using his influence as a go-between; and when the matter hung fire, with Tchaikovsky hesitating at Kamenka while his anxieties began piling up once more, she offered him her house at Brailov for a few weeks. Gratefully, Tchaikovsky accepted. To Modest he wrote a coolly appreciative account of the estate, finding the grounds less attractive than the house; but to Mme von Meck he pitched his enthusiasm high, waxing lyrical over the beauty of the garden, describing himself walking in its shady paths, picking mushrooms, lying in the green undergrowth watching the birds and insects. He toyed with her harmonium, enjoyed the excellent food and service, and wrote to her daily with the account he felt she would wish of his life in her house. He contemplated a *Romeo and Juliet* opera, completed his *Liturgy of St John Chrysostom* which he had planned earlier in the year, and added to the original Andante of the Violin Concerto two other minor pieces which he offered to his absent hostess as *Souvenir d'un Lieu Cher*. On 7 June he wrote to Modest, 'I played the whole of *Eugene Onegin* from beginning to end. The author was the sole listener. I am half ashamed of what I am going to confide to you in secret: the listener was moved to tears, and paid the composer a thousand compliments. If only the audiences of the future will feel towards this music as the composer himself does!' Four days later he left for Moscow.

# The Mature Composer
## 1879–84

Restored in health and in spirit by his long absence, and with two works of genius, the Fourth Symphony and *Eugene Onegin*, composed in the aftermath of the crisis, Tchaikovsky should have been returning to Moscow in the mood of a conqueror. Yet no sooner had he arrived than he found himself once more enmeshed in difficulties. He was nervous of facing Nikolay Rubinstein; as ill luck would have it, Rubinstein's birthday was being celebrated that week and there was no escaping the courtesy, observed with particular strictness in Russia, of calling and of joining in the birthday party. It proved an awkward occasion. Tchaikovsky was warmly welcomed by his friends after his eight months' absence, but in Rubinstein's eyes he read (or thought he read) disapproval for his rejection of the appointment as delegate to Paris. Obviously he was rather guilty about the episode, and knew that in any case Rubinstein did not take his prolonged nervous illness very seriously; but it also seems that, like many autocrats, Rubinstein did not care for people refusing his

kindnesses. 'He does not like those who do not feel in his debt,' Tchaikovsky told Nadezhda von Meck; 'he would prefer everybody around to be regarded as his creations.'

Far worse than the embarrassment of meeting Rubinstein were the troubles with the divorce. From the birthday party he had to go to see the Clerk of the Consistory, and was appalled at the corrupt farce to which he seemed obliged to subject himself in order to obtain the necessary papers. A confrontation with Antonina was part of the ritual; but she never appeared, and could not be found. Already reduced to a state of nerves by the strain, he retreated to Lev Davidov's estate at Verbovka, near Kamenka, leaving matters in the hands of the faithful Jürgenson. When Antonina was eventually run to earth, she merely told Jürgenson that she did not fancy a divorce after all; she now believed herself the victim of a complicated plot, with Jürgenson a disguised lawyer and Tchaikovsky's family and Rubinstein conspirators who had planned the divorce before the marriage had even taken place. When she declared that if the matter were brought to court she would deny Tchaikovsky's 'adultery' – the only grounds for divorce in Russia at the time – Jürgenson saw that he dared not call the bluff: he must have had at any rate strong suspicions about the real reasons for the marriage's impossibility, and was too loyal a friend to risk what might, with a woman of Antonina's unbalanced temperament, prove a major public scandal. Tchaikovsky was forced to write to Nadezhda von Meck declining her offer of sufficient money to pay for the divorce; a third of that, he learned from Antonina, would be sufficient to persuade her to leave Moscow while a regular allowance was arranged. For her part, Mme von Meck was no doubt relieved to forget about Antonina, and to pass from even the topic of Tchaikovsky's health, about which he always supplied her with lavish detail, to the subject about which she could never have enough information – his methods of working. But when he gave her the full

ove *Tchaikovsky with some of his relations. The photograph includes (seated, left to right) composer, Nikolay, Lev and Alexandra Davidov, and Anatoly*

*Tchaikovsky's father in old age*

Opposite *The Nevsky Prospekt in the centre of St Petersburg*

accounts, together with a description of all the tension involved, which have already been quoted, she wrote in some alarm begging him not to overstrain himself. His reply was that only in his work did he feel himself fully a man: he admitted his tendency to laziness, his hypochondria, but he insisted that it was only in the work he sometimes had to force himself to do that he really had his existence.

From Verbovka, Tchaikovsky went on to Brailov where he worked on the sketches of his First Suite; then, pausing in Kamenka for a few days, he travelled north in mid-September to St Petersburg. Part of the purpose of his visit was to see his father and Anatoly; he also discussed plans for the future, and returning to Moscow took his first class of the new term at the Conservatory. At the beginning of October, Nikolay Rubinstein returned from Paris, and at the dinner given in his honour he paid generous tribute to Tchaikovsky and to the great success his music had won in the Russian concerts (one of which Nadezhda von Meck had attended). It was an embarrassing scene, the more so since Tchaikovsky had finally made up his mind on a course of action which he went to explain to Rubinstein the following morning: he had decided to leave the Conservatory. Having found a replacement, he was even able to detach himself sooner than the end of the term. After a farewell dinner which Rubinstein, Albrecht, Kashkin, Taneyev and Jürgenson gave him on 19 October, he left for St Petersburg; and three weeks later he was back at Kamenka.

This time, however, Kamenka was only a temporary halt. He found the calm, after the strain of severing his connections with Moscow, conducive to work, and sketched the last two movements of the First Suite. To his dismay he found that he had left the earlier movements in St Petersburg. His real destination was to be Florence, where Nadezhda von Meck was herself staying and where she now tele-graphed to say she had rented a flat for him. They planned the visit carefully: he was welcomed with a cordial note that included the times of her morning walks so that he could avoid her, and replied with enthusiastic praise for the comfort and the peaceful conditions for work. Once, it chanced, they did meet face to face, for the first time, though the short-sighted Mme von Meck seems not to have realized it; and subsequently they saw each other in the distance at musical functions; but they never spoke, and tried to avoid one another despite the warm comments they exchanged by post about each other's appearance and behaviour. News of the Fourth Symphony's triumph in St Petersburg cheered him; he worked on scoring those parts of the suite that he had with him; he gave lessons to her current domestic violinist, Vladislav Pakhulsky; but the real task in hand was a Joan of Arc opera, to be based on Schiller's *Die Jungfrau von Orleans*. On learning of this Nadezhda von Meck sent him Henri-Alexandre Wallon's *Jeanne d'Arc*, which moved him to tears. Visiting Paris briefly with the idea of doing some research on Joan of Arc for the opera, he travelled on to Clarens, where he settled in to the Villa Richelieu on 7 January 1879 to concentrate on the opera.

Using Zhukovsky's translation of Schiller, Tchaikovsky began work upon his own libretto, groaning at the difficulty of finding suitable rhymes and of fitting the right words together. Each evening he wrote as much of the text as he felt he could set to music next morning, keeping in his head the general design of the whole work. Not even the unexpected arrival of the missing sketches of the First Suite distracted him. For relaxation he read *Little Dorrit* in translation, conquering with difficulty the temporary dislike of all things English which had been inspired in him by Disraeli's handling of the situation in the aftermath of the Russo-Turkish War. 'Have you read this work of genius?' he asked Anatoly. 'Dickens and Thackeray are the only single people I forgive for being English. I should go on to add Shakespeare, but he was of a time when this vile nation had not yet sunk so low.' Work on *The Maid of Orleans* absorbed him totally, and as always he was swept with the enthusiastic conviction that he was composing his operatic masterpiece. On 18 February he arrived in Paris, continuing to work hard at the opera and going out only to a few

concerts; he avoided even Turgenev, explaining to Nadezhda von Meck that, as in the case of his acquaintanceship with Tolstoy, he only really enjoyed the company of close friends and found that in most cases the books or music of famous people were more interesting than their personalities. On 5 March he finished *The Maid of Orleans.*

Though Tchaikovsky based his text chiefly on Zhukovsky, retaining some of the original Russian verses, he also drew on Wallon's book, on Auguste Mermet's libretto for his own opera for the opening scene and on Jules Barbier's tragedy for the Finale (Verdi's opera, which he had got hold of, he thought 'extremely bad'). He abandoned Schiller's dénouement, with Joan escaping from her captors and meeting a glorious end on the battlefield, though shortly before his death he was contemplating yielding to Modest's insistence that this would be better; and he devised for himself a libretto that fell quite neatly into four acts.

> ACT I: In the square before the church, Joan and the village girls are decorating a sacred oak. Her father Thibaut presses her to marry Raimund, who loves her. When she insists that she is destined for a different fate, Thibaut reproves her for consorting with evil spirits. Villagers fleeing the marauding English appear, and one of them, Bertrand, laments the miserable state of France. Joan prophesies the defeat of the English and announces that Salisbury is already killed; the villagers are astonished to have this vision confirmed by a soldier newly arrived from Orleans. Alone, she realizes that her hour is at hand and, supported by her angel voices, she bids farewell to her home.
>
> ACT 2: In the Castle of Chinon, the King, with Agnes Sorel and Dunois, is being entertained by minstrels' songs and the dances of gypsies and jesters. In spite of Dunois's urging, the King refuses to leave Agnes and join battle with the English. Lauret,

*The coronation procession and Joan of Arc from Act 3 of* The Maid of Orleans

wounded, is brought in with news of another defeat, and dies. Agnes consoles the King. Suddenly the crowd is heard hailing a victory by a 'saviour maid' who has taken command of the French army. Joan appears and, picking out the King from his courtiers, tells him his secret prayers and relates her own story. She is acclaimed as an emissary of heaven.

ACT 3, *Scene* 1: Close to the English camp near a battlefield, the Burgundian knight Lionel is being pursued by Joan. She defeats him, but when she sees his face lit up by the moon, she spares him; and they find themselves falling in love. When Dunois appears, Lionel surrenders to him and joins the King; Joan faints from her wounds. *Scene* 2: As the coronation procession leaves Rheims Cathedral, Thibaut denounces Joan as an agent of hell; she feels unable to protest her purity because of her guilty love for Lionel. When he steps forward to defend her innocence thunder rings out. The people believe it to be the voice of heaven; Joan is banished from Rheims, and repudiates Lionel as the cause of her ruin.

ACT 4, *Scene* 1: Sitting in a wood, deserted by her family, the King and the people, Joan admits her love for Lionel. He now appears, but their reunion is interrupted by angel voices declaring that Joan will atone for her sin by suffering and death. English soldiers appear, kill Lionel and seize Joan. *Scene* 2: Crowds are gathered in the square in Rouen; shouts of sympathy for Joan are heard. Seeing the pyre prepared for her, she momentarily loses her courage, but she is strengthened and blessed by the priest. The fire is lit.

It was to the character of Joan herself that Tchaikovsky was attracted above all here. Wallon's book had aroused in him an 'infinite sorrow for all mankind'; and just as it was around Tatyana's Letter Scene that the whole of *Eugene Onegin* had grown, so from the Act 2 scene of Joan's narrative and her acclamation came the whole of *The Maid of Orleans*. Yet touched as he was by her fate, and moved more deeply by her example as a heroic, misunderstood figure brought to destruction by her guilty love, he was unable to enter very fully into her emotional life. Her farewell at the end of Act 1, the only portion of the opera to have survived in the repertory as an occasional concert item, is fine, if less characteristic than the Act 2 scene. There are some attractive strokes to suggest the fundamentally simple girl caught up in a complex and powerful set of forces. But all that makes her more than this eludes him altogether, and even in this aspect of her he cannot do much to give her any individuality, any exceptional quality of the kind that drew men to her leadership. She is too distant from his understanding, and he would have done well to have heeded his own advice about the remote feelings of Egyptian princesses when contemplating *Onegin* before he gave himself to the subject. 'Medieval dukes and knights and ladies captivate my imagination but not my *heart*,' he once said, 'and where the heart is not touched there can't be any music.' The dukes and knights in *The Maid of Orleans* are but empty suits of armour.

Since he managed to make so little of the character of Joan, his devotion to the idea of the opera may seem hard to understand. Probably the answer lies in the new situation in which he now found himself. He had recently severed his professional ties with Russia, and was living abroad with no immediate plans to find a permanent home of his own. He was forever drawn to opera as a medium, but found little encouragement in Germany, whose opera was in any case associated too closely with Wagner for his taste; and however much he loved Italy and sensed his Russian operatic roots to lie there, he was unsympathetic to Italian opera even in the hands of Verdi. Yet just before leaving Russia he had learned of the recent triumph of his music in Paris. French music was an old love and a powerful formative influence in his art; perhaps he had his eyes on a success in the country of his beloved *Carmen*. Certainly *The Maid of Orleans*, even apart from its French subject, shows every sign of one of the most pervasive but treacherous of all nineteenth-century operatic influences, that of Meyerbeer. Here are the familiar crowd effects, the grandiose coronation, the processions, the culmination in a scene that would make a tremendous spectacle on the vast stage of the Opéra. There is even the essential French condition of a long Act 2 ballet neatly fulfilled; while some of the gentler lyrical passages reflect Tchaikovsky's often expressed admiration for Massenet – whose pale lyricism he sometimes reflects here – and even for Gounod. *Faust* was an opera he deeply respected, and which influenced him not least in its ballet music, though he told Taneyev that *Polyeucte* was, 'the worst opera I have ever seen'; not until 1889 does he seem to have heard *Roméo et Juliette*, a work whose remarkable qualities might have impressed him when he came to write a love duet for his own projected opera on the subject later that year. Yet hardly was *The Maid of Orleans* completed than he was toying with another operatic subject, this time wholly Russian, Pushkin's *Poltava*; and he does not seem to have retained very powerful loyalties for the work. Of all his half-forgotten operas, *The Maid* is the one that most deserves its neglect.

Tchaikovsky remained in Paris for only about a week more. The day after finishing the opera, *The Tempest* was due to be played at one of Colonne's concerts. It was not a success, and though upset by the poor reception and by the superior smile on the faces of some of the orchestral players, he blamed himself for the work's failure, reproaching himself in a generous note to Colonne for the music's diffuseness of form while praising the excellence of the performance. Within a few days he had left for home; and though delayed for a while in Berlin – he had overspent on clothes and other luxuries in Paris, and had to wait for the arrival of funds from Nadezhda von Meck before he could pay his hotel bill – he was in St Petersburg by soon after the middle of March. Hardly had he reached home when he was summoned to Moscow. *Eugene Onegin* was in rehearsal for its performance by students of the Conservatory. The soloists might have been better, the composer felt, but he had only praise for the chorus and the orchestra. Nikolay Rubinstein declared that he had fallen completely in love with the music, and Taneyev, trying to express his enthusiasm, found himself in tears. To the première itself came Modest and Anatoly, and also Anton Rubinstein; and when he went backstage before the

*The Davidov family, with Alexandra and Lev seated between Vera and Anna, Tatyana a*
*Natalya standing at the back, and Vladimir (Bob), Yury and Dmitry in fro*

performance, Tchaikovsky found to his surprise the entire staff of the Conservatory. He was presented with a wreath, and managed to make some kind of a speech in reply. But at the performance itself, the applause was thin and only for him, which he read as a friendly tribute to the composer but not to this one of his works. At a café afterwards, where he was dragged against his will, more speeches and toasts followed, though Anton Rubinstein was conspicuously silent; not until four in the morning, with a splitting headache, was he able to escape to bed. To avoid travelling with Anton Rubinstein (who privately told his wife that *Onegin* was hopelessly deficient in grand opera style) he took an early train for St Petersburg, and was back at work when the Press notices appeared. Though on the whole favourable, they were guarded; only one foretold *Onegin*'s future position as one of the most popular works in the entire operatic repertory.

Meanwhile, he learned, a lady had been seen watching the house, and once or twice had called. It was, of course, Antonina. One day he returned to find her waiting for him. With Anatoly listening anxiously from the next room, he tried to reason with her, but she was only calmed when he gave her money to go to Moscow; she would not hear of a divorce, and continued to reiterate her pathetic fantasies at Modest and Anatoly, whom she alternately abused and flattered, and at the bemused Tchaikovsky, protesting the undying love which he really had for her and which only vile schemers, themselves merely jealous, were trying to prevent. She moved into another part of the house where he and Anatoly were lodging; and when he went to Moscow, she pursued him and forced her way in upon him. Thrown into a complete panic, he fled to his usual refuge, Kamenka.

In the country, calm and the ability to work returned. He visited Brailov and Nizy briefly, and continued work on the orchestration of *The Maid of Orleans* and on completing the First Suite. The *Liturgy* was performed, but immediately confiscated by the director of the Imperial Chapel under a regulation giving that institution rights over all religious music. Jürgenson boldly sued for damages, and won the case. There was encouraging news from abroad: Colonne was resolved not to be deterred by the failure of *The Tempest* from playing more of Tchaikovsky's music; in Wiesbaden the Rococo Variations had been enthusiastically received by an audience that included the greatly impressed Liszt; and Bülow had been winning triumphs on his tours with the First Piano Concerto.

While Nadezhda von Meck was at Brailov he went for a short stay at Simaki, a small house on the estate; but he found her proximity upsetting, and when it was suggested that Pakhulsky might bring Milochka over to see him, he replied immediately and firmly that he did not want any alteration to the friendship which had by now settled into a firm convention of never meeting and never making any attempt to bridge the gap of distance. To meet Milochka, he felt, would disrupt this, and besides it would be difficult to explain to her why he never went to see her mother. Nadezhda von Meck took this point; and though he did accept her invitation to come over to Brailov one day when she was out, so that he could see the house when it was in a state of full occupation, he assumed that they would be able to conduct their friendship along its accustomed lines. The shock was the greater, then, when by a miscalculation over meal times he found himself face to face with her as their carriages passed on a narrow road through the woods. Both were confused. The moment he reached home, Tchaikovsky wrote apologizing for his carelessness and hoping that he had not caused a flood of questions from Milochka about the mysterious inhabitant of Simaki; but Nadezhda von Meck answered candidly that she was delighted by the incident, since it made her feel that living close at hand to her was indeed the real Tchaikovsky and not merely the remote correspondent of her imagination. As for Milochka: the child was told that the reason for Tchaikovsky's seclusion was that he was writing beautiful music and must not be interrupted.

Although, consciously or unconsciously, Nadezhda von Meck was trying to encourage their friendship to move onto a plane of greater reality – and there is no reason to suppose that, with her delicacy of understanding and her quickness of response to his feelings, something of the sort might not have been manageable – she again accepted his refusal to alter matters. She was forced to turn any thoughts of closer contact aside; though her real feelings are revealed by her next suggestion, in which she sublimated the thought that must have been somewhere in her own mind by proposing the idea of a marriage between one of her children and one of the Davidovs. Tchaikovsky was not opposed to the plan himself; and there ensued a correspondence between them in which she argued that a marriage based on passion had a worse chance of enduring success than one in which love grew, on the basis of a selection made by the partners' parents, from mutual appreciation of moral qualities. For Nadezhda von Meck to abandon the romantic ideal of marriage in favour of this strictly practical approach reflects only too clearly her own past experience and present state of mind. And she could restrain herself from revealing it no longer that autumn after a performance of 'our' Fourth Symphony. From Brailov in September she wrote pouring out all the feelings that had been pent up in her since Tchaikovsky's marriage, confessing that she had been almost broken-hearted when he had married, that she could not prevent herself from feeling satisfaction that he was unhappy with Antonina, that she loathed Antonina for making him unhappy but would have hated her more if she had made him happy, that she is not so idealistic as he seems to think, that she loves and prizes him more than anything in the world; and touchingly she asks, for the only time in their correspondence, for him to acknowledge this letter. He did so, carefully fastening on her confession that the symphony was to blame for this sudden outburst; his reply is gentle and kindly, but she must have understood his meaning when he wrote that his love for her was so great that it could only be expressed in music.

Meanwhile, with the opera scored, Tchaikovsky completed his other summer task, final work on his First Suite. He was to compose four suites in all. To Taneyev, in connection with the Third Suite, he once said, 'I meant to write a symphony, but the title is of no importance.' They are attractive works that give full rein to his skill in the short genre piece and in orchestration without posing the challenge of symphonic form. Brahms, also haunted by the ghost of Beethoven, was glad to find a similar outlet in his serenades, which play a comparable role in his output by providing a medium for pure orchestral music more relaxed than had become possible in the post-Beethoven symphony. In its final form, Tchaikovsky's First Suite comprises six movements; but this was reached only by way of a five-movement version, which went through various modifications, and at quite a late stage had a Divertimento movement added when Tchaikovsky realized that the entire suite would otherwise be in duple time. He duly added what he described as a minuet, though this Divertimento is really another waltz movement. Like the Scherzo, which was the germ of the whole suite, it is more substantial than his ballet music in manner, and could indeed have taken its place in a symphony planned on the lines of one of his first three. But after the Fourth Symphony, he clearly felt that a return to that world was no longer possible. He begins, therefore, with an Introduzione e Fuga which is slow and as solemn in content as anything in the early symphonies, with a decently worked fugue. After the Divertimento comes an Intermezzo, originally subtitled 'Echo du bal', a graceful if sentimental piece of Slav Soul, and a delicious little Miniature March (originally 'March of the Lilliputians') in the manner he was to make entirely his own with *Nutcracker*; and to conclude, after the Scherzo, comes a charmingly ungainly Gavotte (which quite apart from its own merits suggests where some of Prokofiev's roots lay). Lying almost exactly halfway between what had become his symphonic style and that of his ballet music, the suite includes some of his most agreeable music. If it does not earn more frequent performance, the reason is to be found not only in its unevenness but in the fact that though Tchaikovsky was here enabled to make use of movements pleasantly contrasted in weight and colour, he had not discovered a method of conferring some kind of unity on their contrast.

Tactfully rebuffed from trying to base their relationship on anything but music, Nadezhda von Meck responded by offering to arrange a performance of the Fourth Symphony in Paris. For all his doubts about its chances there, Tchaikovsky agreed; and while she set off to open negotiations with Colonne in the course of her travels, he paid a visit to Moscow – where he spent a drunken evening with Nikolay Rubinstein and Jürgenson – and then returned to Kamenka. With Alexandra's house for once empty of guests, he enjoyed the quieter domestic routine, even to the extent of joining the ladies at hemming towels and marking the linen; but fretting at his idleness, he began work on his Second Piano Concerto. In November he visited Moscow and heard Nikolay Rubinstein give a fine performance of the Piano Sonata – a work he now found 'dry and complicated' – and passing briefly through St Petersburg, he set off for Paris. Here work on the new concerto continued; he went to concerts and to the opera, finding Colonne's performance of the second part of *Les Troyens* feeble and boring; and he kept up his correspondence across the city with Nadezhda von Meck, remaining in the city only three weeks before she returned to Russia and he went on to Rome, with neither of them having stayed to

*The first fire-engine arriving at the Winter Palace after the attempt on the life of Alexander* II *in* 1880

hear the performance of the symphony. In Russia, assassination attempts upon Alexander II had led to an atmosphere of alarm in which even *The Oprichnik* fell under official scrutiny for subversive tendencies, and its projected revival had to be postponed; but though he lamented that there was no hope for a better future for his beloved country until some form of democracy could be evolved, Tchaikovsky was personally content to settle into rooms in Rome in time for Christmas in the company of Modest, Kolya Konradi and Alexey Sofronov. Not even the news of his father's death at the age of eighty-five seriously upset him; for though he had always been fond of the old man, it was a relationship based on friendly affection, involving none of the intensity of his feelings for his mother. In an effort to arouse enthusiasm for the Tsar, the government decided to stage a set of tableaux for the twenty-fifth anniversary of his accession; to his dismay, Tchaikovsky drew as subject, 'Montenegrin villagers receiving news of Russia's declaration of war on Turkey', for which, he told Anatoly, he was unable to manage anything more than the most frightful bangs and crashes.

From abroad, however, the news of his music was nothing but good. Despite the predicted failure of the Fourth Symphony in Paris, other works were making their way steadily in the repertory there, in Germany and even across the Atlantic. He was on the verge of real international success, so much so that he felt encouraged to ask Nadezhda von Meck to desist from her efforts with Colonne and allow his music to make its own way. The material fruits of success meant nothing to him. Improvident to the last, he spent any money that appeared on clothes, or on some trivial possession that took his fancy, or on a gift for a friend in trouble; and so far from relishing fame, except as private satisfaction, he was acutely embarrassed by public acclaim and by having to respond to attentions from the aristocracy or official organizations. Only in the interests of advancing *The Maid of Orleans* would he agree to wait upon government officials, when he returned from Rome, or dine with Grand Dukes. Yet he had a natural relish for the popularity of his music, which was by no means finally assured, and this overcame him when in April he thankfully escaped from Moscow for Kamenka. Admitting to Mme von Meck that the model for his *Italian Capriccio* was Glinka's Spanish pieces, he declared that he expected it to have a fine future; and composing with an eye to popularity drove him to the lowest common multiple of what he believed to be most effective in his art. The *Capriccio*'s assembly of several Italian folk and street songs and bugle calls, at times almost suggesting a parody of the simplest Verdi, haphazardly constructed and blatantly scored, has indeed come to adorn the repertory, but not his reputation.

The impetus for the Second Piano Concerto, the other work which he was now able to complete, was more prosaic. Fretful and bored, as he told Nadezhda von Meck, when he had no work on hand, he set himself the task of writing a successor to the Piano Concerto which was now beginning to make its way with the public. His regular habits of work were by no means the enemy of inspiration – quite the contrary, as he had already described – but in this case he was led into somewhat routine gestures. In the absence of the essential 'lyrical idea', he is committed to going through procedures which he sometimes handles with real invention and distinction, but which lack the conviction of the work's predecessor. Whatever the formal awkwardness of the First Piano Concerto's opening passage, it is a whole-hearted musical gesture. The equivalent in the Second Concerto has a note of more deliberate calculation, and though the movement has ingenious and effective ideas – notably the devising of a second subject that lies naturally in two strains across first wind and then piano – there is a sense of grandeur being consciously sought rather than resulting from a genuine musical impetus. The length of the movement is such that it can accommodate some attractive episodes, and find room for a third theme that cleverly leads back to the first; but the quest for magnificence leads Tchaikovsky into undertaking a larger structure than either his ideas can support or his formal skill handle. Without sufficient lyrical impulse, there comes to seem a strenuousness, and merely a strenuousness, in the struggle between piano and orchestra which Tchaikovsky described in a letter to Nadezhda von Meck as an essential element of piano concertos:

> There is no tonal blend, indeed the piano cannot blend with the rest, having an elasticity of tone that separates from any other body of sound, but there are two forces possessed of equal rights, i.e. the powerful, inexhaustibly richly coloured orchestra, with which there struggles and over which there triumphs (given a talented performer) a small, insignificant but strong-minded rival. In this struggle there is much poetry and a whole mass of enticing combinations of sound for the composer . . . To my mind, the piano can be effective in only three situations: (1) alone, (2) in a contest with the orchestra, (3) as accompaniment, i.e. the background of a picture.

This was written in the October of that year, 1880, as part of a reply in which he turns down her request for piano trio on the grounds that there is no tonal blend between piano, violin and cello; and it is surprising not only in view of the Trio he was later to write, but because the Andante of the Second Concerto is virtually a triple concerto, written for piano, violin and cello against the background of the orchestra. It is an attractive movement, and, with good reason, Tchaikovsky himself particularly liked the closing section in which the piano rejoins the solo violin and cello; the Finale has plenty of spirit and a certain formal ingenuity. Yet as a whole the concerto lacks the sense of identity which informs its predecessor; and this once more struck Nikolay Rubinstein when Tchaikovsky, encouraged to bury any hatchets by Rubinstein's brilliant performances of the First Concerto, sent him the new work asking for comments. This time, however, Rubinstein was cautious, and though he suggested that perhaps the piano part was episodic and too much engaged in dialogue with the orchestra, he hedged his opinion with tactful reservations about his lack of thorough knowledge of the work. When Taneyev gave the first performance in May 1882, the general opinion was that the work was too

long; and Tchaikovsky agreed, wryly adding that he wished that those whose opinions he had sought had said this earlier. Clearly he had conveniently forgotten the scenes over the First Piano Concerto.

July found him back at Brailov, where he examined Nadezhda von Meck's library of music with a good deal of gloom as far as his own works were concerned but with delight when he came to the volumes of Glinka: 'How astonishingly original is his *Kamarinskaya*, from which all later Russian composers (and indeed myself among them) continue to this day to derive obvious methods of harmonic and contrapuntal design whenever they are required to develop a Russian theme of dance character.' He resolved to spend more time revising his own compositions and writing histories of music or studies of other composers – a sure sign of creative inertia. Moving to Simaki, a house he had come to love, he spent a blissful time enjoying the hot summer days, until sharply interrupted by a letter from Antonina. She now agreed to a divorce, yet still refused to accept adultery as the condition. She further accused him of spreading malicious gossip about her, while remaining silent about his own 'dreadful vices'. He turned to work for distraction, copying out some vocal duets and some solo songs he had recently written (Op. 46 and Op. 47), and correcting proofs of *The Maid of Orleans*. He renewed his study of English in greater earnest, so as to be able to read his three favourite English authors, Dickens, Thackeray and Shakespeare; by the end of his life he was fluent enough to be able to manage *The Pickwick Papers* and *David Copperfield*. He played through his beloved *Carmen*, with all his former enthusiasm. Back at Kamenka, he was repeatedly pressed by Nikolay Rubinstein for a piece for the Silver Jubilee Exhibition, and he settled for a subject on Napoleon's invasion. The Ceremonial Overture, *1812*, was duly finished on 7 November, shortly after the Serenade for Strings on which he had been working.

Tchaikovsky's view of the two works' comparative merits was short and to the point:

> The Overture will be very loud, noisy, but I wrote it without any warm feelings of love and so it will probably be of no artistic worth. But the Serenade, on the contrary, I wrote from inner compulsion. This is a piece from the heart and so, I venture to say, it does not lack artistic worth.

The Serenade is, indeed, one of the most charming of his shorter works, characteristic of him in the elegance of the scoring, in the handling of the opening Pezzo in Forma di Sonatina in which a slow Introduction returns at the end, in the tunefulness of the waltz (one of his most memorable) and of the Elegy, in the somewhat boisterous Finale, a piece based on a lively Russian folk tune to which a slower Volga hauling tune acts as introduction. Possibly the relief of turning from the bombast of *1812* to a lighter companion encouraged his most relaxed side: certainly there is throughout the work a freshness and charm which he often found difficult to sustain when larger artistic issues were involved.

Left *Playbill for the first performance of
Eugene Onegin at the Bolshoy Theatre, Moscow*

Above *Pavel Khokhlov as Onegin in* 1881

Nadezhda von Meck had meanwhile acquired a new domestic musician, an eighteen-year-old French student (who had been recommended to her by Antoine Marmontel of the Paris Conservatory): Claude Debussy. For three summers he was to be a member of the Von Meck household, acting as duettist with Nadezhda herself, as accompanist and teacher to several of the children and as pianist in a trio with Pakhulsky and the cellist Danilchenko; he was also called upon to make arrangements for piano duet of parts of *Swan Lake*, and, whether or not out of tact, he showed the greatest enthusiasm for the music of his employer's mysterious friend, declaring roundly that not even Massenet could have equalled the fugue in the First Suite. The Von Mecks grew very attached to the visitor who brought a heady whiff of Parisian sophistication into their lives, mimicking Gounod, Ambroise Thomas and other eminences, delighting them with his rapid wit, enchanting them with his conversation and labelling them all with affectionate nicknames; they in turn used to call him their little Bussy, or Bussik, or Petrushka. There was even a mild flirtation with Sonya, in the course of which Debussy actually proposed, though not, it seems, very convincingly. Tchaikovsky, kept informed of his patroness's delight in her new discovery, was for his part somewhat wary of what may well have seemed like a new musical plaything threatening to replace the old.

In November he visited Moscow and St Petersburg, where his music was now making its way with great success. He missed the première of the *Italian Capriccio*, over which only a few critical voices dissented from the general enthusiasm, but he attended rehearsals of *Eugene Onegin* at the Bolshoy and saw *The Oprichnik* there, the censor's ban having now been lifted. He was delighted with the performance of his *Liturgy* in Moscow, and apparently unruffled by the only serious attack upon it, made in an article by 'an old Moscow minister of the Church' who was in fact none other than the Metropolitan of Moscow; and it was no less a pleasure to find that his songs and piano pieces had become part of the repertory of domestic singers and pianists. The chief disturbance of the visit was the call he felt obliged to pay on his much-loved servant Alexey Sofronov, who had been called up for military service and whose living conditions he found appalling. The Moscow première of *Eugene Onegin* was satisfactory, if not the hoped-for triumph; but Tchaikovsky's attention was centred on the première of *The Maid of Orleans* due in St Petersburg. Here all was far from well. The directors of the Maryinsky were saving on the production, having overspent on a new ballet, the singers were quarrelling, and Nápravník – 'that knight of the baton and the blue pencil', as Gerald Abraham has described him – was as usual plying the pencil as vigorously as the baton on Tchaikovsky's score. With an uneven cast that included, in the role of Dunois, Stravinsky's father Fyodor, *The Maid of Orleans* was quite cordially received on 25 February; and unaware that hostile criticism, headed by Cui, was about to lead to the work's withdrawal, Tchaikovsky set off for Italy.

In Rome, a letter reached him from Jürgenson with news that Antonina was reported to have taken a lover and had a child. Yet though now free to sue for divorce himself, he never did so. Wisely, he must have argued to himself that her own guilt was the most effective seal that could be set upon her importunities; in the glare of a divorce suit she was still capable of blurting out counter-accusations of his own 'vices', and he preferred to let the matter rest and quietly continue to contribute to her maintenance. Other news from home was less comforting. The assassination of Alexander II on 13 March deeply distressed him, though less through his

*A crowd running to the place where the Tsar was assassinated in St Petersburg*

personal devotion to the Tsar than for his dislike of feeling himself at a distance
from his own country at a time of national crisis. Worse, his fears for Nikolay
Rubinstein's health, which had concerned him on his St Petersburg visit, were
confirmed by a telegram from Jürgenson. Rubinstein was dying in Paris; and within
a few hours there followed the news of his death, on 23 March. Two days later
Tchaikovsky was in Paris, resolved to pay his respects to the man who had meant so
much to him and yet, as he admitted with shame, afraid of the distress he would
surely feel at the sight of the body. He arrived only in time for the service, and to be
part of the group who saw to the dispatch of the coffin to Moscow in a luggage van
from the Gare du Nord.

He felt bitterly the ironies attendant upon death. Nikolay Rubinstein had been
to him a friend and counsellor, sometimes – as over the matter of the First Piano
Concerto – a hard mentor, latterly a less close associate, but always a man representing musical authority, whose views and reactions carried great weight. The Rubinstein brothers stood in a parental relationship to Tchaikovsky's career, and it was
their good opinion for which he cared more than that of anyone else; there is,
indeed, something in the whole story of his friendship with them of the insecure
child desperately trying to please his parents and taking refuge in temper and despair

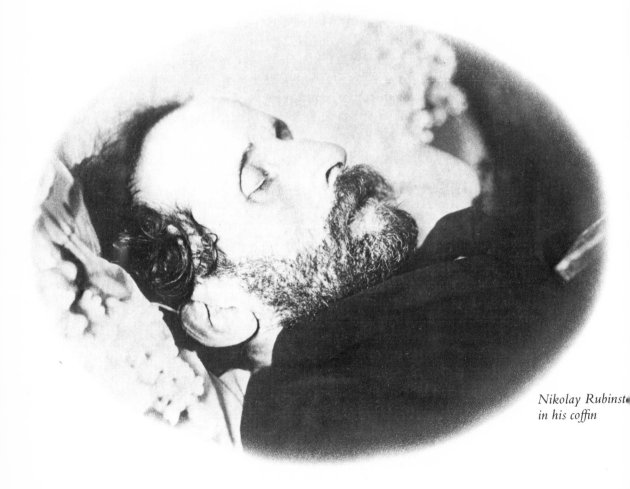

*Nikolay Rubinst⊙*
*in his coffin*

*The new Tsar: Alexander* III

if he fails to do so. Now to see Nikolay's body dispatched in a guard's van to Moscow affected him deeply; and he took some kind of comfort in a long letter to Nadezhda von Meck on the subject of belief, voicing his longing to be able to feel the Christian truths more strongly in his condition of painfully slow movement towards the faith whose security he craved.

There was depressing news of a material kind in the rumour that reached him of Nadezhda von Meck's financial setbacks. When he wrote to her about it, she confirmed the reports, but refused to hear of his own pension being affected. Nevertheless, he was unsettled, though he remained firm when the post of Director of the Moscow Conservatory, fallen vacant on Nikolay Rubinstein's death, was offered to him. His own candidate was Taneyev. At Kamenka, lacking ideas for music, he continued with various tasks for which he had little taste, such as the editing of the works of Bortnyansky. When Nadezhda von Meck came to hear of this, she tried to prevent him from taking on such tasks purely for the money involved; but he had promised Jürgenson to do the work, and felt, moreover, obliged to help in what way he could the man who had been so good a friend to him with these evidently sound publishing ventures. A successful appeal to the new Tsar for 3000 rubles gave him extra freedom for work, and for the planning of a new opera on Pushkin's *Poltava*. The Violin Concerto belatedly reached its first performance in Vienna on 4 December, with Adolf Brodsky as soloist and Hans Richter conducting; and in gratitude for learning it, and continuing to champion it against ferocious opposition, Tchaikovsky rededicated it to Brodsky. Auer, like Rubinstein with the First Piano Concerto, lived to repent his first opinion, and took the work up enthusiastically; it was he, indeed, who became responsible for teaching it to the senior generation of twentieth-century virtuosos who have remained loyal to it, among them Heifetz and Elman.

The loss of Rubinstein is mourned in a work for a combination which Tchaikovsky had previously declared he detested, piano trio. Begun in December, it was finished early in February 1882 and dedicated, 'To the memory of a great artist'. Tchaikovsky told Nadezhda von Meck that he was moved to write for these instruments partly in order to please her and partly so as to overcome the difficulties he felt to be inherent in the combination. He is by no means always successful, and there are passages in which the string instruments have some difficulty in making themselves effective against Tchaikovsky's typically weighty piano textures. It is an unusually constructed work, consisting of two movements with the second subdivided into a theme and variations and then a so-called Variazione Finale e Coda. The first movement is entitled Pezzo Elegiaco, with a graceful, plaintive string tune unfolding over a rocking piano accompaniment, and this returns with beautiful effect in the Coda; but the real memorial to Rubinstein is contained in the Variations. According to Kashkin's *Memoirs*, Tchaikovsky made use of a folk theme as token of Rubinstein's delight in Russian folksong, and particularly as souvenir of an occasion one beautiful spring day when Rubinstein had sent for wine and sweetmeats for a group of local peasants, who in turn had entertained him and his friends with songs and dances. This variation movement, supposedly based on episodes in Rubinstein's life, stimulates the best invention from Tchaikovsky, not least in a charming 'musical clock' variation; and the scoring has an aptness and charm in most of the Variations which disappear in favour of a heavier manner when larger formal issues are involved in the other movements.

For all the success which his music was now increasingly enjoying, Tchaikovsky remained depressed about his career and his creative abilities: to Jürgenson he complained that *The Maid of Orleans* and *Onegin* were being dropped; that no one would perform the Second Piano Concerto; worst, that the theatre directors were refusing to spend any money on *The Maid* yet making lavish allowances for a production of Rimsky-Korsakov's *Snow Maiden*, a subject Tchaikovsky regarded as his own. The necessity of joining in the family celebrations of Anatoly's wedding in Moscow irked him; and not even the cheering news of Richter's success with the Violin Concerto in London, of Taneyev's enthusiastically received première of the Second Piano Concerto, even of Anton Rubinstein's high praise of the Serenade when he conducted its first performance, could do more than palliate his mood of gloom. Brailov and Simaki had been sold; his first summer destination was Grankino, where he began work on his *Poltava* opera, *Mazeppa*, with little pleasure. A visit to Moscow for a concert of his works in connection with the Exhibition festivities was almost the only interruption to work on the opera at Kamenka, where he moved with Modest: 'Never has any important work given me such trouble as this opera', he wrote in September, and even the scoring, usually a pleasure, proceeded 'at a snail's pace'. Correspondence was resumed with Balakirev, who as usual had plans for a new work Tchaikovsky was to write: the subject, *Manfred*, was at this stage unwelcome, and he further told Balakirev that he now found his *Tempest* and *Francesca da Rimini* extremely cold, false and weak. *Mazeppa* remained a burden, still heavy on his shoulders by the time he arrived in St Petersburg at the end of December. Nápravník had by now seen some of the work; and profiting by previous experience, Tchaikovsky asked him to make his comments before work on the second act's orchestration went any further. On 9 January 1883 he left for what had become his annual foreign visit. As usual he enjoyed the opera in Paris, finding *Figaro* so rewarding that he went to seven or eight performances; he even found his interest in *Mazeppa* briefly rekindled. However, work had to be interrupted for the sake of some commissions, for an arrangement of the 'Slavsya' chorus from *A Life for the Tsar* to be sung in the open air by 7500 students, for a cantata, *Moscow*, in honour of the coronation of Alexander III, and for a march for the coronation celebrations. There was good news in the sale of the Trio, Violin Concerto and some other music at a high price to a Paris publisher, and in the report of the belated performance of his *Six Pieces* by their dedicatee, Anton Rubinstein. But the most welcome event was the completion of *Mazeppa* at the end of April.

Viktor Burenin's libretto for *Mazeppa* was originally written for Karl Davidov, Director of the St Petersburg Conservatory; for lack of time, he passed the subject on to Tchaikovsky, who was satisfied rather than excited by it. Preserving the outline, he made several changes to the actual libretto, inserting where possible some of Pushkin's own verse from the first two cantos of *Poltava* which are the matter of the opera.

> ACT 1, *Scene 1*: In the garden of the rich Cossack Kochubey, girls are telling fortunes by throwing wreaths into the river. When they have left, Kochubey's daughter Maria (sop.) reveals her love for their guest, the elderly Mazeppa; she is unmoved by the young Cossack Andrey's (ten.) declaration of love for her. When they have gone, Mazeppa (bar.) himself appears with his host, Kochubey (bass), and his hostess, Lyubov (mezzo), and the guests and the rest of the household, who are entertained with singing and dancing. When they are alone, Mazeppa asks for Maria's hand, but is refused because he is too old and is, moreover, her godfather. The discussion develops into a quarrel which brings back the others; Mazeppa summons his retainers and, calling on Maria to decide, carries her off. *Scene 2*: Maria's abduction is being lamented in Kochubey's house by her parents and friends, among them Andrey and Iskra (ten.), the Governor of Poltava. When Kochubey agrees to his wife's urgings for revenge, Andrey willingly offers himself to act as messenger to the Tsar with information about Mazeppa's intrigues with the Swedes.
>
> ACT 2, *Scene 1*: Kochubey is chained to a pillar in a dungeon of Belotserkovsky Castle, the Tsar having taken Mazeppa's word against his. Orlik (bass) demands Kochubey's treasure, and when he is refused summons a torturer. *Scene 2*: Mazeppa is sitting in his castle, gazing into the starlit garden. Orlik tells him of the failure of the torture on Kochubey. Maria, who knows nothing of her father's fate, is distressed by Mazeppa's

recent aloofness; he tells her his plan to set up a separate Ukrainian state with himself as its head. When he has gone, Lyubov arrives and reveals the truth about Kochubey to Maria, pleading with her to ask for his life. *Scene* 3: A crowd, including a drunken Cossack (ten.), is gathered by a scaffold, to which come Mazeppa and Orlik with executioners and Cossacks. Kochubey and Iskra are brought to execution.

ACT 3: After the symphonic picture 'The Battle of Poltava', the curtain rises on Kochubey's garden, now overgrown and ruined. Andrey and his men are pursuing the fleeing Swedes; he pauses, alone, and then hides as he hears horsemen approaching. It is Mazeppa and Orlik; Andrey attacks them, but is shot by Mazeppa. Maria, now deranged, appears as Orlik drags Mazeppa away, and believing herself once more a child cradles Andrey's head in her lap as she sings a lullaby over him. (In the original version, Tchaikovsky concluded with a scene in which the chorus re-enter and Maria, remembering the wreaths of the first scene, casts herself into the river.)

As ever, Tchaikovsky composed very early, if not actually first, a single extended scene in which the central character or characters are fully portrayed; without this sympathetic identification, he found it hard or indeed impossible to fill out a drama with music around them. In this case the scene was the duet between Mazeppa and Maria in Act 2. Each is a more absorbing and complicated character than can emerge in any summary of the action, or indeed emerges in Tchaikovsky's musical characterization. Mazeppa himself is one of Pushkin's Byronic *âmes damnées*, a dark figure, devious and calculating yet a violent natural force, who is intended to excite our sympathy as well as our awe, whose prime characteristic is his fascination and who, in his resolve to reach his fullest potential as a human being by trampling down society's restrictions, foreshadows Dostoyevsky's gambler Alexey and even Raskolnikov. But if Mazeppa is a character fundamentally divided against himself, the division is not one that matches Tchaikovsky's own personal dilemma, and in portraying him the composer reflected not so much Mazeppa's dual nature as a bewildering inconsistency. The man who can on the one hand scheme his treacherous way to power and compass the torture and judicial murder of those who stand in his way, and on the other rhapsodize about the beauty of the night and his love for Maria, need not be beyond the understanding of music, as he is not beyond that of poetry; but a substantial act of creative sympathy is demanded. Tchaikovsky portrays his cruelty in the powerful figure which opens the whole work and permeates the Introduction, and his gentler side is reflected in the arioso in which he declares his love of Maria to Kochubey, and particularly in the scene, which matches the beauty of Pushkin's poetry, when to eloquent woodwind scoring he contemplates the starry night. Yet if Tchaikovsky was trying to suggest Mazeppa's Faustian nature, he did not elaborate upon it very thoroughly, and even in Mazeppa's musing over his love for Maria (an aria which was inserted later) and in their duet, the central number of the opera, there is little sense of where the key to this difficult, dark character is to be found.

*Emilia Pavlovskaya* (1853–1935) *suggested* Onegin *to Tchaikovsky, who wrote the part of Tatyana for her.*

Nor did Maria fulfil what he knew to be the essential proviso of 'touching him to the quick'. Her sorrows make her kin to Tatyana, indeed place her among the suffering heroines so popular in the Russian imagination, with Katya Kabanova or Maria Bolkonskaya or Turgenev's Tatyana Shestov; but she has too few of their positive characteristics to engage his invention. Occasionally, as in her first aria, there is a suggestion that Tchaikovsky was trying to rekindle his feelings for Tatyana, or at any rate to reproduce the manner of their expression, and her final lullaby has an effectively macabre simplicity; but for the most part her role is rather lamely drawn, and certainly she lacks the quality to awaken the love of the powerful Mazeppa. There is still less dramatic life in the other characters: Andrey merely tenorizes suavely, and Kochubey, potentially one of the intransigent old men we also meet as a type in Russian novel and opera, never recaptures the sombre strength of his soliloquy chained to the pillar in his dungeon: Tchaikovsky's feeling for the 'colour' of a scene here enables him to portray vividly the truculent old man *in extremis.*

Everything, Tchaikovsky wrote near the start of work on *Mazeppa*, seemed routine and *remplissage*; and he confessed to Nadezhda von Meck that he was not very attracted to the characters. He was going through a long creative fallow period, and though he found it vital to keep on working for the sake of his peace of mind, and though he followed his prescription of settling regularly to work, composition gave him little pleasure and the necessary angel remained aloof. It is not surprising, then, that the most rewarding aspects of the opera conceived under such difficulties are almost incidental – the delightful opening chorus in quintuple time, the famous *hopak*, indeed most of the episodes in which the chorus play a part in contributing local colour or a background to the action. The 'Battle of Poltava' Intermezzo is an effective piece of programme music, vehement enough in Tchaikovsky's *1812* manner (he even requotes the liturgical chant used in the overture, together with an old military march and the 'Slava' theme familiar also from *Boris Godunov* and Beethoven's Second Razumovsky Quartet) to appeal to programme-builders seeking alternatives for their audiences. There are, furthermore, some successful dramatic ideas, not only Maria's final lullaby but the grim contrast of the drunken Cossack's song with the ritual of execution, in which the brilliantly sinister glitter of Pushkin's account meets a vivid musical response; and Tchaikovsky's hand does not fail him in scoring for lyrical scenes or for the popular songs and dances. But with the centre of the opera lacking in real character, these incidentals fail to achieve their real dramatic potential and become little more than agreeable interludes between scenes of ostensibly greater dramatic power.

Back in St Petersburg by the end of May, having heard and enjoyed *Lohengrin* in Berlin on the way, Tchaikovsky nevertheless avoided the performances of the works he had written specially for the coronation celebrations. The new Tsar had liked *Moscow*, he was told, and had ordered him to be suitably rewarded; though he had previously refused a fee, he was depressed to find it taking the form not of money but of a diamond. This he promptly pawned, hardly less promptly losing both pawn ticket and the money advanced. In his current state of financial uncertainty, he was further upset to receive a letter from Jürgenson offering 1000 rubles for *Mazeppa*, a sum which he insisted, successfully, be increased to 2400. *Mazeppa* was enthusiastically accepted by the new director of the Bolshoy, however, and though his distaste for the work remained, he was much cheered to find this new evidence of his music now being in such demand. Withdrawing to Kamenka, he completed the work which had been occupying his spare time from *Mazeppa* revisions and proofs – a Second Suite.

This time Tchaikovsky confined himself to five comparatively brief characteristic pieces, without attempting anything ambitious in the way of form. The opening movement, subtitled 'Jeu de sons', derives from the idea of contrasting themes arising out of the character of string and wind instruments; and the Finale, misleadingly entitled 'Danse baroque', is based on Dargomizhsky's orchestral piece *Kazachok*. It is the middle movements that contain the most characteristic music, and Tchaikovsky himself, writing to both Anatoly and Modest to express his satisfaction with the suite, added to Modest, 'I'm pretty certain that the Scherzo (with the accordions) and the Andante ("A child's dreams") will give pleasure.'

*Ippolit Altani (1846–1919), who conducted several first performances of works by Tchaikovsky, including* Mazeppa

The accordions are not essential, as Tchaikovsky made clear, but their sudden wild blare towards the end adds an entertaining texture to a movement of abrupt contrasts and hectic pace. It is a good example of Tchaikovsky's brilliant ear for original effect, though it is less typical in its use of that quality of obstreperous Russian humour that seems constantly on the verge of violence. The waltz is less personal than either this amusing movement or the very touching Andante, in which Tchaikovsky gives rein to his sense of the lost happiness of childhood and, with the appropriate degree of wistfulness, decorates his melody with pretty woodwind flourishes.

The winter of 1883–4 was largely taken up with journeys connected with performances. Despite his continued misgivings about his talent, which he felt had expired, his music was by now a staple part of the Moscow and St Petersburg repertory; and despite parallel misgivings about money, which led to his trying to persuade the theatre directorate that *Mazeppa* should be treated as a four-act work and thus paid at a higher rate, his income was reasonable and still supplemented by Nadezhda von Meck. Having survived the crisis of 1877, he now seems to have experienced the not uncommon psychological crisis of a man in his early forties, which in his case took the form not only of self-doubt and the fear that he was played out as a creative force but of a need to find greater security and greater stability than the present life of perpetual travel permitted. He continued to find public life painful, and the now warmly applauded appearances he made after performances merely embarrassing. Though he went to St Petersburg for the wedding which Nadezhda von Meck had at last brought about between her son Nikolay and his niece Anna Lvovna Davidova (and from which Mme von Meck absented herself), he was only too thankful to escape from the city, where *Mazeppa* was in the trusted hands of Nápravník, for Moscow, where a rival production was due under the less experienced Altani. The preparations taxed his energy and still more his nerves; and he sensed, rightly, when he was called before the curtain at the end of the performance that the applause was more for the singers and for himself than for the new work. He refused to return to St Petersburg for the *Mazeppa* première there, for which Alexander III, who was present, expressed his 'extreme surprise' and on which Jürgenson firmly blamed the work's failure, and without even remaining to hear the offended Erdmannsdörfer conduct the première of his Second Suite on the day of his departure, he wrote brief notes of thanks to his principal singers and set off for Berlin and Paris. 'At my age and station,' he wrote to Modest on receiving Jürgenson's reproaches, 'when it is hard to hope for the future, any even *relative* failure assumes the dimensions of an ignominious fiasco.'

The Tsar, however, forgiving the absentee composer of his beloved *Eugene Onegin*, dispatched after him a summons to appear to receive a decoration. Having duly returned and spent a day in bed with a chill, Tchaikovsky dosed himself with bromides and managed to make his punctual appearance at ten o'clock at the Gatchina Palace. Here he had conferred on him the Order of St Vladimir (Fourth Class). Later he wrote his enthusiastic impressions of the Tsar to Anatoly: 'I think that anyone who even once in his life has the opportunity of seeing the Emperor face to face will remain forever his passionate admirer; for it is impossible to express the charm and sympathy of his presence and his whole manner.' Much encouraged by this encounter, by the signs that *Mazeppa* was not such a failure as he had been led to suppose, and by the release of Alexey Sofronov from his military service, he set off in April once more for Kamenka. To Nadezhda von Meck he confided his shame at having been so easily depressed, and declared that, deeply moved by a reading of Tolstoy's privately circulating *A Confession*, he was profoundly grateful for the simpler mind and more readily found faith which had been granted him.

On the crest of this renewed wave of confidence, he began contemplating ideas for a piano concerto and a symphony. The time was not ripe, however: he quickly recognized the symphony's material to be better adapted to a suite. The abortive piano concerto eventually absorbed the suite's original first movement as the second movement of the Concert Fantasia. He was not entirely content with the ideas, but at least he was working; and as recreation he was pursuing his study of English, finding his pleasure at being able to understand Dickens somewhat dashed when he could not follow a word spoken by the Davidov's English governess. The suite, the study of English, and above all the company of his nephew Vladimir – the beloved Bob, or Bobik, of his later years – were the three delights of the summer at Kamenka; and it was with reluctance that he joined Modest at Grankino in mid-June. From here, three months later, he moved to the estate with which Nadezhda von Meck had replaced Brailov, Pleshcheyevo. He played through *Khovanshchina* and *Parsifal* on the piano, signally failing to appreciate either. Having completed the suite at the end of July, he was able to finish the Concert Fantasia as well a week after arriving at Pleshcheyevo.

Even shorn of its first movement, the Third Suite remains a long work, and one that is proportionately unbalanced by the famous Theme and Variations occupying

*Vladimir Davidov* (1872–1906)
*Tchaikovsky's beloved nephew 'Bob'*

half its length. The present first movement is the charming Elegy, one of Tchaikovsky's most relaxed inspirations but a movement that would better take its place as contrast to a stronger opening movement, particularly so as one of three interlude movements before the long Finale. Nevertheless, the Valse Mélancolique is an agreeable piece in Tchaikovsky's now familiar vein and the Scherzo a vigorous and quick-witted piece of virtuoso scoring. The substance of the suite remains with the admirable Variations. Any doubts Tchaikovsky was, genuinely or superstitiously, nursing about the extinction of his talent should have been dispelled by his success here; and indeed he wrote one of his facetious letters to Jürgenson on 2 July exclaiming, 'I work contentedly and diligently. There never yet was a work of greater *genius* than the new Suite!!!! Such is my usual disinterested attitude towards my offspring.' The theme is simple, but stimulates his liveliest and most diverse invention, a sure sign that creative confidence was returning; it ranges from studies that arise from the technical characteristics of the theme to a group of brilliant little sketches in which the theme is subjected to various manners, chorale and folk ballad and folk dance, and ends up with a superb polonaise, the rhythm traditionally associated by Russians with irresponsibility and frivolity on their western frontier.

Like its predecessor, the Third Suite was to begin with a 'Contrasts' movement; but already by 23 May Tchaikovsky was describing the theme noted in his diary as 'detestable'. When he cast it out of the suite, he decided that it could find a place in the new Concert Fantasia, not least since the design of the whole piece was so empirical. The first of the two movements was an attempt to break away from the

*Tchaikovsky in* 1884

sonata form which Tchaikovsky found a shackle unless he had some emotional programme in his mind. Entitled 'Quasi Rondo', it attempts to combine sonata and rondo forms by first expounding two themes as if in sonata form, then abandoning them for a central section as if the episode in a rondo, and finally bringing the opening music back in rondo fashion but with the material modified in sonata fashion. The middle section, moreover, is for piano solo, and thus also takes on the nature of the cadenza in a sonata movement. It is an ingenious scheme; though hardly a formal innovation for general use, it is justified by the material and by Tchaikovsky's comparatively lightweight handling of it. He seems, however, to have been uncertain how to continue (if at all, for there is in the score an alternative ending of a dozen rather flashy pages to be played if the second movement is omitted). The 'Contrasts' movement in fact answers the problem quite well, and is based on another innovation the contrast of two themes both in sequence and simultaneously. There are various smaller episodes, but this is the burden of a movement for which it is difficult to share Tchaikovsky's distaste. The whole work, indeed, deserves better than its neglect.

After this fruitful summer, the autumn return to St Petersburg was harder than ever. He tidied up Pleshcheyevo carefully, leaving everything in order for Nadezhda von Meck's return, though he had to confess that he had wound up his bedroom clock so vigorously one night that he had broken the weights. By late October he was in St Petersburg preparing for the first performance on the imperial stage of the Tsar's favoured *Eugene Onegin*. It was a triumph. For all his usual panic at being required to receive applause, he was delighted and strengthened in his new confidence; he went to two performances, became more sociable, was able to enjoy his growing fame, and made the visit the occasion for renewing his friendships with

Balakirev and Stasov. The strain told on his nerves as usual, however, and he was glad to escape abroad, partly for a rest and partly to visit Kotek, who was seriously ill in Davos. Balakirev had by now revised the plan of the *Manfred* he had required of Tchaikovsky, who dutifully took note of the new instructions and, much more drawn to the subject, acquired a copy of the poem for his journey. This he broke briefly in Berlin, where he greatly enjoyed a performance of *Oberon*, before reaching Davos. Having assured himself that Kotek's condition was not grave – falsely, as it turned out, for within a few weeks Kotek was dead – he moved on to Paris. Here his homesickness and his longing for a house of his own welled up more strongly than ever. Earlier in the year, at the beginning of May, he had written to Nadezhda von Meck of his wish to settle and of his requirements:

> I do not need any land, i.e. I want only a cottage with a pretty garden – *not new*. Certainly a *stream* is desirable. If it were near a forest, so much the better, though of course I mean someone else's forest, for, I repeat, I want to own only a cottage and a garden. It is essential for this little *dacha* or farmhouse to be an extremely open property, not beside a neighbouring *dacha*, and above all, indispensably, that it be not far from a station, so that I can always get to *Moscow* at any time. I cannot afford more than two or three thousand rubles.

Left *Playbill for the first performance of* Eugene Onegin *in Petersburg*

Above *I. M. Pryanishnikov, who sang Onegin*

*Design for Act 2, Scene 2, of* Eugene Onegin *in St Petersburg, 1884*

Deeply involved with her own property difficulties, Nadezhda von Meck did not respond to this wish as perhaps she might have done a few years previously. To Modest, who had been keeping an eye open on properties for him, he wrote again from Paris, 'I must at all events have a *home*. Whether in Kamenka or Moscow, I can't go on with this wild, peculiar life of a wandering star.' The need to settle and make a home continued to preoccupy him on his return; he advertised without success, and his thoughts were seldom far from the idea of finding his ideal country house even in the turmoil of preparing for the first performance of the Third Suite. Von Bülow was in St Petersburg, and having corrected the lamentably inaccurate score and parts Tchaikovsky hurried there to hear him conduct the work. It was another triumph: 'for such moments', he told Nadezhda von Meck, 'it is worth living and toiling.' *Eugene Onegin* was again enthusiastically received; and keen as usual to return to opera, Tchaikovsky listened with interest to Modest's suggestion of Shpazhinsky's play *The Sorceress*. There was no one, the dramatist replied when approached, with whom he would rather collaborate. Then, at last, he heard of a small furnished property at Maidanovo, near Klin. By mid-February, Alexey Sofronov had been dispatched to view it and given a favourable report, and negotiations with the owner of the land had been concluded. So keen was Tchaikovsky to settle that he made the arrangements before even seeing the place, knowing and loving the district of old. As soon as he saw it, he realized his mistake in trusting to his servant's taste in interior decoration; but he was relieved to have found somewhere, and satisfied with the cook, houseman and laundress whom Alexey had engaged. At last he had a home of his own. To Modest he wrote, 'I am fortunate, contented, pleased, peaceful.'

Right *Tchaikovsky's des*

Overleaf *The main living and working room at Kl*

Klin lies some fifty miles from Moscow, on the main railway line providing the link with St Petersburg that was essential to Tchaikovsky. In retreating to the country, he was not at first proposing to sever himself entirely from public life. He was pleased to see his real friends, to show them with pride his new surroundings and the possessions that he gathered about him, and he was very willing to make sorties into an urban life which had become the more tolerable now that he felt he had a secure home of his own to which he could withdraw. He loved the district; and though he still hankered after a property he could actually own, he took great pleasure in the countryside in which he found himself. As Modest put it, 'Tchaikovsky was so enamoured of the scenery of Great Russia that he was quite satisfied with a birch or a pine wood, a marshy field, the dome of a village church and, in the far distance, the dark line of some great forest.' Already in 1885 the district had lost some of its former rural isolation through the building of country houses by wealthy landowners who also found it convenient to reach either capital quickly; and since then industry has further altered the neighbourhood. Yet the country-side's broad sweep and the charm of its woods remain as at any rate some indication of the appeal it had for Tchaikovsky. Maidanovo itself lies close to Klin, its manor house set on a bank overlooking the River Sestra. At the time of Tchaikovsky's arrival, the property had fallen into some decay; Modest describes the remains of a rose garden and an orangery, together with other traces of what had once been a well-laid-out park. Apart from the advantage of its seclusion, it provided a pleasant variety of the walks which Tchaikovsky found necessary to the working out of his ideas for music.

After brief visits to Moscow and St Petersburg, Tchaikovsky duly settled into his new home in February 1885. His first task was the revision of his early *Vakula the Smith*: '*C'est un menu surchargé de mets épicés*', he now complained, and accordingly wrote some new scenes (amounting to 112 pages of new music) and, as he told Emilia Pavlovskaya, 'all that was bad I threw out, all that was good I kept, I lightened the massiveness and weightiness of the harmony – in a word, I did whatever was necessary to rescue the opera from the oblivion which it really has not deserved.' Renaming the work *Cherevichki* (from the red morocco slippers sought by Vakula), he completed what had now become a 'comic-fantastic opera in four acts' at the beginning of April; and after a visit to Moscow he went to St Petersburg to see Polonsky, the librettist, about the publication of this revision and to attend, to his delight, the meeting of the opera directors at which Vsevolozhsky overrode doubts and ordered a sumptuous new production. He celebrated his forty-fifth birthday with a dinner at his brother Anatoly's and a party given him by the Conservatory. Three weeks in May were spent in Moscow at the annual examinations of the Conservatory, when he went thoroughly into the institution's present situation in the aftermath of Nikolay Rubinstein's death, and to his great satisfaction managed to carry the election of Taneyev to the position of Director. In the middle of June he was able to return home and settle down to the major task that was to occupy his summer, the composition of *Manfred*.

During his second visit to Russia in the winter of 1867–8, Berlioz had conducted his symphony *Harold in Italy*. The work caused a considerable stir: its subject was greatly to the taste of a nation whose enthusiasm for Byron had not yet had time to exhaust itself as much as in the rest of Europe, and its handling in a four-movement programme symphony made a strong impression on musicians. The immediate outcome was Rimsky-Korsakov's Second Symphony, *Antar*, of 1868; and at about the same time Stasov sent Balakirev a fairly detailed four-movement programme, closely modelled on *Harold* but based this time on *Manfred*. Balakirev did not feel attracted to the idea himself, but he could not resist first sending it on to Berlioz, only hinting that it was not wholly his own; fourteen years later, he remembered the plan which the dying Berlioz had rejected. When writing to Tchaikovsky to thank him for the dedication on the revised score of *Romeo and Juliet* (a year late), and heaping praise on *The Tempest* and *Francesca da Rimini*, he submitted the idea as a subject ideally suited to Tchaikovsky's talents. Having expressed polite curiosity, Tchaikovsky was promptly sent detailed invoices for music, from the careful outline of the programme down to precise instructions about keys, a solemn warning to avoid 'vulgarities in the manner of German fanfares and *Jägermusik*' and even orders about the layout of the flute and percussion parts.

Clearly somewhat bemused by this, Tchaikovsky replied that the subject seemed too close to the Berliozian model for anything but an imitation which he could doubtless screw out of himself, but which would hardly have any inspiration or originality behind it. So there the matter rested until 1884, when Balakirev returned to the attack with a revised version of the original Stasov programme plus his own annotations. Having read Byron, Tchaikovsky began to feel that perhaps there was indeed a subject here for him; however, his suspicion of programme music made him wary, and though he was not reluctant to put an inner, personal programme into a symphony, he made a sharp distinction between this process and the use of a literary programme for music. 'Composing a programme symphony,' he told Taneyev, 'I have the sensation of being a charlatan and cheating the public; I am paying them not hard cash but rubbishy bits of paper money.' Yet to Emilia Pavlovskaya he wrote a little later, 'The symphony has turned out to be huge, serious, difficult, absorbing all my time, sometimes to my utter exhaustion; but an inner voice tells me that my labour is not in vain and that this work will be perhaps the best of my symphonic works.' He devoted the entire summer to *Manfred* – with scarcely a break to consider the other subject in mind, his Shpazhinsky opera *The Sorceress* – and finished it at the beginning of October.

Of all Tchaikovsky's major neglected works, it is *Manfred* which has least deserved its fate. Whatever his doubts about programme music, he was in fact better able to handle large forms when there was behind the music the impulse of an emotional idea, and he felt one sufficiently, if not in Byron's poem, at least in the programme as presented to him, for the outcome to be a work of great originality and power. Berlioz remains the father-figure of the work, but for all the similarity of the general plan to *Harold in Italy*, Tchaikovsky has well understood how the subject could be made his own. Though he did not feel the need to identify his hero with a solo instrument as Romantic outsider, observing but never taking part in all the vivid action, as in the case of Berlioz's viola, he did make use of a motive which recurs in all four movements; and he accepted the merit of Berlioz's design of a lengthy, reflective, melancholy first movement, two colourful interlude movements, and a Finale in which Berlioz's Brigands' Orgy becomes (without any such hint from the poem) a Bacchanal.

The first movement is prefaced:

> Manfred wanders in the Alps. Weary of the fatal questions of existence, tormented by hopeless longings and the memory of past crimes, he suffers cruel spiritual pangs. He has plunged into the occult sciences and commands the mighty powers of darkness, but neither they nor anything in *this* world can give him the *forgetfulness* to which alone he vainly aspires. The memory of the lost Astarte, once passionately loved by him, gnaws his heart and there is neither limit nor end to Manfred's despair.

It is not hard to see how these carefully selected elements of Manfred would appeal to Tchaikovsky; and freed from the necessity of making some reconciliation with sonata form for this first movement, he constructs a form of his own which is remarkably successful as an expression of his programme. The powerful opening motive associated with Manfred himself both expresses the strength and gloom of his character and can return at various crucial points to identify his part in the action; but beneath this is a musical structure which does not deal in the classic recapitulation of themes of traditional sonata form, but succeeds in moving forward without loss of unity or merely turning into a succession of episodes. It is a musical portrait, as strongly drawn as Berlioz's Harold, of the guilty, doomed sensibility which was perhaps the aspect of Byron which most vividly appealed to Russians and which had a close contact with Tchaikovsky's own predicament.

In the two middle movements, firstly 'The Alpine fairy [Byron's Witch of the Alps] appears before Manfred in the spray of a waterfall', and secondly a Pastorale

depicts 'The simple, free and peaceful life of the mountain people'. Both are, in effective structural contrast to the drama of the first movement, genre movements in which mood rather than description dominates. The waterfall gives Tchaikovsky the chance for one of his longest and most beautifully worked out scherzos, scored with a delicacy that Berlioz himself would surely have admired; Tchaikovsky's Alpine experiences may well have stood him in good stead here, though when the Fairy herself appears, in the Trio section, her features prove unmistakably Slavonic. The third movement, 'Scène aux champs' – Balakirev had hoped for a Russian version of the *Symphonie Fantastique* – is a more conventional idea, but the skill of its handling saves it from banality. Based on two simple melodies, one graceful and the other more roughly rustic, it has in its static nature an expressive point before the activity of the Finale, suggesting an idealized retreat from the turmoil of Manfred's life in the identical manner that Berlioz's Abruzzi mountaineers did with Harold; and the idea encourages from Tchaikovsky some of his most ravishingly decorative instrumentation. The Finale again reflects *Harold in Italy* in the somewhat factitious exuberance of the revelling; but there is room for an excellent fugue, for a well-judged return of Astarte, and at the end for a finely conceived death scene. For all his distrust of programme music, and for all the work's kinship to the Berlioz original that Tchaikovsky did not wish to repeat, *Manfred* proves Tchaikovsky's capacity to recharge another composer's example with his own personality, always provided that the emotional matter of the work found response in him. *Manfred* is one of the great programme symphonies of the nineteenth century.

With *Manfred* completed early in October, Tchaikovsky was able to put the finishing touches to Act I of *The Sorceress*, at which he had been working in the time he could spare from the symphony. To Nadezhda von Meck he reiterated his devotion to opera, though the reasons he gives are still that the stage is the most effective way of reaching a wide circle of listeners with his music and thus of letting it 'penetrate as far as possible into the heart of humanity'. When Mme von Meck held to the traditional view of her upbringing that opera was essentially a vulgar art beside the exalted nature of symphonic and chamber music, he implicitly agreed with her when he reminded her that the only contemporary composer who, from the highest ideals, had refrained from writing opera was Brahms and added, 'All the same, he is a hero. This heroism is not in me, and the stage with all its tawdry nevertheless attracts me.' As for *Manfred*, so unconvinced was he that the public would ever accept it that when Jürgenson approached him, also making an offer on behalf of the Paris publisher Félix Mackar, Tchaikovsky replied that though he regarded the work as his finest, he refused to accept any payment for something which he could not believe would ever repay his publishers' investment.

Settled at last into a home of his own, with no longer the need to find summer retreats as the guest of his family or of Nadezhda von Meck, Tchaikovsky found the year very fruitful for work. Maidanovo continued to delight him, and though never a real countryman or domestically very accomplished, he took the greatest pleasure in his new establishment. In fact, the organization was entirely in the hands of Alexey. Apart from the stocking of his library, his contributions to the household tended to be haphazard and misguided: he once bought a pair of horses which had to be disposed of, with great difficulty, and an English clock that did not go. Visitors noticed, however, the pride with which he would speak of 'my' cook, 'my' silver, 'my' tablecloth, and the fact that most of his possessions were plain and somewhat ill assorted counted for less than the actual ownership. He was, nevertheless, intensely conventional about the arrangement of his rooms, which Alexey had to repeat on their subsequent moves. Pride of ownership in the cook extended, his visitors noted to their dismay, to the cooking itself, which he would invariably praise: 'as he was always very abstemious and plain in his meals', notes Modest, 'it often happened that his guests, instead of complimenting the cook, felt inclined to do just the contrary.'

Here at Maidanovo Tchaikovsky also formed the habits of work which remained with him almost as a ritual for the rest of his life. He got up between seven and eight; drank tea and read the Bible between eight and nine; and studied his English or read some other book before setting off for a walk lasting about three-quarters of an hour. It was noticed that if he talked at his morning tea or took a friend with him on his walk, he did not intend to compose that day but would occupy himself with letters and business affairs. Latterly at Klin the company of anyone but Alexey came to fret him; it was Alexey's complete indifference to music that allowed him to come and go about his work as if invisible, and when once Alexey burst out with enthusiasm for the chorus of village girls in the third scene of *Onegin*, which was being played on the piano, Tchaikovsky was horrified at the unexpected intrusion. Between half past nine and one, he would work, always trying to get the unwelcome tasks out of the way before settling down to something he enjoyed; this meant dealing first with his correspondence, which sometimes amounted to as many as thirty letters a day, then his detested proof-reading. Lunch was at one and was followed, wet or fine, by a walk. Having read that in order to keep healthy, a man should walk for two hours a day, he took this with ritual scrupulousness, refusing to return even five minutes early. It was on these walks that the work of composition was initiated, ideas tried and jotted down in the little exercise books which were carefully preserved at Klin or even on the backs of envelopes or bills; these were subjected to critical scrutiny at the piano the following morning. The second sketch at the piano was always very full, since he did not trust his memory, with indications of orchestration (as part of the 'lyrical idea') marked in when neces-sary. When scoring, he wrote out a neat draft to which few alterations were usually made. By four o'clock he was ready for tea, perhaps to read the papers or see a friend; from five to seven came more work; and at eight, after another short walk, came dinner. The evenings would be spent playing duets with friends, perhaps Laroche or Kashkin, or at cards or listening to someone reading aloud; alone, he tended to become easily bored, though he would read historical books or play patience. By eleven he would retire to his bedroom, write his diary, and read a little more before going to sleep. 'Habit', he once quoted Pushkin to Nadezhda von Meck,

> is sent us from above
> In place of happiness.

It was chiefly for the steadiness and calm of this routine that he enjoyed the coun-try; yet his pleasure in the scenery was intense, not to be disturbed with casual exclamations of pleasure from friends, and his interest in village life genuine. Accustomed to tip the local children whom he met on his walks, he was naïvely surprised to find remarkable numbers of them unexpectedly bumping into him. When he altered his usual route on his walks, there were still large numbers of children happening to be about. Even their elders took to waiting with expectant smiles as he came on his way through the forest. His reaction to the children was always kindly; and discovering that they had no school, he inquired with the priest. He was told that the expense was too great; whereupon he offered money himself, and continued to subsidize the school until his death. Established so securely in his country life, he was glad to renew his lease, and as well as planning the usual foreign trip for next summer he was able to face the idea of a stay in St Petersburg with something approaching enthusiasm. Even the lack of plans there for a performance of *Manfred* and the postponement of *Cherevichki* failed to cast him into his former

despair at such setbacks; and though nervous, he survived without difficulty the first performance of *Manfred* at a Moscow concert in March dedicated to the memory of Nikolay Rubinstein. A visit to St Petersburg for a successful concert at which Bülow played the First Piano Concerto was, his diary noted, accompanied by 'social successes'.

At the beginning of April, he set off on his summer travels. He spent two days at Taganrog, on the Sea of Azov, where his brother Ippolit's ship was posted, and thence set off through the Caucasus. The dramatic beauty of the road between Vladikavkaz and Tiflis made as strong an impression upon him as it had on Lermontov, whose description of it at the beginning of *A Hero of Our Time* is reflected in Tchaikovsky's enthusiastic letter to Modest. He arrived to a heartening welcome from his brother Anatoly, and to vigorous acclaim from the public when he appeared at some concerts at which his works were played. The success of his music in a distant part of Russia, far from the centres of musical life, was particularly pleasurable. He took ship early in May, quickly finding his travelling companions tiresome but enjoying the visits to Trebizond and Constantinople and being much excited by the

Tchaikovsky in 1886

Left *A self-portrait of Pauline Viardot Garcia in her youth*

sight of Etna in eruption as they steamed through the Straits of Messina. Marseilles was reached in mid-May, Paris a few days later. Here he resumed his now familiar round of theatres and the opera, working from time to time on Act 3 of *The Sorceress*. He called on Pauline Viardot, who enchanted him with her conversation and her stories of Turgenev and who allowed him, to his profound emotion, to examine the manuscript score of *Don Giovanni* which her husband owned. He attended a dinner given in his honour by Marmontel, though the subject of Wagner seems to have broken the evening up. He met Fauré and Lalo; Delibes called and left his card; Ambroise Thomas was friendly; Colonne and Lamoureux showed interest in giving concerts of his music; and only by a chance absence did he fail to make contact with his admired Gounod. His success in Paris seemed complete; but the note that he made in his diary as the train left was, 'Anniversary of mother's death'.

He was pleased to be home again, and to find, as he told Nadezhda von Meck, that the snow had melted and the house was surrounded by flowers. Their correspondence was maintained, though with less intensity than formerly; his diary had begun to take some of the place his letters once occupied as the receptacle of his confidences, not only those concerning his private life and the oblique references to 'This' and what he described as the sensation 'Z' but also his reflections upon literature and music. There is the long passage in which he shares the dismay of his contemporaries at the course Tolstoy was taking in the years following the completion of *A Confession* in 1882; he regrets that when once, 'the highest love for mankind, the highest pity for its helplessness, limitations and insignificance could be read between the lines' of the great novels, now 'a cold wind blows from all his present writings'. Deciding not to follow the example of Tolstoy's reticence about his fellow writers, Tchaikovsky also records his views of other composers: Beethoven strikes into him the awe he felt as a child towards the Old Testament God, whereas his love is reserved for the Christ of music, Mozart (a comparison he hastens to disclaim as blasphemous). Bach he regards as able to provide the entertainment of a good fugue, Handel a fourth-rater, Gluck attractive, and he likes some of Haydn. But it is in Mozart that he finds the sum of all that is good in other composers.

For all the security of his life, however, and the knowledge of his success as a composer, he remained prone to the nervous attacks that had beset him all his life and had once come near to causing a total breakdown. Few composers have been so much at the mercy of their own nervous systems in their actual illnesses. Like Nadezhda von Meck, he was a sufferer from what it seems clear were migraines, the blinding headache and sense of mental disarray which are certainly connected to some kind of nervous hypertension. He had had a sudden and violent cold the day before his investiture by the Tsar, but been apparently all right on the actual day. When Antonina wrote to him again this July, her letter had the effect of causing another brief illness with sharp pains from piles. And later in the year, when terrified at the idea of conducting *Cherevichki*, he went down with a ten-day headache that cleared up the moment he sent word of his inability to attend. 'Isn't this a curious pathological case?', he wondered to Modest. Yet when engaged on a major work, he would not spare himself. The enormous effort of composing a large piece of music, even of merely writing out the full score, is something few people not professionally connected with music can understand; but the nervy, weak, easily upset Tchaikovsky showed the creator's true resilience, and ruthlessness with himself as well as with others, when it came to the necessity of composition.

It was, however, not manly resolve but vodka which enabled him to screw up his courage to mount the rostrum for the first rehearsals of *Cherevichki* in December. To his relief he found that the respect of the orchestra and their willingness to obey his wishes gave him the confidence to conduct with a good deal of success. Probably Russian orchestral players of the day were as suspicious as any others of the newcomer, but to the respected musician and especially to the composer-conductor they would reveal beneath their notorious toughness their real devotion to music and their capacity for taking endless pains to satisfy the highest standards. Now that he was a major figure in Russian music, any shortcomings in stick technique or in handling the orchestra would be readily forgiven; and though he did make a number of mistakes, he gained sufficient confidence and even pleasure in conducting to encourage him to repeat the experience. Despite the shock of hearing of the death of his niece Tatyana Davidova before the second performance of *Cherevichki*, he seems to have managed very creditably, and to have impressed his ideas successfully upon both singers and players. As further concerts in the first months of 1887 showed, he never overcame his fears about standing before an orchestra, but in the event he proved a decisive and effective conductor of his own music. Work on *The Sorceress* was also forging ahead, and by the middle of May he was able to note in his diary that it was all finished.

The crowded action of *The Sorceress*, as Shpazhinsky (an inexperienced librettist) arranged it, could barely be compressed into four acts.

ACT 1: In a squalid inn on the banks of the River Oka, near Nizhny-Novgorod, Foka (bass) and the vagabond monk Paisy (ten.) are joined by Foka's niece Nastasya (nicknamed Kuma, or 'gossip') (sop.) and her friend Polya (mezzo). As Prince Yury (ten.) and his huntsman Zhuran (bass) pass on their way back from a bear-hunt, Kuma's reflectiveness suggests that she is in love with Yury. When Lukash (ten.), one of the drinkers, reports that Yury's father Prince Nikita Kurlyatev (bar.) is on his way to investigate scandals about the inn together with the puritanical clerk Mamirov (bass), Kuma alone keeps her head and succeeds in charming the Prince on his arrival with her beauty and simplicity of manner. She plies him with wine and even induces him to join in the dances of the tumblers, to the rage of Mamirov.

ACT 2: In the garden of the Prince's house, his wife Princess Evpraksya (mezzo) is being consoled for his now daily visit to Kuma by Mamirov's sister Nenila (con.). Her son, Yury, tries to discover the cause of the trouble, and Paisy is ordered to spy on Kuma. There is a furious scene between the Prince and Princess. Yury pacifies an angry crowd who have pursued one of the Prince's men into the garden demanding punishment for his crimes. When Paisy returns with news that the Prince has gone to Kuma, Yury realizes the reason for his mother's grief and swears to kill the 'sorceress' who has thus bewitched his father.

ACT 3: The Prince is wooing Kuma in her hut, but she declares she would die rather than yield to him. When he has gone, Polya and Foka warn her of Yury's resolve. But when Yury himself arrives with Zhuran, he is readily convinced of her innocence, and left alone they fall into one another's arms.

ACT 4: Hunting horns sound from a dark forest on the river bank, and the wizard Kudma (bass) retreats into his cave as the hunt approaches. Zhuran meets Yury and learns of his plan to meet Kuma here and run away with her. When they have re-joined the hunt, Paisy and the Princess arrive to get poison for Kuma from Kudma. Kuma is now set ashore with her belongings, and, not knowing the Princess, is persuaded by her to accept a drink that contains the poison. Yury returns in time for Kuma to die in his arms; he rounds on his mother with curses as she departs rejoicing. The Prince now appears in pursuit of Kuma and Yury, and, refusing to believe that she is not being hidden, kills his son in jealous rage. Yury's body is borne away; left alone in the dark forest, with thunder and lightning and peals of the wizard's laughter all about him, the Prince goes mad.

If he had been gifted with a real flair for the stage, Tchaikovsky would have immediately seen that there was little chance of a successful opera in this farrago. He was, as ever, enticed into accepting it by the imaginative appeal of one scene, in this case the meeting between Kuma (as Nastasya is generally referred to in the opera) and Yury. Presumably it was the idea of love overcoming hatred that was at the root of his attraction to the scene; for when his intended Nastasya, Emilia Pavlovskaya, reacted with distaste to the play, which she had gone to see on hearing that the sub-

*Act* 1 *of* The Sorceress: *a drawing by Nikitin*

ject was mooted, he wrote her a long letter declaring that he could imagine no other Nastasya but her and going on to expound his view of his heroine.

> Of course she is a *loose* woman, but her charm does not consist in the fact that she talks *delightfully and entirely to please*. This quality is enough to attract to her inn *le commun des mortels*. But for *this alone* to force the young Prince from being a bitter enemy, come to kill her, into a passionately devoted lover? The fact is that in the depths of this loose woman's soul there is a *moral power and beauty* which until now have had nowhere to display themselves. *This power is love*. She is a strong womanly nature capable of falling in love only once and of sacrificing *everything* to this love. While her *love* is only in embryo, Nastasya squanders her *power* on small change, i.e. she amuses herself by making one and all whom she comes across fall in love with her. She remains simply an attrac-tive, sympathetic though corrupt woman; she knows she is *charming* . . . and pursues the sole aim of a gay life. But then there appears the man who has the power of touching the sleeping better chords of her instincts, and she is transformed. Life for her is a *trifle* if she cannot achieve her goal; *the power of her charms*, hitherto working elementally, uncons-ciously, now becomes an indestructible weapon which in an instant overcomes the hostile force, i.e. the Prince's hatred.

Going on to declare 'the fundamental requirement of my soul to illustrate in music, as Goethe put it: *"das Ewigweibliche zieht uns hinan"*', Tchaikovsky compares the theatrical interest of 'womanliness long covered under a cloak of sin' with Carmen and Violetta; but it seems that what he really had in mind was the kind of character which Tolstoy was to embody in his Maslova, a strong and attractive peasant girl whose qualities of character and capacity for love survive all manner of squalor, betrayal and suffering. Unfortunately his conception of Nastasya as described to Pavlovskaya far transcends his musical portraiture of her. He was demanding a great deal of himself, particularly as a man with no real experience of women, when he accepted a heroine whose devastating charm conquers every man she meets, to such an extent that she is regarded as, in the opera's title, a sorceress. Occasionally she reveals an individual charm in certain turns of phrase, and she is affecting in the love duet with Yury; but too often she sings in the tones of sentimental French opera, and there is little sense of the animal attraction and high-spiritedness that makes her a popular figure in the inn or of the exceptional qualities that set her above the rest of the crowd.

Apart from occasional felicitous strokes, Tchaikovsky does not help the portrait of his central character by giving the men any distinctive personalities or above all any strength that would be the more impressively overthrown by her charms. Yury is hardly more than a French tenor – the key scene when he is conquered by Nastasya's beauty carries little conviction – and his father a Russian bass; their personalities are outlined, in fact, more by suitable music for their voices than by much

*Tchaikovsky writes in French to Félix Mackar regretting that he cannot supply newspaper notices of his concert as he reads only one paper and giving his forwarding address in Tiflis.*

Left *Nikolay Kondratyev* (1832–87), *a Kharkov landowner and close friend of Tchaikovsky's*

Right *Tchaikovsky surrounded by teachers from the Tiflis Music School*

in the way of characterization. The Princess lacks the power which Tchaikovsky should have had it in him to suggest, and the minor characters are hardly more than the stereotypes of Russian opera. As an opera *The Sorceress* is a bad muddle. It is significant of the nature of Tchaikovsky's failure with the real matter of the work not only that he permits a first act thin in action to be unbalanced by a last act which can hardly accommodate all its action, but that the finest music comes in the first act with all the colourful scenes of singing and dancing. At their best these are tuneful and scored with an expert light hand (there is also a delightful chorus of girls in Act 2, worthy of *Onegin* and exquisitely scored). But the orchestration can also become rather garish, and the introduction of ten principals to sing a decimet with chorus begins well but turns into little more than a self-conscious operatic feat. There is some good music in the introductions and the entr'actes; but the centre of the opera is, fatally, missing, and without it all the multifarious action collapses into meaninglessness.

With *The Sorceress* finished in the middle of May 1887 Tchaikovsky set off for St Petersburg to see Nikolay Kondratyev, who was mortally ill. He spent six days there, making daily visits to his friend's bedside, before having to leave for Moscow and the annual examinations at the Conservatory. This task out of the way, he left for a holiday he planned to spend in Tiflis and Borzhom with Anatoly and Parasha.

He greatly enjoyed the trip down the Volga, was captivated by Borzhom, took the waters for some liver complaint he was discovered to have, and began sketches for a sextet and the scoring of his new suite, *Mozartiana*. Hearing that Kondratyev was going to Aachen in the hope of a cure, he decided to join him; but he found the dying man difficult and demanding, and though Tchaikovsky's motives were of pure kindness, he does not seem to have survived very well the trials of attending patiently to an irritable and suffering man. He was, in any case, going through one of his most introspective, and therefore for him self-reproachful, phases. In Aachen he would sit regretting that his life was passing with too little achieved, and that he ran away too easily from real problems and serious issues. In his diary he cites his present situation: 'Everybody admires my *sacrifice*. But there is no sacrifice. I sit here calmly, stuffing myself at the *table d'hôte*, do nothing, spend my money on trifles, when others are in need of the plain necessities of life. Am I not a pure egoist?' As ever with him, a certain relish in self-reproach went together with a genuine self-awareness and a cutting honesty. Undoubtedly he enjoyed the exercise of beating his breast, and shared to the full the Russian tendency to luxuriate in confession; but for all the histrionic note one may detect as he kneels before himself in his diary, observing the impression he is making upon himself, the comments are sharp and unsparing.

At Aachen he managed also to find time for work, and to finish his Suite No. 4, *Mozartiana*. His choice of pieces fell upon four, a little gigue and a minuet, both for keyboard, a so-called Preghiera that is taken from Liszt's transcription of the motet 'Ave verum corpus', and a set of variations that Mozart wrote on a theme from one of Gluck's operas. Apart from 'Ave verum corpus', they are obscure pieces; and indeed Tchaikovsky's aim was partly to extend knowledge of Mozart, as his note in the score suggests:

> A large number of Mozart's excellent small compositions are, for incomprehensible reasons, little known not only to the public but to many musicians. The author of the suite of arrangements entitled *Mozartiana* wishes to see new cause for more frequent performance of these pearls of musical composition, undemanding in form but filled with incomparable beauty.

He managed to complete the piece on the 100th anniversary of the first performance of *Don Giovanni*; and to Jürgenson, while work was in progress, he wrote suggesting that he might compose more such suites if this one met with the approval he expected for a work which, he felt, was successful in its choice of music and in its originality. 'The past in a contemporary work' was, he claimed, a novel idea; but the music in fact falls hopelessly between two stools. It is neither a reworking of an earlier master by a modern composer in his own style, such as was in Stravinsky's hands to become the matter for original music, nor does it do anything to enhance Mozart. The gigue and minuet are efficiently scored in Tchaikovsky's lighter style; but the pieces are slender for such treatment, and their choice for his opening movements suggests that

like many of his contemporaries he made insufficient distinction between Mozart's lighter and more profound sides. The glutinous arrangement of 'Ave verum corpus' does nothing to upset this view; and it is only really in the final variations that he comes near success, when he can happily indulge his gift for colourful scoring that neatly characterizes in his own manner some aspects of the theme Mozart took. Even here the brief variations carry a strong feeling of variations in the ballet sense. Mozart seems, to Tchaikovsky, still to represent the prettiness of the baroque, a style that attracted him partly by very reason of its remoteness: his inability to see the real power and variety of Mozart was part of his psychological need to regard the past with wistfulness, to associate it with lost purity and felicity, and this inevitably commits him to a view that is merely sentimental.

The *Pezzo Capriccioso* for cello and orchestra, written in a week while he was still trying to cope with the dying Kondratyev's sufferings and demands at Aachen, belies its title by being a sombre piece in the same key (one Tchaikovsky did not use very prominently) as the *Pathetic Symphony*. It is capricious not in any sense of lightheartedness, but in its fanciful toying with various aspects of the simple theme; and throughout, despite some rapid passages and a turn to the major key, the basic pulse and the basic sober mood are preserved. Written for Tchaikovsky's cellist friend Anatoly Brandukov, it is another of the minor concert works that well deserve rescue from neglect.

With the arrival of another of Kondratyev's friends from Russia at the beginning of September, he felt able to leave for home. A month later Kondratyev was dead. Tchaikovsky felt his loss and the distressing circumstances of his Aachen visit acutely, and told Modest that for some time the whole episode was the subject of nightmares. He began looking for a house to buy, without success, and even considered building. But his time was fully occupied with rehearsals for the first performance of *The Sorceress*. Nápravník had prepared the work well, and the soloists, who included Tchaikovsky's favourite baritone Ivan Melnikov, Fyodor Stravinsky (as Mamirov) and of course Pavlovskaya, were greatly to his liking. Yet though he at first believed the work a success, he was soon forced to admit that the public had not taken to it: 'I am unshakably convinced that *The Sorceress* is my best opera', he wrote as usual to Nadezhda von Meck, adding that nevertheless it would quickly vanish into the archives. By the seventh performance, the half-empty house was proving him right. However, he included a selection in the concert he was preparing of his own works for the Russian Musical Society: this also included *Francesca da Rimini*, the Concert Fantasy, *1812* and the première of *Mozartiana*. It was an immense success, and was immediately repeated the following day. Despite the failure of *The Sorceress*, this seems to have confirmed his confidence in his now widely established fame and in his ability to overcome his nerves sufficiently to act as a successful conductor of his own music. He was conducting better than ever before, he told Nadezhda von Meck, and never had he encountered such enthusiasm or had such a triumph. Already a national figure, he was ready to travel in Europe and even America on the crest of a popularity that he was to find had become international.

Right *Self-caricature by Fyodor Stravinsky of himself as Mamirov in* The Sorceress

Overleaf, left *Tiflis (Tbilisi), a city Tchaikovsky loved and where his music had an early succe*

Overleaf, right *The Aragvi Valley in the Caucasus where the composer enjoyed travelling*

Page 208 *Tchaikovsky thought this portrait by Nikolay Kuznetsov, painted in January–February 1893, 'in its expressiveness, vividness and reality really wonderful'. Modest also praised its authenticity, recognizing his brother's 'cold, dark, intense gaze'.*

Дъякъ Мамыровъ
оп. „Чародѣйка" П. И. Чайковскаго.
Ө. Стравинскаго
1889 г. 22 Марта

*Désirée Artôt in later years*

During his European tour in 1888 Tchaikovsky kept a special travel diary. He was conscious of acting as a musical ambassador; for as he proudly noted, apart from one concert which Glinka gave in Paris and Rubinstein's tours as a virtuoso, he was the first Russian to introduce his works personally abroad. For this reason his belated discovery of his competence as a conductor was important to him, and he begins the diary with a summary of his conducting experience. He knows that he has 'no positive gift for conducting'; he pours as much scorn on a critic for praising his conducting as for deploring his lack of talent as a composer; and he is candid in describing his nervousness, his weakness of character and his lack of self-confidence, all of which made it impossible for him to be seriously considered a good conductor. 'Only one thing . . . was of importance to me: to be able to conduct my own works no worse than any other mediocre conductor would have done.' Confident, or at any rate capable, of now being able to stand in front of an orchestra without (as he had once feared) literally losing his head, he accepted with pleasure invitations to tour Europe in concerts of his own music and that of other Russian composers.

His first stop, at the end of December 1887, was Berlin. He spent some time and money in the bookshops, visited picture-galleries, and went to a performance of Berlioz's Requiem, at which he noticed a middle-aged lady of distinguished appearance. It was Désirée Artôt. They had not met since their romance in 1869, and seem to have been delighted to see each other and to renew what had, fundamentally, never really been more than a friendship. From Berlin he travelled on to Leipzig, where his concert tour was to begin. He was welcomed by Siloti and Brodsky, who bore him off from the station in a little sledge to a family meal. The next day, returning for lunch, he heard some unfamiliar music being rehearsed. It was Brahms's recent Piano Trio, and the composer himself was at the piano. Tchaikovsky found him very sympathetic and excellent company, continuing privately to regret his own inability to like Brahms's music. They never became close friends, for Brahms seems to have been aware that Tchaikovsky was unable to do more than respect his music, but the diary gives a pleasing picture of Brahms's appearance, compared to that of 'a handsome, benign, elderly Russian priest', and of the warmth and good nature of his character. On the same occasion Tchaikovsky met Grieg, whom he recognizes as a much lesser composer than Brahms and one whose nature he feels is probably much closer to his own. Then:

> after the Christmas Tree, while we were all sitting round the tea-table at Brodsky's, a beautiful dog of the setter breed came bounding into the room and began to frisk round the host and his little nephew, who welcomed his arrival. 'This means that Miss Smyth will appear directly', everybody exclaimed at once, and in a few minutes a tall English-woman, not handsome but having what people call an 'expressive' or 'intelligent' face walked into the room . . .

Ethel Smyth was making a return visit to Leipzig. Perceptively, Tchaikovsky recognized her as 'lonely'; and he declares the eccentricities from which no English-woman is free to be in her case dogs, hunting and Brahms. He attended the Gewand-haus concert that included the first performance of Brahms's Double Concerto, with Joachim and Haussmann and with the composer conducting, though it failed to make any impression on him; he was made uncomfortably aware of the low stan-dards in Russia by the singing of some Bach motets by the choir of the Thomaskirche, and he found Reinecke's tempos in Beethoven's Fifth Symphony aggravatingly slow.

The next morning at ten o'clock Tchaikovsky himself was introduced to the Gewandhaus Orchestra and formally handed his baton by Reinecke. He spoke a few halting words of appreciation in such German as he had, and set off with the First Suite. Once the orchestra, and he, had settled down, the rehearsal went well, and at the public rehearsal which followed, the Leipzig students were loud in their enthusiasm; what Tchaikovsky treasured, however, was a card left by Grieg with a few words of high praise for the suite. The concert itself was also a success, and at a recital of his chamber music Tchaikovsky was delighted with the playing, and later with the personality, of the young violinist Karel Halíř, who had done much to win a place in the repertory for the Violin Concerto. When, shortly afterwards, Tchai-kovsky heard Halíř in the work, he declared it to be 'a memorable day'.

Pausing briefly in Berlin, he travelled on to Hamburg, where his concerts were also well received. The aged chairman of the Philharmonic Society, Theodor Avé-Lallement, charmed him with his kindness, no less so when the old man, almost with tears in his eyes, besought him to leave Russia, doubtless responsible for all that bar-barous scoring, and settle in Germany since there was still a chance of belatedly correcting the misfortune of having been born in the wrong country when he had in him 'the makings of a really good German composer'. Tchaikovsky was so touched by the old man that, with perhaps the slightest salting of malice, he dedicated the Fifth Symphony to him. He was attacked in similar terms by the local critic, Josef Sittard, but was so impressed by the care Sittard had taken to learn his scores thoroughly and the real feeling and thoughtfulness in his arguments that the two became friends. What he regarded as the Brahms cult continued to pursue him with particular force in Brahms's own city; he could only argue that the enthusiasm sprang from the fact that for many people he was the best alternative they had to Wagner.

Moving back to Berlin, Tchaikovsky heard a new symphony by Bülow's latest protégé, Richard Strauss; what now seems a mild, classically inclined work struck him as talentless and pretentious. He had a great success with his concert, especially with the work he regarded as mediocre and had only included at the insistence of the President of the Philharmonic Society, *1812*, and with a brilliant performance of the First Piano Concerto by Siloti. Returning through Leipzig, he seized the oppor-tunity of hearing *Das Rheingold* and *Die Meistersinger*, the latter of which he had specially requested when the concert due in his honour had to be cancelled. He was particularly impressed by the thirty-two-year-old Artur Nikisch, of whom he has left a vivid comparison with Bülow:

> In proportion as the latter was mobile, restless and showy in his style of conducting, which appealed to the eye, Herr Nikisch is elegantly calm, sparing of superfluous movements, yet at the same time wonderfully strong and self-possessed. He does not seem to conduct, but rather to exercise some mysterious spell; he hardly makes a sign, and never tries to call attention to himself, yet we feel that the great orchestra, like an instrument in the hands of a wonderful master, is completely under the control of its chief.

Tchaikovsky also met and admired Busoni, while regretting that like other Italians he seemed to be doing violence to his real nature by trying to be too German. His own reputation in Germany received charming recognition when one morning, notwithstanding an anti-Russian speech of Bismarck's, a military band arrived under his hotel window and proceeded to deliver an aubade beginning with the Russian national anthem, while Tchaikovsky, gratified but embarrassed and very cold, stood on his balcony with his head bared, vividly aware of the other puzzled guests appearing at their balconies in various states of undress.

From Leipzig he moved on to Prague, not without some apprehension that his visit might be made use of for anti-Austrian demonstrations in the current atmosphere of political tension. But Czech Slavophilia was concerned chiefly to honour him as the representative of the greatest Slav nation, not to associate him with agitation for independence. He was fêted at the station on his arrival, serenaded, cheered and treated more like visiting royalty than a composer; his concerts were a triumph, and he seems positively to have enjoyed the act of conducting that only a matter of months ago had been a source of anguish. He made immediate friends with Dvořák, who presented him with the manuscript score of his Second Symphony; and his departure for Paris was in a railway carriage loaded with flowers.

The new French policy of friendship towards Russia – moving towards a commercial *entente* that also represented a mutual insurance against the common threat of Bismarck – saw to it that Tchaikovsky was received as the man of the moment. Everything Russian was the fashion in the most fashion-conscious of Europe's capitals, and he was whirled from soirée to concert to reception to dinner, renewing his acquaintance with Fauré, meeting and being much impressed by the young Paderewski, receiving calls from Gounod and Massenet among a host of other musicians and a stream of the smart and wealthy, anxious not to miss adding him to their season's collection. The applause for his two concerts was tumultuous, and indiscriminate; and the Press, which had begun by fastening with enthusiasm upon his presence and praising him to the skies at his private soirées, discovered after the public concerts (from Cui's book *La Musique en Russie*, according to Modest) that he was not so Russian as had been at first thought, and so began deploring the lack of

real audacity that was considered the essential Russian spice. Exhausted and disillusioned, he considered returning home. As he wrote to Jürgenson, he had expended a good deal of energy and expense on acquiring some celebrity, but had come to the conclusion that it was far better to live quietly at home without fame. However, he had promised to conduct in London, and after a bad Channel crossing and a train journey that was at one point brought to a halt by snow, he arrived to a welcome that was, in contrast to that of Paris, cool for him personally but very warm and appreciative for his music. His four days were the foundation of the popularity in England which has never waned. 'Thus . . . ended', he wrote to Nadezhda von Meck, 'my torments, terrors, agitations but, one must truthfully say, also *joys*.' Relief was certainly a dominant emotion at concluding a concert tour which would have exhausted many a more robust man and would have been totally unthinkable for Tchaikovsky a few years previously. Pausing briefly in Vienna, where he survived only two-thirds of an act of *The Mikado*, he reached Tiflis, for a brief stay with Ippolit, early in April. He was anxious to be home. He was still looking out for a good opera subject, though he rejected the idea of a libretto on *The Queen of Spades*, on which Modest had been working for another composer, Nikolay Klenovsky. He was resolved to spend the summer writing a new symphony.

Early in May he went to inspect the new home which Alexey Sofronov had been making ready for him at Frolovskoye, near Klin. He describes it as picturesque, set on a wooded hill and remote from summer visitors. He loved the view and the surroundings, so much so that he found his walks growing longer than he intended, and he took great pleasure in his garden, which boasted a pond and a tiny island. With all the enthusiasm of the new gardener, he describes his adventures with his seeds and his planting and his difficulties with the weather, worrying over the fate of his flowers in the cold nights and himself catching a chill by pottering about too late in the damp. Work was slow at first, though by June he was writing to Nadezhda von Meck with the news that he was beginning to make some progress on the symphony. He was also busy writing an overture on the subject of *Hamlet*. But it was the symphony that really absorbed his attention. At the end of May he had told Modest that he was having to 'squeeze it out of my dulled brain'. 'Now that the symphony is nearing its end', he wrote to Nadezhda von Meck on 19 August, 'I regard it more objectively than at the height of work on it and I can say that it is, praise be to God, no worse than its predecessors. This knowledge is very sweet to me!'; to Shpazhinsky he wrote on 26 August, as he finished the work, 'My symphony is ready, and it seems to me that I have not blundered, that it has turned out well.'

In one of his notebooks, Tchaikovsky left a rough programme of the first movement of the new symphony.

> Introduction. Complete resignation before Fate, or, which is the same, before the inscrutable predestination of Providence. Allegro. (1) Murmurs, doubts, plaints, reproaches against xxx. (2) Shall I throw myself into the embraces of faith ???

In the ten years that had elapsed since his Fourth Symphony, Tchaikovsky had not only established his reputation abroad as well as at home but had matured from the tormented neurotic brought to the verge of suicide by the 1877 crisis into a state of comparative security. Yet that the change was one of degree, and less marked than outward circumstances would suggest, is indicated even by this brief programme, and confirmed in the symphony itself. Whether or not xxx refers to an actual person, there can be little doubt that Tchaikovsky is alluding to the only matter that was ever concealed under secret signs in his diary, his homosexuality. The phrase 'complete resignation' suggests that he had, somewhat ruefully, come to accept his nature. 'Fate', in the Fourth Symphony a violent battering theme, has now become identified with the workings of 'Providence' which must be accepted, and in the new symphony it thus takes the form of a gentler theme, beginning quietly, repeating its simple phrase, and then adding two falling scales that carry already a feeling of resignation. The harmony is essentially no more complex than two alternating chords followed by converging scales. 'Providence', Tchaikovsky's note suggests, is now associated with the more religious acceptance which his final comment proposes. He had moved some way towards belief, certainly continuing to try to reason his way into the state of faith which he desired emotionally yet to which he could not wholeheartedly commit himself. If the jerky little tune of the Allegro section, after this introduction, represents the 'murmurs' and (with the outbursts

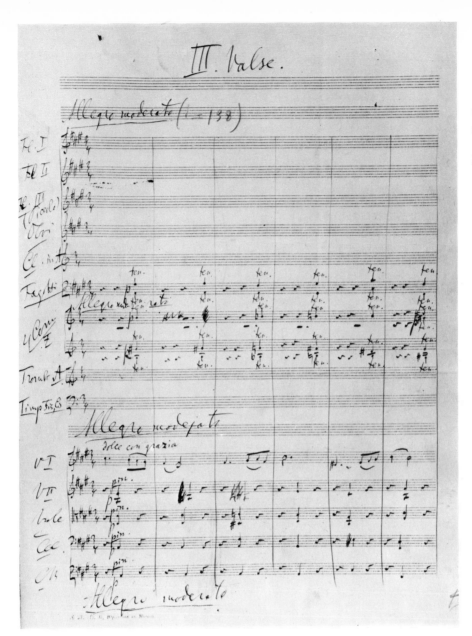

that follow) the 'doubts, plaints and reproaches', then the sudden soft theme on strings with its delicate woodwind answer could equally mean the 'embraces of faith'. Certainly, though the nature of his method in his last three symphonies precluded literal programme representation after the fashion of his own *Romeo and Juliet* or *Francesca da Rimini*, there is every indication that the thematic material was coloured by association with emotional states, and that the symphonic process was related to their implications.

No further clues to the course of the symphony survive, though Tchaikovsky is said to have written over the famous horn melody which opens the Andante

Cantabile, 'O que je t'aime ! O, mon amie ! O, how I love . . . If you love me . . .'
Certainly he composed few more explicit love scenes in the whole of his music. The
tune is marked 'dolce con molto espressione', the atmosphere one of great tenderness
and longing that rises to ever new pitches of intensity; the tempo is very flexible,
with constant urges forward succeeded by passionate rallentandos into the original
tempo; and over the music is set a host of instructions, so that in the first section there
are hardly three or four bars at a time without some new marking, *animando,
ritenuto, sostenuto, animando* again and so on. The steadiness of the first movement
has been succeeded by a fervent outpouring of emotion which seems almost on the
verge of speech. There is little respite in a contrasting section in which the woodwind
utter a quaint little phrase, for almost at once this develops into a shattering statement of the 'Providence' theme, now carrying as strong an atmosphere of hostile
Fate as anything in the Fourth Symphony. Even when the music resumes, after an
appalled silence, with the horn theme now on violins and decorated with a charming oboe melody, the emotional tension quickly mounts again, the 'Providence'
theme interrupts once more, and the movement ends with the secondary theme
played dolcissimo on strings over pulsing horns and bassoons. Even without any
surviving hints, no music could more vividly suggest a tragic love scene frustrated
by Providence, with the outcome the renewal of 'complete resignation before Fate'.

The answer, in the third movement, is escape. The world of the ballet was for
Tchaikovsky an enchanting unreality that could provide consolation and temporary
respite in illusion. The waltz which follows the love scene belongs to this world,
but in its gentle feminine endings and falling phrases it is brought into proper
emotional contact with the matter of the symphony by suggesting wistfulness
within the grace of the melody (it is related to a street-song Tchaikovsky had heard
sung by the boy singer in Florence). Though there is a contrast in a curious little
theme on bassoon, and another section based on running violin scales, there stirs
under all the charm, variety and elegance a more serious undertone in the accompaniment, and a brief growl from Providence near the end confirms that any escape
is temporary and illusory.

Though the Finale returns to sonata form, with as its two subjects a strong,
jabbing chordal theme with a somewhat nervous oboe answer, and a more serene
flowing woodwind phrase, these are less the matter of the movement than their
relationship to the 'Providence' theme. Once again this provides an introduction,
now 'andante maestoso' and in the major key. Over the other music, this theme
proceeds to assert its influence more and more powerfully, returning to open the
development section in which the most crucial progress of the music takes place,
and towards the end of the recapitulation building up towards the climax: this is a
triumphant coda, in which marching chords and flourishes of woodwind precede
the entry of 'Providence' into the centre of the symphony. There are references to
the earlier themes, and the final thematic allusion is to the first subject of the first

movement, perhaps (if Tchaikovsky's notes on the movement are correctly understood) finally sweeping aside the 'murmurs, doubts, plaints, reproaches'.

Resignation was to be the keynote of the symphony, and here is triumph. Yet one cannot but feel it to veer in the direction of bombast, as the rhythms pound and the brass blares after the fashion of *1812*, and find the assertions ringing hollow for all their emphasis. It is not that Tchaikovsky has misjudged the use of his motto theme in the earlier movements, where it returns with admirable dramatic timing as grim interruption or as reminder, nor that he has avoided the issue of Providence by brushing it aside, as in the Fourth Symphony. Yet, especially after the sorrowful warning that intervenes towards the end of the 'escape' waltz, the victory comes to seem too easily won. Nothing has occurred to alter the issue of resignation before Providence; hitherto the symphony has proposed a personality unhappy but attempting to come to terms with Providence; yet now the music suddenly flings this aside with claims that cannot fail to seem overstated and false. Even so, there is a certain courage behind all the empty show; from Tchaikovsky's effort to assume an emotional attitude that he could not really carry through, there inevitably follows a musical process that faithfully reflects this strenuousness, which is that of someone heroically trying to convince himself of something he desperately fears may not be true. Not until his last symphony was Tchaikovsky finally to concede his real relationship to his Fate.

Within a few months, having conducted performances in St Petersburg and Prague, Tchaikovsky himself had come to dislike the work. To Nadezhda von Meck in December he wrote:

> I have become convinced that this symphony is unsuccessful. There is something repulsive about it, a certain excess of gaudiness and insincerity, artificiality. And the public instinctively recognizes this. It was very clear to me that the ovations I received were directed at my previous work, but the symphony itself was incapable of attracting them or at least pleasing them. The realization of all this causes me an acute and agonizing sense of dissatisfaction with myself. Have I already, as they say, written myself out, and am I now only able to repeat and counterfeit my former style? Yesterday evening I looked through the Fourth Symphony, *ours*! What a difference, how much superior and better it is! Yes, this is very, very sad!

No specific programme survives for the other work which occupied him during the summer and autumn, the Fantasy Overture *Hamlet*. However, the subject had first occurred to him as early as 1876 – Hamlet was, indeed, a character who absorbed Russians more than any other of Shakespeare's – and a letter of that year to Modest outlines his plans for a work that seemed to him to fall naturally into three parts: '1. Elsinore and Hamlet, up to the appearance of his father's ghost. 2. Polonius (scherzando) and Ophelia (adagio). 3. Hamlet after the appearance of the ghost. His death and Fortinbras.' He found the play, in his own words, 'devilishly difficult', and no more was heard of his plans until 1888. But certainly some of the original idea has survived into this admirable piece. There is an obvious love theme, presenting Hamlet as something of a Lensky; and clearly the charming, plaintive oboe melody represents Ophelia. The design of the work in something approaching sonata form enables the march theme that approaches from a distance and obviously represents Fortinbras to appear twice, matching the play: once Fortinbras 'craves the conveyance of a promis'd march' across Danish territory, and he returns at the end 'with conquest come from Poland'. But the essence of the work is the dark brooding atmosphere cast by Elsinore; and rather than an enactment of the events of the play, or even a presentation of its key characters, the Overture follows the example of *Romeo and Juliet* and *The Tempest* in using certain characteristics or emotional situations of the parent play to foster an abstract musical structure of great strength and potent atmosphere. It is a work that deserves much wider currency.

Meanwhile Tchaikovsky had also orchestrated an overture sketched by Laroche, which he liked, and there was reassuring news of the new symphony's reception among his Moscow friends, Taneyev in particular, to set against personal worries. His niece Vera Davidova was seriously ill, Nikolay Hubert was dying in Moscow; Tchaikovsky made two trips to see his old friend, then, in great grief, returned for a third time to attend Hubert's funeral. However, he was able to complete his set of *Six French Songs* during the autumn and to prepare for a heavy round of conducting engagements that included the premières of the Fifth Symphony and *Hamlet* in St Petersburg. From here he hurried on to Prague, where he was due to repeat the St Petersburg concert that had included the symphony and the Second Piano Concerto as well as to rehearse *Eugene Onegin*. Through various pieces of mismanagement the concert was poorly attended, and the irritated composer directed that his meagre share of the profits should be given to a musicians' charity; *Onegin*, however, was warmly received, and on Tchaikovsky's request for an opinion Dvořák wrote a warm letter declaring that, 'None of your other works has given me so much pleasure as *Onegin*.' The news, which reached him in Vienna on his way home, of Vera Davidova's death depressed him further in the wake of the loss of Hubert; and it was in a state of profound gloom that he reached Frolovskoye.

Work seemed the antidote, and he plunged himself into plans for a ballet on a scenario first proposed to him in May by Vsevolozhsky on *The Sleeping Beauty,* to which Petipa had added a very detailed list of suggestions for music. He continued his conducting appearances, being particularly pleased with his success with *Hamlet* in a concert at which Rimsky-Korsakov was what he called 'the principal actor'. Christmas was spent at home: Jürgenson had imaginatively arranged with Alexey Sofronov for Tchaikovsky to be given a little Christmas tree – perhaps tales of Leipzig the previous Christmas had reached him – together with as complete an edition of Mozart as could be obtained. When not working on the ballet, he spent his time reading Otto Jahn's life of Mozart side by side with the music. There was a

Left *A photograph of Ivan Vsevolozhsky (1835–1909) inscribed to Tchaikovsky*

Right *The ballet-master Marius Petipa with his son and his daughter Maria*

carefully selected stream of visitors, chief among them Jürgenson, Siloti and Taneyev, and discussions about Tolstoy and Mozart. Tchaikovsky was himself reading Dostoyevsky and was much impressed with a new young writer, Chekhov. His visitors tried to encourage him about his Fifth Symphony, but he remained sceptical about its merit and more interested in *The Sleeping Beauty*. By the beginning of February enough of it was ready to make possible a rehearsal of some excerpts and a discussion with Vsevolozhsky and Petipa. But completion of the score had to be postponed until he had made another international tour.

After the success of his first visit to Germany he was a welcome guest, and several new towns and cities were now included in his itinerary. In Cologne his reappearance at the end of the concert to take a bow was accompanied by a special fanfare from the orchestra; Frankfurt, with a reputation for coldness and for a devotion to the classics and Brahms, gave him the greatest ovation with which it had greeted any composer of late except Strauss; Dresden was less of a success, with a poorer orchestra that he did not feel he had handled well, though they, too, gave him a fanfare; and in Berlin, where he spent every one of his five days with Désirée Artôt, the reception was divided, with the majority enthusiastically on his side. His

*Johannes Brahms*

last professional port of call in Germany was Hamburg. On arrival he was delighted to find that the next room in his hotel was occupied by Brahms, the more so when it transpired that Brahms had postponed his departure by a day so as to hear the Fifth Symphony. At rehearsal there was a note of coolness from the orchestra, which Tchaikovsky, still very ambivalent about the work, understood only too well. When at lunch next day Brahms candidly said that he liked the Fifth Symphony except for the Finale, Tchaikovsky was at first put out; but Brahms's warmth and his transparent honesty so impressed him that he could not take serious offence over a judgment he himself shared, and, exchanging candour for candour, he found it possible to admit that he for his part could not greatly care for Brahms's work. He was, nevertheless, drawn still more to the nobility of character he found in Brahms, and was deeply disappointed when his hopes of persuading Brahms to come to Moscow to conduct were dashed. Old Avé-Lallement was unhappily too ill to hear the performance of a symphony that would have put some strain on his tact, but the work was generally liked, and its success persuaded the hesitant composer that he himself was pleased with it.

Moving on to Paris, he saw old friends and attended the opera, including performances of Lalo's *Le Roi d'Ys* and his beloved Gounod's *Roméo et Juliette* and concerts that included his own works and what he regarded as Berlioz's masterpiece, *La Damnation de Faust*. At Pauline Viardot's he heard an opera, *Le Dernier Sorcier*, that she had composed twenty years previously with Turgenev, performed by her daughters and pupils. In London, where once again he concluded his tour, he was depressed by a fog such as he had never encountered before, though there was enthusiasm for the First Piano Concerto, which Sapellnikov played, and for the

*Sergey Taneyev (seated) with the conductor and director of the Moscow Conservatory, Vasily Safonov*

First Suite. But he was glad to leave for home early in April, and after a journey from Marseilles to Batum, during which he worked at *The Sleeping Beauty* and saw the sights of Constantinople in company with a Moscow student and a boy with whom he had made friends, he spent a few days in Tiflis enjoying the radiant spring with particular pleasure after the London fog, and then turned his steps for home.

In Moscow the Conservatory was in a state of turmoil following Taneyev's resignation, with Safonov making his nomination conditional on the resignation of Albrecht. Tchaikovsky supported Albrecht, but could not delay his departure beyond the annual examinations as he had undertaken to be on the committee in St Petersburg celebrating Anton Rubinstein's fiftieth jubilee as a pianist. He spent a convivial evening with Rimsky-Korsakov, Lyadov and Glazunov at a restaurant until thrown out at two in the morning, but he was glad to escape to Frolovskoye. He was anxious to finish *The Sleeping Beauty*, and throughout June he laboured at the scoring, a task he usually enjoyed but which on this occasion gave him much difficulty. He took much pleasure in the company of the three-year-old daughter of his friend Kondratyev's servant Legoshin, spending hours with her and delighting in her clever chatter; she was ideal company for him as he let his mind dwell on his fairy-story ballet. The diary for the month is filled with notes of the long hours he put in on it – for one day in June, 'I work, I work and I work' – though he does not forget the anniversary of his mother's death. When he reached the end of August and the end of the whole ballet almost simultaneously, he felt, he said, as though a huge mountain had fallen from his shoulders.

Ivan Vsevolozhsky, an immensely talented and intelligent man with a wide knowledge and understanding of the arts, had been appointed to the Imperial Theatres in St Petersburg in 1881. He found that the standard of the ballet had sunk to a deplorable level, with the skill of the dancers and the expertness of the ballet-master only serving to exalt execution above any creative approach to ballet. The costumes and décor tended merely to form a background to the displays of virtuosity which delighted an uninformed public, and the music itself was hardly allowed to stray beyond this supporting role. In 1886 Vsevolozhsky had approached Tchaikovsky as the obvious composer to collaborate in an enterprise that would raise the

general standard and make some attempt to unify dancing, plot, décor and music in
a proper danced drama; but the proposed subject, *Undine*, failed to interest Tchaikovsky in spite of, or perhaps because of, his own former commitment to it. He
returned to the attack in May 1888 with the idea of a ballet on Perrault's *La Belle au
Bois Dormant*, proposing a *mise en scène* in the style of Louis XIV with music 'in the
spirit of Lully, Bach, Rameau, and so on and so forth'. By August Tchaikovsky had
received the scenario and thought it 'superlative'; later he told Nadezhda von Meck
that he found it excellent for music.

After the experience of *Swan Lake*, however, he was wary of the world of ballet
and its rigid sets of conventions. At his request, Petipa furnished him with a very long,
detailed scenario which not only outlined the action and divided it into dances but
even set out suggestions for the music in meticulous detail at certain key points,
requesting, for instance, 'broad, majestic music', 'graceful 3/4', 'Coda – rapid 2/4
(vivace) – 96 bars'. Like many ballet and film composers since his day, Tchaikovsky
seems to have found these precise instructions a stimulus rather than a hindrance to
his ideas, and an excellent discipline. He set to work with a will, and in the growing
belief that into this ballet he was putting some of his best music. With Vsevolozhsky
resolved to astonish the public by the richness and exquisite taste of his designs and
Petipa equally determined to devise a strong structure for a full-length ballet that
would extend the normal range of choreography, the enterprise was an epoch-
making one. Now, when *The Sleeping Beauty* has long since passed into history as
one of the most successful and popular ballets ever composed, it is difficult to think
of it in such terms. But the public of the day had no experience of anything so elaborate artistically; and it was a brilliant notion of Vsevolozhsky's to devise a full-length
work in which the fairy-tale subject would seem completely disarming, the designs
would be relevant while not failing in prettiness, the choreography would see to it
that there were sufficient occasions for virtuosity in the course of the simple plot,

and the music would be by the composer who had by now won the enthusiasm of the public for his tunefulness and for his mastery of dance rhythms and colourful orchestration.

PROLOGUE, The Christening: After a short Introduction, the curtain rises on the Grand Hall at the Court of King Florestan XIV, in the seventeenth century; celebrations are in progress for the christening of Princess Aurora. 1 *March* – The guests are shown to their places by Catalabutte, the Master of Ceremonies. The King and Queen enter and prepare to receive the six Fairy Godmothers. 2 *Scène dansante* – They now arrive with their pages, who dance with the Royal Maids of Honour. 3 *Pas de six* – (a) Intrada. (b) Adagio, by the six Fairies and the Pages. (c) Variation 1: Candite (a kind of phlox, in the Language of Flowers symbolizing Beauty). (d) Variation 2: Fleur de Farine (a kind of convolvulus: in the Language of Flowers, Grace). (e) Variation 3: Miettes qui Tombent (the 'falling crumbs' are those by Russian custom sprinkled on a cradle by the godmother to ensure that her godchild shall never go hungry). (f) Variation 4: Canari qui Chante (the gift of eloquence). (g) Variation 5: Violente (the gift of energy). (h) Variation 6: La Fée des Lilas (the gift of wisdom, which in Russian folklore a child will acquire if it is placed under lilacs). (i) Coda. 4 *Finale* – Just as the Lilac Fairy is approaching the cradle, the Wicked Fairy Carabosse arrives, uninvited, in a carriage drawn by rats. Her gift to the baby is for her to fall into everlasting sleep if she should prick her finger. When Carabosse has gone, the Lilac Fairy, who was about to bestow her own gift, now says that this shall be for Princess Aurora to be able to be roused from her sleep by a Prince's kiss of true love.

*The principals of the first production of* The Sleeping Beauty, *with Carlotta Brianza as Princess Aurora in the centre*

Right *Alexander Glazunov, by Repin*

Overleaf *Design by M. A. Shishkov for Act 3, Scene 5, of* The Sleeping Beauty

ACT 1, The Spell: 1 *Scene* – In the gardens of the Royal Palace, villagers are gathering to celebrate Aurora's sixteenth birthday. Catalabutte confiscates some knitting needles which, against the King's strict ban on all sharp implements, he sees some villagers using. The King arrives with his Queen, and discovering the crime threatens the culprits with death, until he accepts the plea that on this occasion there should be nothing but rejoicing. 2 *Waltz* – This is performed by the villagers with garlands of flowers. 3 *Scene* – The Four Princes come as suitors make their claim to the King; when Aurora arrives, they are presented to her. 4 *Pas d'action* – The Princes try to win her favour. (a) Adagio: in this 'Rose' Adagio each presents her with a rose. (b) Dance of Maids of Honour and Pages. (c) Aurora's Variation. (d) Coda: as the Maids of Honour resume dancing, Aurora joins the onlookers, where a bent old hag shows her a spindle; delighted with it, she dances, waving it in the air. 5 *Finale* – suddenly she pricks her finger; she dances ever faster, but abruptly falls to the ground. The old hag reveals herself as Carabosse, and threatened by the Princes, disappears in a cloud of smoke. The Lilac Fairy orders Aurora to be carried into the Palace. She must sleep for a

hundred years, and all the Palace with her; they are frozen in the attitude in which they find themselves; trees and bushes grow swiftly up to hide the castle and its silent occupants.

ACT 2, The Vision: 1 – A hundred years have passed. On the banks of a river, huntsmen appear with a group of villagers, and then Prince Désiré and his tutor Gallison. 2 *Colin-maillard* – During this game of Blind Man's Buff, the Prince stands aloof and uninterested in the girls' attentions. 3 (a) Scene: Gallison sets the dancers in their places. (b) Dance of the Duchesses. (c) Dance of the Baronesses. (d) Dance of the Countesses. (e) Dance of the Marquises. 4 *Farandole* – (a) Scene: the ladies propose a farandole such as the peasants dance and in which they can join. (b) Dance, in which all join. 5 The hunt is resumed by all except the melancholy Prince. The Lilac Fairy arrives in a boat of mother-of-pearl and, finding that he is not in love, tells him of Aurora; he is enraptured, the more so when she conjures up the vision of Aurora before him. 6 (a) *Pas d'action*: The Prince is hindered from approaching Aurora by her fairies. (b) Aurora's Variation. (c) Coda: the visions disappear. 7 *Scene* – The Lilac Fairy agrees to take the Prince to Aurora. 8 *Panorama* – They journey to the kingdom of the Sleeping Beauty. 9 *Entr'acte*. 10 (a) Symphonic entr'acte and Scene: the Fairy leads the Prince through the forest and the Castle to Aurora's bedside; he kisses her. (b) Finale: The spell is broken, the forest vanishes, and King, Queen and courtiers awaken.

ACT 3, The Wedding: 1 *March* – Catalabutte leads in the nobles and courtiers, and the King and Queen take their places on their thrones. 2 *Polacca* – Other guests arrive, among them fairy-tale characters. 3 *Pas de Quatre* – (a) Intrada: the Silver, Gold, Sapphire and Diamond Fairies arrive. (b) Variation 1: Gold Fairy. (c) Variation 2: Silver Fairy. (d) Variation 3: Sapphire Fairy. (e) Variation 4: Diamond Fairy. (f) Coda. 4 *Pas de caractère* – Puss-in-Boots and the White Cat. 5 – Blue Bird. Originally a *pas de quatre* for Cinderella and Prince Fortuné with the Blue Bird and Princess Florine, now usually a *pas de deux* for the latter pair. (a) Adagio: Blue Bird and Princess Florine (b) Variation 1: Blue Bird (c) Variation 2: Princess Florine (d) Coda. 6 *Pas de caractère* – Red Riding Hood and the Wolf. 7 *Pas berrichon* – Hop o' My Thumb 8 – Cinderella and Prince Fortune. 9 *Pas de deux* – Princess Aurora and Prince Désiré. (a) Entrée. (b) Adagio. (c) Variation 1: Prince Désiré. (d) Variation 2: Princess Aurora. (e) Coda. 10 *Sarabande*. 11 *Finale* – (a) Mazurka. (b) Apotheosis.

So much praise has, with the best of reasons, been lavished on the tunefulness and the *ballabile* quality of this famous score that it is easy to overlook the skill with which it is all constructed. Even a melodist of Tchaikovsky's distinction needs more than merely the occasion for good tunes: for all their instrinsic charm, they will not make their true effect unless they are well placed and skilfully presented in a sound musical design, and for all their brilliant aptness as material for dance they will risk losing some of their real character and point if they are not properly arranged into a choreographic design that gives them meaning. The plot here forms a simple and attractive framework, part of the strength of which (from the ballet point of view) is its flexibility, so that the story introduces, with no straining at logic in the magical

Above *Playbill for the first performance
of* The Sleeping Beauty *in* 1890

Right *Maria Petipa as the first
Lilac Fairy*

context and the dance medium, plenty of opportunities for solo virtuosity. Each of the four acts (if we count the Prologue as an act) is based on a narrative opening and close (except for the Finale, where there is obviously only the need for a final token 'Apotheosis'). Each also includes scenes in which a dance forms a natural part of the plot – the Scène dansante of the Prologue, the immortal Waltz in Act 1, the Farandole in Act 2, the Polacca in Act 3, together with other examples. Each is further designed so that at its centre lies a set of solo variations with only the merest connection to the plot. There is thus satisfied the need for a plot to give coherence to a full evening's entertainment, the need for company numbers and for numbers in which a characteristic dance grows out of the temporarily halted plot so that the attention is turned towards dance, and finally the need for solo numbers in which to pure dance that is virtually unrelated to the plot there is added the element of personal virtuosity.

To this subject, and this design, Tchaikovsky responded with some of the most delightful music he ever wrote. To escape into the artificial world of ballet, with its detachment from troubling reality and its emotions presented entirely in terms of *le joli*, was always a pleasure to him; and as we have seen, so far from regarding the task as intrinsically inferior, he had the highest regard for ballet music and the ambition to satisfy his highest standards in writing it. With a scenario as attractive as Vsevolozhsky's and a choreographic plot as detailed as Petipa's, he clearly felt himself to be in the company of experts of the greatest professional skill. His own would not be less; and he was indeed the ideal composer to handle the intricate pattern they proposed to him. His symphonic experience enables him to control the narrative scenes and to confer a sound musical design upon whole acts; and his hand never betrays him in producing for himself the expectation of a short number or sequence of numbers in which the music reflects with unfailing charm the mood or situation or simply the choreographic need of the moment. This was a plot and a medium that asked for a constant succession of varied 'lyrical ideas' such as Tchaikovsky delighted to provide, and it tapped in him his freshest flow of melodic inspiration. The *facture* that irked him so much in symphonic music is here of a kind that came naturally to him, depending as it did less upon the working out of ideas to form a substantial symphonic structure than upon the cunning balance and contrast of a sequence of melodic ideas presented in attractive orchestration to match the lightness and prettiness of the fairy-tale subject. For all his avowed debt to Delibes, he was as no other composer of his day the master of the art of music that, while being captivating in its own right, still needs completion in dance, containing as it does such a strong and infectious sense of physical movement. In *The Sleeping Beauty* he rose to his greatest heights.

That he took the task as seriously as that of a symphony or an opera is shown in his reaction to the Tsar's comment after the dress rehearsal in St Petersburg the following January. '"Very charming"!!!', he quotes; 'His Majesty treated me in a very offhand manner. God be with him.' For all the care lavished upon the work by Vsevolozhsky, in a costly production with the finest dancers (among them Maria Petipa as the Lilac Fairy and Enrico Cecchetti as the Blue Bird), the public did not respond, finding even this score confusingly elaborate and symphonic; and its subsequent history, which includes a famous revival by Diaghilev in London in 1921 for which Stravinsky orchestrated some numbers eventually omitted by Tchaikovsky, has been surprisingly erratic, with the stagings of separate acts or versions of the work greatly exceeding performances of the original.

*No. 24 Fontanka, the house in St Petersburg in which Modest Tchaikovsky had a flat, and where Tchaikovsky met Chekhov and also began* The Queen of Spades

This was, for Tchaikovsky, the climax of a winter season into which he put much energy and time. Now secure enough materially and within himself to face urban life, he took a flat in Moscow for the winter; and having mastered his fear of conducting he was ready to put himself at the service of other men's music as well as his own. He conducted the first performance of a revival of *Onegin*, concerts that included his concertos, and, at a concert including the Russian première of his *Pezzo Capriccioso*, he even conducted Beethoven's Ninth Symphony. At the beginning of December he was in St Petersburg for the Rubinstein jubilee, conducting an all-Rubinstein concert at which the great man seated himself at the piano for the first performance of his *Conzertstück*. On the following day he again conducted a Rubinstein programme that included a performance with 700 singers of *The Tower of Babel* ('a martyrdom', he told Mme von Meck). He was, of course, glad to be able to show this respect to a man whom he continued to regard as a master and whose approval he needed more than that of any musician. Modest describes how his brother had first pointed out Rubinstein to him at a play, which was entirely forgotten while 'his eyes followed his "divinity" with the rapt gaze of a lover . . . This feeling . . . practically lasted to the end of Tchaikovsky's life. Externally he was always "in love" with Rubinstein, although – as is always the case in love affairs – there were periods of coolness, jealousy and irritation.' Hero-worship was part of Tchaikovsky's temperament, and that Rubinstein never professed admiration for his music was a source of pain for him. Yet he always denied with great heat the suggestion of well-meaning friends that Rubinstein was jealous; and though Rubinstein indeed ignored all music after Schumann, there is some evidence that he privately liked much of Tchaikovsky's music in a manner that Modest compares to Wotan 'secretly rejoicing in the success of Tchaikovsky-Siegfried, and sympathizing in his heart with Tchaikovsky-Siegmund.' When he must have seen how much a word of approval would have meant to his adoring ex-pupil, who never ceased to be grateful for the artistic standards Rubinstein had implanted in him, it is difficult to acquit Rubinstein wholly of jealously resisting the success of Tchaikovsky's music when few works of his own were held in much more than the respect due to a great musician.

*One of Tchaikovsky's sketch-books, showing the melody Hermann's Act 1 aria declaring his love for L*

At the end of January 1890 Tchaikovsky set off abroad without any precise destination. Leaving Alexey Sofronov behind to tend his sick wife, he took with him Modest's servant; and after a brief stay in Berlin, departed for a city he loved, Florence. He was, as usual, preoccupied with ideas for opera. Earlier in the season, he had met Chekhov, who had dedicated a volume of stories to him, and they discussed plans for an opera on Lermontov's *Bela* (the first part of *A Hero of Our Time*, a tantalizing theme for a collaboration on this romance set in the Caucasus they both loved). However, the subject which the theatrical authorities, still in a position to dictate even to Tchaikovsky, had approved was *The Queen of Spades*; and it was upon Modest's version of this that he set to work. Apart from the need for revisions to the libretto, the composition went fluently and the opera was sketched complete by the middle of March. He was increasingly excited by the subject, and by the end of the month was writing to his brother with his usual enthusiasm, once an opera was nearing completion, to declare that this time he really had written his masterpiece, and that the history of the world was henceforth divided into two periods, before *The Queen of Spades* and after. He began the scoring in Italy, working with great pleasure on it, and by mid-June, back at Frolovskoye, had finished the entire opera.

It was, once more, Vsevolozhsky from whom the initial idea of the new work had come. Pushkin's tale had long been popular, and only two years after its appearance in 1834 there was staged in St Petersburg a version by the then popular playwright Prince Alexander Shakhovskoy entitled *Chrysomania, or The Passion for Money*. At least two operas, by Suppé and by Halévy (to a Scribe libretto, Paris 1850) had been written on the subject, and a further dramatic treatment, *The Card-Player*, by Dmitri Lobanov very probably influenced Modest Tchaikovsky, himself by 1890 well established as a minor dramatist, when he came to write his libretto. However, it was not he but a member of the theatre directorate, Vasily Kandaurov, who was first asked to write a libretto for the composer of Vsevolozhsky's choice, Nikolay

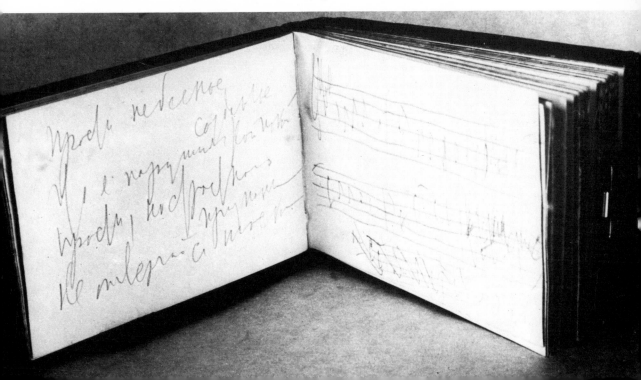

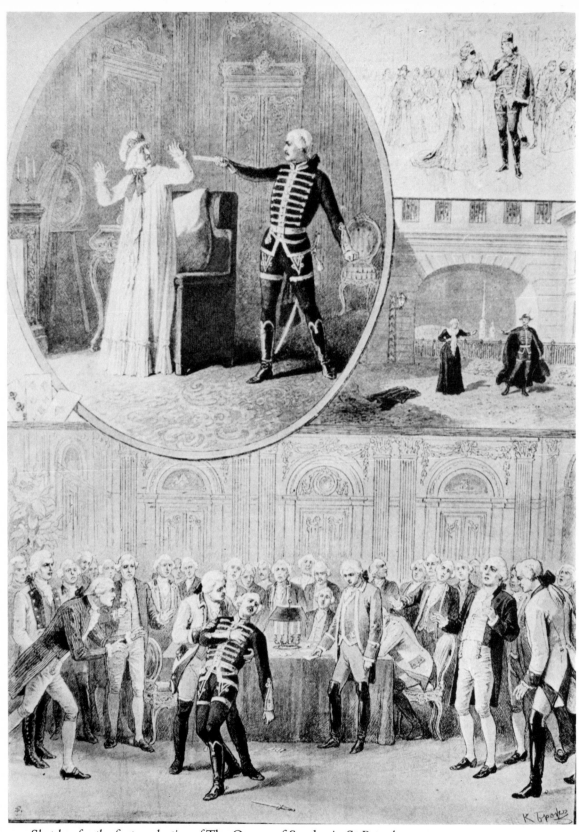

*Sketches for the first production of* The Queen of Spades *in St Petersburg*

Klenovsky, a pupil of Tchaikovsky's who had helped in the first performance of *Eugene Onegin* and was the author of a number of ballets. What Vsevolozhsky had in mind was another spectacle to follow up the enterprise of *The Sleeping Beauty*, with exquisite rococo sets and music that would similarly play a decorative function; it is presumably for this reason that he did not immediately approach Tchaikovsky. When Klenovsky failed to make any progress with the work, Kandaurov sent his material to another minor composer, known chiefly as the writer of little salon pieces, A. A. Villanov. But Vsevolozhsky reacted unfavourably to Villanov's plans, and in 1888 sent Klenovsky to Modest Tchaikovsky. At this stage, it will be remembered, Tchaikovsky himself was not interested in writing the music; but when the Klenovsky/Modest Tchaikovsky collaboration was suddenly broken off in 1889, he found himself 'catching fire' at the idea.

The libretto which was eventually agreed upon fell into three acts, with originally two scenes in each act.

ACT I, *Scene* 1: In a public garden in St Petersburg, children are playing with their nurses and governesses, and everyone is enjoying the sunshine. Count Tomsky (bar.), with Chekalinsky (ten.) and Surin (bass), meets the young officer Hermann (ten.), who confides that he is love with an unknown beauty. When Prince Eletsky (bar.) appears, they congratulate him on his engagement, to a girl who now is seen approaching with her grandmother: it is Lisa (sop.), Hermann's beloved, and the Countess (mezzo). While they are talking, Tomsky tells the other men the story of how in her youth the Countess learned from a lover in Paris the secret of three cards that would infallibly win at *shtos*, or faro, and how she had confided the secret to her husband and to a young protégé, but had then been warned by the ghost of her original seducer that the third man who approaches her for the secret will bring her death. A thunderstorm disperses the company, leaving only Hermann brooding on the story. *Scene* 2: Lisa and Pauline (con.) are singing and dancing in Lisa's room, but are reproved and made to stop by the French governess (mezzo). Alone, Lisa reflects that instead of loving Eletsky she is fascinated by the mysterious officer who looks like

*Medea and Nikolay Figner as Lisa and Hermann in Act 1, Scene 2, of* The Queen Of Spades *(1890)*

*Maria Slavina as the Countess in* The Queen of Spades (1890)

a 'fallen angel'. Hermann himself now appears at her balcony window; he persuades her not to rouse the household, and when the Countess enters to investigate the noise she has heard, Lisa hides him; he is reminded of the three-card story. When the Countess has gone, Hermann renews his pleas of love, and Lisa yields to him.

ACT 2, *Scene* 3: At a masked ball, Eletsky is troubled to find that Lisa seems uninterested in him, and though devoted to her is unwilling to force himself on her. Surin and Chekalinsky, aware of Hermann's growing preoccupation with the three-card story, whisper 'ghostly' suggestions in his ear about it. A 'pastoral interlude', *The Faithful Shepherd*, is now performed for the amusement of the guests, with Prilepa (sop.) (Tchaikovsky rejected the idea that this should be played by Lisa), Milozvor (played by Pauline) and Prilepa's rich admirer Zlatogor (played by Tomsky). Lisa gives Hermann the key to the garden door so that he can come to her by night, through the Countess's room; he is by now wholly preoccupied with the thought of the three-card secret, which will bring him the wealth to enable him to elope with Lisa. It is announced that the Empress has decided to honour the ball with her presence, and all prepare to greet her as the curtain falls. *Scene* 4: Hermann conceals himself in the

Countess's bedroom. She enters, and is prepared for bed, musing on her young days in Paris and softly singing an air by Grétry. Hermann emerges from hiding and demands the secret; when he tries to frighten her into revealing it, she falls back dead. Lisa hurries in, and realizes that Hermann's passion for the secret of the cards has by now become stronger than his love for her.

ACT 3, *Scene* 5: In his room in the barracks, a few days later, Hermann is reading a note from Lisa in which she declares that she has perhaps blamed him unduly for the Countess's death and asks to meet him by the canal opposite the Winter Palace. Hermann is still obsessed by the secret, and recalls how at the Countess's funeral she seemed to wink at him. The ghost of the Countess appears and reveals the secret, for Lisa's sake, she says – it is to play Three, Seven, Ace. *Scene* 6 (inserted by Tchaikovsky against the advice of Modest and Laroche so as to tell what becomes of Lisa and also so as to provide contrast in an otherwise almost all-male act): Lisa is waiting by the canal; but when Hermann comes, he is less interested in her than in hurrying to the card game to try out the secret. When she tries to claim him, he thrusts her aside, and realizing that he is indeed a murderer and has no real care for her, she throws herself into the canal. *Scene* 7: At the gaming house, Eletsky has unexpectedly turned up. After a break for supper, when Tomsky sings to them, they return to the tables. Hermann rushes in, looking distraught, and stakes a huge sum on the Three; he wins. He stakes again on the Seven; he wins again. Chekalinsky now resigns the bank, which passes to Eletsky, who has come to see how he may avenge the loss of Lisa. Hermann stakes a third time, and claims a win on the Ace; but Eletsky points out that the card he holds in his hand is the Queen of Spades. The ghost of the Countess herself, the Queen of Spades, appears once more to Hermann, whose reason snaps; he stabs himself, and in his last lucid moment sees a vision of the forgiving Lisa.

Possibly Modest had Pushkin's six short chapters in mind when he arranged his original version into three divided acts; but if he was concerned with the framework of the story, he paid less attention to its real atmosphere and point. Pushkin's writing is deliberately dry and ironical, telling the Hoffmannesque tale with the flatness that has bewildered many readers, especially outside Russia, but which has a particular point and a sense of delayed action. Whether or not his Countess was based on a real person, Natalya Petrovna Golitsin, as tradition has it, she is an exactly described figure from the society of Catherine's day; she, and the life of gambling and dancing and all the nicely observed details of manners, are the geography of the tale that also conditions those who live in it. But Hermann is the arrogant man of will, superstitious like most men who believe in a destiny designed for them, and yet it is the supernatural element unexpectedly occurring which compasses his destruction. His German name suggests the faintly ridiculous serious-mindedness which Russians traditionally associate with Germans in their literature, together with a certain stupidity (the very word for German, *nemetsky*, derives from the ancient supposition that because they spoke no Russian they were therefore dumb). These are the only two real forces in the story; the other characters are décor, and even Lisa, once her role is finished, merely vanishes without explanation. It is a weird, oblique, yet haunting piece of work, difficult to reinterpret in operatic terms.

How much of Kandaurov's first attempt was taken over by Modest is not clear; the original is said to have been very loquacious, and anachronistic in dialogue in an attempt to satisfy Vsevolozhsky's wish for a period piece to match the story's setting in the eighteenth century, in the latter years of the reign of Catherine the Great. Certainly Tchaikovsky had cause to reproach his brother for the wordiness of the text, and there have survived into the final libretto many genre and period scenes. He contributed a number of verses of his own, those of the dance-song with which Pauline sets her companions dancing in Act 1, Prince Eletsky's aria, the final chorus of the Pastorale, the introduction to the brief final chorus of the same ball scene welcoming the Empress, and a considerable part of Lisa's scene by the canal opposite the Winter Palace which he insisted on inserting. But the libretto also includes a number of verses by earlier poets. The duet between Lisa and Pauline is taken from Zhukovsky's 'Evening'. The Romance which Pauline sings to her own accompaniment is the 'Inscription on a Shepherd's Coffin' by Zhukovsky's contemporary Konstantin Batyushkov (1787–1855), the poet of his generation most imbued with eighteenth-century feeling and a love of the classics. The Pastorale itself is taken from Pyotr Karabanov (1765–1829); while from Gavril Derzhavin (1743–1816), Catherine's own favoured poet and one universally admired in Russia and honoured by Pushkin himself, come three pieces: the first chorus in the ball scene, Tomsky's *couplets*, and the final chorus of Act 2 in which the Empress is welcomed with music that is in fact a ceremonial polonaise by the Polish composer Józef Kosłowski, to words by Derzhavin, celebrating one of Potemkin's victories. A fourth Derzhavin poem was eventually dropped.

These are not the only ingredients in the opera which link it both to the time of Pushkin and still more to the age in which he set his story; and even if Modest failed to see the real point of the story, he did sense its peculiar feeling for period. Everything was once better, the libretto emphasizes at various points: the old men grumble that it was so, the old women complain that manners were better and even that the spring was earlier and the sun warmer. So it often is with the old, but the point is reinforced by the Countess musing upon her young days in Paris, when she saw the Pompadour dance and she herself, the beautiful young Venus of Moscow, once sang to the King. And she drifts reminiscently into her little French song, an aria from Grétry's *Richard, Cœur de Lion* (though in fact it dates from 1784, by when she would have been past her first youth). There is a backward look, a regret for past elegance and the kingdom of manners, which is part of the essence of the story and becomes one of the main ingredients of the opera.

Nothing, of course, could have appealed to Tchaikovsky more than a Pushkin subject that combined a feeling for the rococo past with a story in which love is frustrated by sinister forces; and it is difficult to see why he at first resisted the idea.

The eighteenth century provides a source of much of the music, most obviously when he can indulge in pastiche, as with the duet for Lisa and Pauline, Tomsky's *couplets* and the miniature opera-within-an-opera of *The Faithful Shepherdess*. In the latter he goes so far as to use, without acknowledgment, a barely altered version of a piece from one of Bortyansky's French operas, *Le Fils Rival*; but for the rest he trusts to his own feeling for the period, which underlies much of the invention and reveals itself openly as how he would have composed had he been a contemporary of Mozart's in the Entr'acte before Act 2. Though they hold up the action, these interpolated numbers contribute essentially to the spirit of the work; and Tchaikovsky was also right, from his own point of view, to wish as usual to strengthen the lesser characters. Possibly the words he wrote for Eletsky, who thus benefited, assuring Lisa at the ball that he will not press her for her love, are an echo of one of Pushkin's most famous lyrics, 'The Confession'; certainly they place Eletsky himself with Tchaikovsky's own Gremin.

Together with this flair for the rococo goes Tchaikovsky's love of French opera. A French spirit of elegance permeates the score as it did that of Catherine's Petersburg, and reveals itself not only in the tones in which the French governess is made to reprove the girls but in Hermann's last act aria and in the whole of the opening scene, whose promenading couples and little boys imitating the soldiers are clearly inspired by the equivalent scene of *Carmen*. Beneath it runs the sense of Fate which is at the centre of the opera. *The Queen of Spades* lies between Tchaikovsky's last two 'Fate' symphonies; and if there are echoes of the Fourth at the opening of the great scene when the Countess is frightened to death and of the Fifth at the start of the whole opera, there are also anticipations of the Sixth. Hermann is associated with a sombre descending scale which gradually reveals itself as his destined death, and its particular contours (a series of descending notes ending in a leap with a succeeding fall) is not only kin to the three-cards phrase which is the opera's main motive, but also to Lensky's aria fearing death at Onegin's hands and to the Finale of the Sixth Symphony with its idea of death. The close association of Lisa's love with this theme drives Tchaikovsky into his most intense and Wagnerian manner, one which does not sit very easily beside the rococo elegance; but he found no incongruity in their juxtaposition, for he was unable to restrain himself from the passionate involvement with his eighteenth-century characters that demanded this side of his idiom. He would describe to his correspondents on the one hand how he was still under the 'horrible spell' of the gruesome scene of the Countess's death, and on the other that the opera would be 'something *chic*'; and to Modest himself he described how on setting the scene of Hermann's death, 'I was suddenly overcome by such compassion for Hermann that I began to cry', which he goes on to admit he found a pleasing sensation since Hermann, visualized by him in the person of his tenor Nikolay Figner, had become so utterly real to him. It is this combination of extreme, hysterical states and sinister supernatural forces with the formality and elegance of the eighteenth

century that most deeply characterizes *The Queen of Spades*, and which, since these two sides of Tchaikovsky's character were most fully expressed here, have made it his second most popular opera.

Among Tchaikovsky's friends, there was immediate enthusiasm for the new opera; and the composer himself was pleased to discover that he was unable to play several passages through since they always reduced him to tears. As a lighthearted relief after the task of the opera, he amused himself with a string sextet, originally begun three years previously, which he called *Souvenir de Florence* as a gesture to the city where he had often been happy and in which he had worked on *The Queen of Spades*. It is an agreeable piece, with a substantial first movement succeeded by three lighter ones in which Tchaikovsky ingeniously contrives an amiable flow of melody from his six voices (he was, he told Albrecht, particularly pleased with the fugue) and shows all his old feeling for instruments in the musical ideas that are suggested by the unusual textures. It has the atmosphere of a recreation rather than a serious creative engagement, and there is a certain slackness in the writing; as he told Nadezhda von Meck, 'I wrote it with the greatest enthusiasm and pleasure, without the smallest effort.'

Having paid a brief visit to Moscow in July, he went on to Lobinskoye, the home of Nikolay and Medea Figner; and to his great pleasure and relief, both were enthusiastic about their prospective *Queen of Spades* roles. The following month he set off for the south, spending six days at Grankino, the home of the Konradis, and a fortnight at Kamenka. But there, he told Nadezhda von Meck, 'everything has grown old, and through everything there sounds a certain note of melancholy, with no trace of the old gaiety of life there.' He was especially worried about his sister, who (he confides in Mme von Meck) he has learned from the doctor has been having attacks resembling epilepsy as a result of taking narcotics (she had consulted a Paris doctor for acute pain from gallstones, and like others of her day she had become addicted to the prescribed morphine). To these she has begun to add alcohol; she has, moreover, been increasing the doses. 'God alone knows how this will all end!!!' He travelled on to Kharkov, with Kolya Konradi, and from there they continued to Tiflis, where Tchaikovsky settled contentedly down in a city he loved with a brother, Anatoly, to whom he was devoted, much relieved to have escaped from the darkening atmosphere of Kamenka.

Then on 4 October, he received a letter from Nadezhda von Meck. A few days before she had written in her usual vein, giving him a new address to which to write, as was her habit. This one, which has not survived, informed him that she was on the verge of bankruptcy and must therefore break off his allowance and, she hinted, their relationship, for she ended, 'Do not forget, and remember sometimes.' Tchaikovsky's immediate reaction was to write in great concern for her. Admitting that the loss of the money was bound to affect him, he assured her that in recent years his earnings had grown sufficiently for him to support himself; his real worry was that she, used to a lavish scale of living, would now have to face hardship. He was, he further confessed, upset that she should have reminded him to remember her, when he owed so much to her kindness and sympathy, quite apart from her practical help. He ended what is one of the most genuinely warm and unaffected letters he ever wrote her in some perturbation but with the promise to write again soon with news of himself. But a worse shock was in store for him. She was in no financial difficulty at all. She merely wished to break off the relationship; and she did so with her usual decisiveness.

*Tchaikovsky with V. Argutinsky and Kolya Konradi*

# Fame
## 1890–3

The shock of Nadezhda von Meck's abrupt rejection was one from which Tchaikovsky did not recover during the three remaining years of his life; and what prompted it, he was never able to discover. Certainly the relationship had altered over the years. After the first enthralled discovery of friendship and the mutual understanding of its peculiar conventions, there had begun a series of attempts on her part testing Tchaikovsky's willingness to move closer, culminating in the semi-accidental confrontation of 1879 when she was at the very least ready for their association to become actual friendship in the person, and perhaps hoped for something more. She accepted his gentle but very firm definition of his position with a good grace, and continued to value his friendship and of course to subsidize him; but the correspondence thereafter took on a note of restraint and over the years showed signs of lessening ardour. It could hardly have been otherwise; for while Tchaikovsky was really only capable of living a romantic friendship that was at least half imaginary, Nadezhda von Meck, though another frustrated Romantic, had a strong degree of feminine realism in her makeup. She saw to it that the new stage of the relationship was run at the old distance and on the old terms, but inevitably it lacked quite the old emotion. They continued to address each other with extravagant affection; but it took the occasion of the break for Tchaikovsky, who was as he admitted always prone to exaggeration and false enthusiasm in his letters, to discover the depth not only of his dependence on her but of his genuine affection for her.

What he did not know, and has not been widely known outside her family, was that both were largely the victims of a chain of misunderstandings. In the first place, Nadezhda von Meck was under more financial pressure than she could have admitted generally, since she was being blackmailed by her son-in-law Shirinsky over the illegitimacy of his wife Milochka. Her sickly son Vladimir was indulging in the wildest extravagances and claiming more of her attention, now belatedly given perhaps with the sense that, as with her charity, it should have begun at home. She herself was increasingly ill. Her daughter Yulia Pakhulskaya's correspondence suggests that she was in an odd mental state, without suggesting any cause, and her tuberculosis had gained ground and was attacking her larynx: within three months of Tchaikovsky's death, she was to die in a choking fit. Further, she had developed an atrophy of the arm which made it no longer easy for her to write; and a continuation

*Nadezhda von Meck
in later life*

of the old relationship, in all its extravagantly expressed terms, would obviously have been difficult through the medium of dictation to a relation or a servant. She knew the relationship had to be altered; but she never intended to break it off utterly, and though at her request Pakhulsky urged Tchaikovsky to write (with the assurance that her feelings really had not changed) he felt at a loss and perhaps unwilling to make further approaches when they might well be met with more of what had seemed silent rebuffs. His own acute sense of the appallingness of being abandoned, remembering as he always did the day when his mother's carriage had borne her away from him, would have made him reluctant to risk further rejection by a woman who was at any rate in part a surrogate mother. He could not have known all that was going on in her life, and had no means either of obtaining information, when the family circle would have had every interest in keeping him out and even the Pakhulskys would have been tactful, or of sensing her state of mind, when he had never really known her. To his miserable imagination, the entire relationship was now corrupted, himself degraded to the position of a rich woman's plaything, a servant to her emotions who had been engaged for a suitable wage and then dismissed.

The sense of outrage dominates his correspondence of the months that followed. Her faith in him as an artist worthy of support was more important to him than the actual money, whose loss in any case was soon made good by *The Queen of Spades*. It was, indeed, the fact that her interest in him seemed to go with the money she gave him that upset him most deeply, the more enduringly when he found that neither his willingness to start repaying the subsidy nor simply to continue the friendship apparently affected her decision. He could not even let her know how distressed

Left *Playbill for the first performance of* The Queen of Spades *at the Maryinsky Theatre*

Above *Broadway, New York, as Tchaikovsky would have seen it on his visit to the States*

and hurt he was, for even now he did not wish to hurt in return someone who had done so much for him, and who had once represented an ideal relationship to him. He was obliged to take what consolation he could that winter in his friends, and in the great public success of *The Queen of Spades*. The dress rehearsal was given in the presence of the Tsar in mid-December; the first performance was followed within a fortnight by the first performance in Kiev, and from there he went on to Kamenka, spending a New Year's Eve at which, for a short moment, all the old gaiety and warmth of the house seemed to be revived.

The other anodyne was, of course, work. He wanted subjects for an opera and a ballet. 'Give a thought to *King René's Daughter*', he told Modest. 'I shall probably go to Italy to compose, and I need a subject by the end of January. And what ballet?' Back in Frolovskoye, he settled down to some incidental music he had promised the French actor Lucien Guitry, who was to make his farewell performance that spring as Hamlet. He found the work distasteful, and resorted to making use of earlier pieces: the Overture was a contraction of the Fantasy Overture of 1888; and of the sixteen pieces, including two songs for Ophelia and one for a gravedigger, two of the entr'actes came from the 'alla tedesca' movement of the Third Symphony and the

Right and overleaf *Costume designs for two clou and a prince in* The Nutcrack

*Snow Maiden*, and a Melodrama came from the Elegy for Ivan Samarin. He completed the work in time for Guitry's Benefit, and having attended the performance returned home to press ahead with the new ballet, *The Nutcracker*. He hoped to finish a good deal of it before departing on what was the most elaborate foreign tour yet planned, which included a visit to America. Having conferred with Petipa and the theatre directorate about the ballet, and had some discussions about the opera, he set out in March.

So keen was he to have *The Nutcracker* out of the way that he worked on it as he journeyed towards Berlin: this, with heavy doses of wine and brandy, helped to keep at bay the homesickness that descended heavily on him. From Berlin, where he heard incognito a concert including some pieces of his own, he moved on to Paris and a huge success with a Colonne concert at which he conducted a programme entirely of his music. He was welcomed by Sapelnikov, Sophie Menter and Modest, who found him very changed; he was morose, bitter and evidently very absorbed in professional contacts, only finding time to relax with his friends in the evenings. To fill in time before the boat from Le Havre, he spent a few days in Rouen; and it was while he was there that Modest received news of Alexandra Davidova's sudden death. Very worried about the effect this would have on his brother, Modest set off for Rouen to break the news to him personally; but finding him touchingly excited and pleased by this unexpected visit, Modest realized that to add to such evident loneliness, and homesickness, the news of the most serious possible bereavement on the eve of a transatlantic journey was pointless and indeed heartless. He pretended that his own homesickness had driven him to seek his brother out once more to say goodbye, and returned to Paris; the news would be less distressing in America in the hurly-burly of a concert tour. But growing still more depressed, Tchaikovsky resolved to return to Paris for a day or two, and in the Reading Room in the Passage de l'Opéra he found a Russian newspaper with the announcement of Alexandra's death. 'I started up as though a snake had stung me', he later told Modest. He spent the evening in the comforting company of Sapelnikov and Sophie Menter. At first he thought he should return at once to St Petersburg, especially since he was worried about Bob Davidov; but eventually he decided to go ahead with the tour, and duly set off from Le Havre gloomily reflecting on 'the absolute impossibility of depicting in music the Sugar-Plum Fairy'.

Matters were not improved by a young man committing suicide as they left; but the ship was comfortable, 'a floating palace', and though seasick he managed to divert himself to some extent on the voyage. He was cordially welcomed in New York, and though put out when he discovered that he would be expected to conduct out of town and to return home later than he thought, he was able to enjoy the surprising experiences of seeing buildings nine storeys high and Negroes in the streets before returning to his hotel to cry himself to sleep. Next morning he was welcomed at a rehearsal under Walter Damrosch, later calling on Andrew Carnegie (whom he

# PROGRAMMES.

## FRIDAY EVENING, MAY 8TH, 1891.

THE SEVEN WORDS OF OUR SAVIOUR, . . . . HEINRICH SCHUETZ
(Seventeenth century.) (First time in America.)

For Soli, Chorus, String Orchestra and Organ.

SOLOISTS, { FRAU ANTONIA MIELKE, FRAU MARIE RITTER-GOETZE,
HERR ANDREAS DIPPEL, HERR THEODOR REICHMANN,
MR. ERICSON BUSHNELL.

TWO A CAPELLA CHORUSES:
a. PATER NOSTER,
b. LEGEND. } (New. First time in America.) TSCHAIKOWSKY

Conducted by the Composer.

SULAMITH, . . . . . . . . LEOPOLD DAMROSCH
For Soli, Chorus and Orchestra.

Soloists, FRAU ANTONIA MIELKE, HERR ANDREAS DIPPEL.

---

## SATURDAY AFTERNOON, MAY 9TH, 1891,

FIFTH SYMPHONY, C MINOR, . . . . . . . BEETHOVEN

SONGS, { "TO SLEEP," . . . . . . WALTER DAMROSCH
"SO SCHMERZLICH," . . . . . TSCHAIKOWSKY

CONCERTO for Piano with Orchestra, B Flat Minor, Op. 23, . . . TSCHAIKOWSKY

 I. *Andante non troppo e molto maestoso. Allegro con spirito.*
 II. *Andantino Simplice.*
 III. *Allegro con fuoco.*

Piano, MISS ADELE AUS DER OHE.

Conducted by the Composer.

PRELUDE,
 FLOWER MAIDEN SCENE, ACT II, } FROM PARSIFAL, WAGNER
For six Solo Voices and Female Chorus.

MRS. GERRIT SMITH, MRS. TOEDT. MISS KELLY, MRS. KOERT KRONOLD,
MRS. ALVES, MRS. MORRIS.
Steinway & Sons' Piano used at this Concert.

---

## SATURDAY EVENING, MAY 9TH.

"ISRAEL IN EGYPT" Oratorio, . . . . . . . HANDEL
For Soli, Double Chorus and Orchestra.

SOLOISTS:

MISS KELLY, MRS. TOEDT, MRS. ALVES, HERR DIPPEL,
HERR FISCHER, MR. BUSHNELL.

Top left
*Programme of one of the concerts which opened the Carnegie Music Hall*

Top right
*Andrew Carnegie, who befriended Tchaikovsky in America*

Above and left
*The front steps and auditorium Carnegie Hall 1891*

thought looked like Ostrovsky); he was pleased to find his reputation so high, but the whirl of American hospitality took him completely by surprise, and flattered though he was by the warmth and kindness of his hosts, he was soon utterly exhausted. 'I am sure I am ten times more famous here than in Europe', he wrote to Bob. 'At first when people told me this I thought it was just their exaggerated kindness, but now I see that it is really so.' He was gratified that several works barely known even in Moscow were being played in New York, and was immensely flattered by all the attentions lavished on him, which struck him very favourably after the self-interest he had always detected in Parisian courtesy; but he found himself, he said, like a man before whom a superb meal is set and then finds he has no appetite. His four New York concerts were well received, though he was irritated to find the critic describing his personal appearance as well as his conducting; two others were given in Baltimore and Philadelphia; he visited Niagara Falls, where much to his alarm he was submitted to the tourist rite of being led behind the falls themselves; and in Washington, which like Baltimore he found delightful, he lunched at the Russian Embassy.

American hospitality rose to a climax for his farewell in New York: he was piled high with presents, lunched and dined extravagantly, subjected to addresses in his honour, compelled to autograph some hundred-odd programmes, and given a lavish farewell at the Composers' Club in the Metropolitan Opera; he replied to the speech in his honour in French, which caused the enthusiasm to redouble and a lady to throw a bunch of roses straight into his face. His most attentive hosts had been Morris Reno, president of the Music Hall Company, and Ferdinand Mayer, of the Knabe piano firm; their attention had been kind and unremitting, and it was with them that, after this last reception, he drank a couple of bottles of champagne before they took him to his boat, due to leave at five in the morning. He bade them an affectionate farewell, and thankfully settled into a luxurious cabin. The crossing was bad; he was forced to abandon sketches for a new symphony, and spent two nights sitting up miserably on a sofa. By the end of May he was in Hamburg, and three days later he reached St Petersburg.

The forests had been felled round Frolovskoye, to Tchaikovsky's distress, and in his absence in America, Alexey Sofronov had moved back to Maidanovo. Here the house had fallen into disrepair, and there was the increase in summer visitors to disturb him further; but he managed to resume work on *The Nutcracker*. In Paris he had heard one of Victor Mustel's new instruments, the celesta, and now hastened to order one through Jürgenson for use in the ballet together with some children's instruments. 'I want you to show it to no one,' he added, 'as I'm afraid that Rimsky-Korsakov and Glazunov will get wind of it and make use of its unusual effect before me.' He finished the first draft of the ballet by early in July, without much enthusiasm. 'The ballet is infinitely poorer than *The Sleeping Beauty* – I am in no doubt of it. We'll see what happens with the opera. If I become convinced that

I can only set *réchauffés* at my musical banquet, then I shall certainly give up composing.' 'The old chap's getting worn out', he wrote in the same letter to Bob Davidov, adding a lurid account of his hair turning white and, like his teeth, falling out, his feet beginning to drag, and his eyes failing along with all his other faculties. His lifelong hypochondria and his love of self-dramatization no doubt contributed to this description; but he had indeed begun to tire more easily, and his friends noticed that he now seemed old at fifty and to have changed very markedly in recent years. When he turned to the opera with the resolve to show what he could really do, he found himself thinking that it was perhaps the ballet after all which was better. He was, as ever, easily depressed about his work and about his life. The theft of the clock which Nadezhda von Meck had given him upset him, and he was further distressed when the thief, discovered and brought before him, implored forgiveness but would not admit to having taken it. He was affronted by what seemed a lower financial offer for a return visit to America. The gathering fear of death, to which he used to refer as 'the flat-nosed horror', was increased by the necessity of making a will. Hitherto he had believed that the rights to his operas would pass on his death to the Imperial Theatres; on discovering that this law had been repealed by Alexander III, he set about making dispositions. He had always been generous, and indeed was this autumn often in difficulties, for he never regarded money as for any purpose except immediate use. He was, moreover, assiduous in helping his friends, sometimes wishing upon Jürgenson, or others, young men who would soon turn out to be hopelessly unsuited to whatever position he had recommended them. He was, therefore, pleased to be able to plan for the well-being of various of his friends after his death.

His self-dissatisfaction deepened as the autumn wore on. With the new opera, now finally entitled *Yolanta*, completed in sketch by the middle of September, he turned to a large orchestral tone-poem, *The Voyevoda*. Based on Pushkin's translation of the ballad by his friend Adam Mickiewicz, Poland's treasured poet, it is a cumbersome piece; and the friendly tone of the critics did not reassure Tchaikovsky about its merits. He conducted in lackadaisical fashion at the first performance, and returned to the artists' room in the interval declaring, 'Such rubbish should never have been written.' Siloti, who was in charge of the rest of the concert, took care to preserve the orchestral parts, so that when Tchaikovsky next day carried out his threat of destroying the score it remained possible to reconstruct the work after his death. To Anatoly he wrote that it was unsuccessful, 'a sign of the decline in my powers', and explaining to Jürgenson what had happened, he added:

> I do not regret *The Voyevoda* – it's got what it deserved. I am not in the least sorry, for I am profoundly convinced that this work would compromise me. If I were an inexperienced youth it would have been another matter, but a hoary old man should either go forward (even that is possible, as, for instance, Verdi goes on developing and he's almost eighty) or else remain on the heights he has already reached. If something of this sort happens again, I shall tear it to shreds, or else completely give up composing. Not for anything in the world do I want to go on dirtying paper like Anton Grigorye-vich [Rubinstein] when everything has long since packed up.

However, with his usual optimism about the actual work in hand, he felt able to write to Siloti the same day to say, 'I am delighted that work is going well. The main feeling of pleasure comes from the fact that I shall probably not tear *Yolanta* to shreds like *The Voyevoda*.' Exactly a month later the opera was finished.

It was in the translation of Konstantin Zvantsyev, a journalist and a co-librettist of Serov's *Judith*, that Tchaikovsky came to know the Danish author Henrik Hertz's *Kong Renés Datter*. Based on a story by Hans Andersen, it had also been popular in England; and there was not too much difficulty confronting Modest in turning it into a one-act opera.

> The time is the fifteenth century. *Scene* 1: Yolanta (sop.), the blind daughter of King René, is picking fruit in her garden. She has never been allowed by her father to know that she is any different from others, and strangers are forbidden on pain of death to approach the castle. *Scene* 2: Brigitte (sop.), Laure (mezzo) and her maids help her to find the fruit, while her nurse Marthe (con.) holds the basket. *Scene* 3: Yolanta is de-pressed and tired; they try to amuse her with songs and flowers, then sing her to sleep and carry her into the castle. *Scene* 4: Marthe's husband Bertrand (bar.) now opens the gates to Almerik (ten.), the King's armour-bearer, who announces the arrival of his master, King René (bass), in company with a Moorish doctor, Ebn-Hakia (bass). *Scene* 5: Having examined Yolanta, Ebn-Hakia announces that she can only be cured if she knows she is blind and wishes to see. The King refuses to allow this. *Scene* 6: Robert, Duke of Burgundy (bar.), now arrives at the castle with his friend Count Vaudémont (ten.); he has been betrothed to her from childhood, but loving another he has come to ask for his release. Neither he nor Vaudémont know of Yolanta's blindness; and when they find her sleeping, Vaudémont is enchanted – literally so, Robert believes, trying to drag his friend away from this haunt of witchcraft. *Scene* 7: Their voices arouse Yolanta,

and Robert goes in search of help. In conversation with her Vaudémont discovers that she is blind, and reveals the fact to her. *Scene* 8: The King, returning, is appalled to discover what has happened, but Ebn-Hakia observes that one of his conditions is now fulfilled. The other is not, for not understanding sight Yolanta cannot wish for it. So the King announces that Vaudémont must pay with his life for entering the castle unless she does see. Having fallen in love with Vaudémont's voice Yolanta willingly agrees to submit to treatment and is led away by Ebn-Hakia; the King explains that this was merely a ruse. *Scene* 9: Robert returns with his followers and all is now explained. Bertrand reports that the treatment is completed, and when Yolanta returns, the bandages are taken from her eyes and she sees.

A marginal amount of historical accuracy lies behind this tale, in that the King, the *bon roi René* still held in affectionate memory in his capital of Aix-en-Provence, did indeed have a daughter, Yolande, who married the Comte de Vaudémont. However, the period flavour can have had little influence on Tchaikovsky, who was shortly to write that 'medieval dukes and knights and ladies captivate my imagination but not my *heart*'; possibly, as Gerald Abraham has suggested, there was an attraction in 'the psychological point that the heroine's physical abnormality can be removed only when she recognizes it and wills its removal strongly enough.'

Certainly Tchaikovsky was pleased with the scene between the wondering Vaudé-mont and the girl who does not know she is blind, and it was this which provided the starting point he had so often liked to have in the form of some crucial scene in his operas. The remoteness of the subject, and its semi-fairy-tale nature, was a further attraction; but the mixture of this distancing convention which had often served him well – and was indeed simultaneously doing so with *The Nutcracker* – and a story centred on the vital and ever-painful subject of love, served to confuse his idiom. There are some captivating passages, especially with the lullaby chorus which is in a vein not quite like anything else in his output, with the opening chorus (a reflection of his Italian experiences), and with the moment when Yolanta gives Vaudémont a white rose. Here and in several other passages the music has a delicacy and grace which is charmingly completed in the orchestration. The fineness of the scoring and the subtle orientalisms also suggest *Oberon* (Weber was a composer Tchaikovsky greatly admired, to the point of arranging two movements from his piano sonatas). Yet there is also a manner present in the work that, however much Tchaikovsky would have disliked the comparison, recalls Wagner, not only in the harmonic tension of the long duet between Vaudémont and Yolanta but in the tendency of the main interest to be centred in the orchestra. There are also phrases and harmonic progressions which anticipate the last symphony in their sorrowful decline and bitter flavour. It is a work that veers between the extremes of delicacy and tension, of prettiness (*le joli* again) and passion. In the process an essential part of Tchaikovsky's own personality seems to have been lost.

Vsevolozhsky's idea was that the one-act *Yolanta* should make a double bill with the two-act *Nutcracker*; but before Tchaikovsky could complete the ballet, he had to undertake a short tour. From Kamenka, where he was overcome with grief at the house without its mistress, he went on to Warsaw. Here the inevitable homesickness descended on him, and only the thought of returning to his beloved Bob Davidov kept him going. He admired *Cavalleria Rusticana* and was fêted by Polish countesses. In Hamburg difficulties over the translation of the recitative passages led to him handing *Onegin* over to the local conductor, who was, he reported, 'not some medio-crity but a man of genius who is longing to conduct the first performance': it was Gustav Mahler, and the performance justified Tchaikovsky's highest expectations. After ten days in Paris, bored and lonely, he was unable to bear any longer his separation from Bob Davidov and 'my adored Mother Russia', and cancelling some concerts in Holland he went home. At Maidanovo he orchestrated parts of the new ballet to make a concert suite to replace *The Voyevoda* at a St Petersburg concert in March; thus the *Nutcracker Suite* was performed before its parent ballet, which Tchaikovsky completed immediately afterwards, at the beginning of April.

Tchaikovsky had first come across E. T. A. Hoffmann's *Nussknacker und Mause-könig* – probably in the version by Dumas *père* eventually used for the ballet – as early as 1882 when it was sent to him by Alexey Bakhrushin, a functionary of the

The Nutcracker: above *Varvara Nikitina and Pavel Gerdt*;
below *the Mouse King's troops and the toys*;
opposite *Fairies and Snowflakes*

Theatres. He liked it, but showed no further interest; this was, however, the version which formed the basis of the immensely detailed scenario which Petipa now sent him.

ACT 1, Tableau 1: 1 *Scene* – It is Christmas Eve in the home of the President of the Town Council and his children, Clara and Fritz. As the parents prepare the tree the children burst in with some friends. 2 *March* – All join in a lively march round the room. 3 *Children's galop and entry of the guests* – Everyone joins in a galop and the guests enter to a polonaise. 4 *Dance scene* – A new arrival, Counsellor Drosselmeyer, alarms the children until they are told he is a kind old man who has brought them presents – a cabbage and a pie, to the children's initial disappointment, which turn out to contain a beautiful doll and a splendid toy soldier. 5 *Scene and 'Grossvater' dance* – To console them for not being able to carry off the toys, Drosselmeyer gives them a huge nutcracker with a human head; they quarrel and break the nutcracker, which Clara picks up. The party ends with a grandfather dance. 6 *Scene* – After everyone has gone to bed Clara comes down to see her nutcracker. Mice appear from every corner, while the dolls spring to life and gingerbread soldiers left over from tea begin to march to and fro. 7 *Scene* – Dolls and soldiers join battle with the mice, who overwhelm the soldiers. The Nutcracker rallies the dolls and fights the King of the Mice; when the Nutcracker begins to be overthrown, Clara hurls her slipper at the King of the Mice, and kills him. The Nutcracker is turned into a handsome prince; he offers Clara as reward a visit to his kingdom.

Tableau 2: 8 *Scene* – Clara and the Nutcracker Prince begin their journey to the Kingdom of the Sweets, which lies through a thick forest; they are guided through the falling snow by gnomes with torches. 9 *Waltz of the Snowflakes* – They are met by the King and Queen, who join their subjects in a swirling waltz.

ACT 2: 10 *Scene* – The travellers are welcomed to the palace of the Kingdom of Sweets
by the Sugar Plum Fairy and her suite. 11 *Scene* – In the great hall the Nutcracker
Prince tells how Clara saved his life. They settle down to a splendid banquet and a
*divertissement.* 12 *Divertissement* (a) Chocolate. Spanish dance. (b) Coffee. Arab dance.
(c) Tea. Chinese dance. (d) Trepak. Russian dance. (e) Shepherds' Dance, or *Danse des
Mirlitons.* A pastoral dance using toy flutes. (f) Clowns. The *divertissement* is concluded by the Old Woman who Lived in a Shoe and her children, with a group of
clowns. (13) *Waltz of the Flowers* – Dance for the Sugar Plum Fairy's attendants. (14)
*Pas de deux* – variation 1: Tarantella, for the Nutcracker Prince. Variation 2: the
Sugar Plum Fairy. (1) *Final Waltz and Apotheosis* – The entire court joins in, and the
curtain falls on a final tribute to Clara.

'I began the ballet with an effort, sensing a decline in my inventive powers,'
Tchaikovsky told Taneyev early during the composition; but a month later he was
sounding more optimistic as he reported progress to Modest. However, he always
felt that it was, as he told Bob Davidov, 'far weaker than *The Sleeping Beauty*'.
Certainly it lacks the sense of overall design which marks that masterpiece and had
been present in *Swan Lake*, and his weariness shows in some of the more perfunctory

narrative music. Yet he had by now set himself standards higher than those which had been attained by any other ballet music, and even at its weakest the score of *The Nutcracker* has a skill and charm which his contemporaries never matched. In the characteristic dances he excelled even his own standards. Brief as they are, each one is a brilliant little invention, entirely original (though the Arab Dance is actually based on a Georgian folksong), and unforgettable in its charm. It is out of the association between a particular tone-colour and its ideal melody that Tchaikovsky contrives this entertainment of genius: the flourish of the *mirlitons*, with the rich yet delicate chords of the three flutes, the frenzied Russian dance with its almost violent orchestration in the manner of the Violin Concerto's Finale, the shrieking flute of the Chinese Dance, above all the enchanting effect of Tchaikovsky's cherished celesta and its soft bass clarinet answer in the Sugar Plum Fairy's Dance, all these are of an aural succulence brilliantly designed to reflect the world of Confiturenburg, the Kingdom of Sweets, and never stay so long as to cloy.

Whatever his own doubts about the work's quality, the conscious reduction of his ballet music here to miniature reveals its essence. At this stage of the history of

*Title-page of the full score of* The Nutcracker, *published by Jürgenson*

ballet no great revolution was possible, and it is one measure of Stravinsky's genius that only just over twenty years later *The Rite of Spring* was to shatter the conventions that had for so long frozen over the art. Tchaikovsky had the genius for the melody that was essential to dance still entirely decorative, together with the fineness of ear to make his orchestration not merely an apt presentation of that melody but another expressive facet of it. Both were required to serve music as the highest form of décor. He did not seriously question these precepts, since for all his high respect for ballet music it was connected to a prettiment of life rather than an interpretation of life. And the decorative attracted him since it actually precluded, for its brief intoxication, any deeper emotional engagement, suggesting the illusion of prettiness as a quality sufficient in itself. It is an art whose limitations are part of its essence; and in a world starved of sweetness there will never fail to be a craving for the music of Confiturenburg.

Having fulfilled a promise to conduct Rubinstein's *The Demon* and Gounod's *Faust*, as well as *Onegin*, in Moscow, he was seen off at the station by the entire opera company; from St Petersburg he left for what was to be the last of his country homes, at Klin itself. It was less attractively situated than Maidanovo, with a small garden and little in the way of a view; the great advantage, in a comparatively modest Russian country house, was the size of the rooms, both for guests and for himself to work in. After his death the property passed to Alexey Sofronov, thence to Modest and to Bob Davidov and eventually into the care of the State. Despite being sacked by the Nazis, it has survived to become a very well-organized museum in which his belongings are preserved in something near the order in which he kept them in his lifetime. For all the profusion of pictures, the well-stocked library (which includes some of his English books), the desk with its array of pipes, cigarette-holders, pens and a pen cleaner made of a toy pig with long bristles, the atmosphere is one of simplicity. It carries a strong feeling of his personality, not least in a tiny, sunny room off one of the main rooms in which it was, in these last days as always, his habit to sit over his morning tea before deciding on the day's work.

Here he began another symphony; but becoming dissatisfied with it as symphonic material, he turned it into the first movement of a Third Piano Concerto, leaving also unfinished an Andante and Finale which Taneyev later rewrote so as to make a complete concerto. And once again he planned a foreign tour; for all his misery on these travels, Modest relates, he would no sooner be home than he would be thinking of another journey, only to regret it bitterly as soon as he had crossed the Russian border. What drove him on, Modest does not claim to understand, though even this most loyal and defensive of brothers observes a despondency and restlessness that would not let Tchaikovsky remain calmly at work in the country; and he suggests that this crisis was another of those dark periods out of which several times previously had come a calm and constructive phase. The unhappy composer visited Berlin and Paris with Bob Davidov, going on to Vichy to take a cure for a so-called catarrh of the stomach. In mid-September he was in Vienna, where he refused to conduct a planned concert that he found was due to be given by a scratch orchestra in a beer-cellar. His old friend Anton Door found him, as others had, old at fifty. Back in Moscow and Leningrad, there were many concerts to attend, small official duties to perform; he was Russia's most famous and popular musician, his music was widely played and studied, and his personal appearances were now always greeted with a storm of applause, yet in his tired and morose condition this appreciation he once so keenly coveted now meant little to him. Besides, there were rehearsals of *Yolanta* and *The Nutcracker* to worry about; and for all his feelings of depression, he was more concerned for their success than for past works which by now, he felt, were well able to make their own way.

The Tsar was once more present at the first performance of *Yolanta* and *The Nutcracker*, and 'was full of compliments'. But, Tchaikovsky also wrote to Yuli Konius, 'The success was not absolute. Apparently the opera gives pleasure, but the ballet not really. And as a matter of fact, in spite of all the sumptuousness it did turn out rather boring.' Not all the Figners' skill and reputation could do very much for *Yolanta*; and both works were soon allowed to fall into neglect. Tchaikovsky disappeared once more to the West. From Berlin he sent a long letter to Bob Davidov declaring his intention of abandoning the projected symphony; yet he still needed to work, if only so as to pass time that burdened him increasingly, he wrote, for how could he forget composition?

He occupied himself with a visit on New Year's Day 1893 to his beloved governess of forty years past, Fanny Dürbach, whom he had just discovered was still alive and living in Montbeillard. He was apprehensive as to how time would have dealt with her; but,

> I knew her at once. She does not look her seventy years, and on the whole has altered very little . . . I had dreaded tears and an affecting scene, but there was nothing of the sort . . . She greeted me as though it were only a year since we had met – joyfully and tenderly, but quite simply . . . The past rose up so clearly before me that I seemed to breathe the air of Votkinsk and hear my mother's voice clearly . . .

He went on to Paris and, for some concerts, to Brussels; his journey home was by way of Odessa, where he supervised a concert of his music and rehearsals of *The Queen of Spades*. This left him prostrate with exhaustion, he told Modest, adding that he wished a tenth of the triumphs he had experienced could be his lot in Moscow and Leningrad: in this dark mood he seemed at once to crave the assurance of success yet to resist it when it in fact came, perhaps being still somewhat unable to believe in the fame he now undoubtedly had in the musical circles of the capitals. 'What I need', he insisted, 'is to believe in myself again, for my faith in myself is terribly shattered, and it seems to me that my role has ended.' But Modest knew his brother better than he did himself: out of this darkness of spirit was to emerge one final phase of creative calm, and with it his masterpiece.

At the time of my journey I had an idea for another symphony, this time with a programme, but a programme of a kind that will remain an enigma to all – let them guess,
but the symphony will just be called *Programme Symphony (No. 6)*; *Symphonie à Pro-*
*gramme (No. 6)*; *Eine Programm Symphonie (No. 6).* This programme is permeated with
subjective feeling, and quite often on my journey, composing it in my mind, I wept
copiously. When I reached home, I settled down to the sketches, and the work went
with such ardour and at such speed that in less than four days I had completely finished
the first movement and clearly outlined the remaining movements in my head. Half
the third movement is already done. Formally there will be much that is new in this
symphony, and incidentally the Finale won't be a loud Allegro but, on the contrary, a
very slow-moving Adagio. You can't imagine what bliss I feel in the conviction that
my time is not yet over and that work is still possible. Of course I may be wrong, but I
don't think so.

Within a week of lamenting to Modest that his role as a composer was ended,
Tchaikovsky was confiding these plans for a new symphony to Bob Davidov.
Seldom had he worked so swiftly and with such confidence, or with such impatience
at interruptions. He began on 16 February, and had completed the sketch by 15
April, having had to break off in order to conduct some concerts in Moscow and
another, attended by the now invariable speeches and receptions in his honour, in
Kharkov. He had always tended to believe, in common with most artists, that the
work in hand was the best thing he had ever done, though this mood was often
chastened by waves of self-doubt. Now his enthusiasm was unclouded, and all his
regular correspondents, Jürgenson, Modest, Anatoly, Bob Davidov and others
were given jubilant accounts of work in hand, from the dry remark to Ippolitov-
Ivanov that this time he probably would not tear it up to the claim to his cousin
Anna Merkling that this was 'the best of my works'.

Having completed the sketch, he turned to other tasks, to a *Military March* for
his cousin Andrey Tchaikovsky, colonel of an infantry regiment, to a set of eighteen
piano pieces with which he occupied himself in answer to a commission from
Jürgenson for as many as he liked to send. Without taking them very seriously –
'I am going on baking my musical *blinis*', he told Bob Davidov – he set out to write
one a day, and to his surprise found the ideas beginning to flow well. The set includes

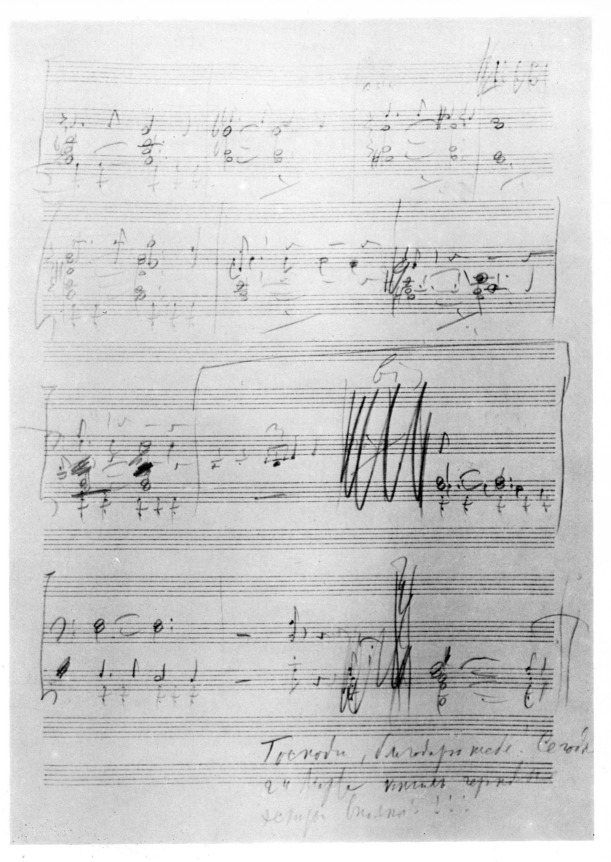

*Last page of the sketch for the second movement of the Pathetic Symphony, with the words,
'O Lord, I thank Thee! Today, 24th March, completed preliminary sketch well!!!'*

*The Tchaikovsky brothers. Left to right: Anatoly, Nikolay, Ippolit, Pyotr and Modest*

a fine Meditation, pieces after the manner of Chopin and Schumann, and a lively waltz in quintuple time. This finished, he turned to a cycle of songs, as usual six in number, to some poems which had been sent to him by an unknown student named Rathaus; they include some of his most beautiful songs, clearly belonging to the world of the Sixth Symphony. He was due to leave on another tour of the West, but delayed his departure so as to finish the songs and to make a transcription of Mozart's C minor Fantasia for vocal quartet, to his own words.

He interrupted this work only briefly so as to go to Moscow to hear the young Rakhmaninov's *Aleko* (he had himself once been approached with a libretto on this subject, Pushkin's *The Gypsies*); and at rehearsals he made a great point of using his reputation to encourage interest in the work and of treating the overawed composer as a colleague on equal terms. Then, after a farewell party given by Rimsky-Korsakov, he departed for England, where he was due to conduct some concerts and to receive a Cambridge doctorate. His letters to Bob Davidov immediately fill with misery. He suffered, he said, from torments which could not be put into words (though he felt he had expressed them adequately in the new symphony), as well as from physical pains. He found London a strain, though he was pleased to see his concerts so well attended; his own music was received with such enthusiasm, he reported, that Saint-Saëns's part in one of the programmes was distinctly overshadowed. Saint-Saëns, however, has left a vivid and generous account of him as 'the gentlest and kindest of men' and a composer of 'talent and astounding technique' in connection with the concert which they shared, together with Bruch and Boito, at Cambridge: Grieg was ill and unable to come. The public orator had evidently been well briefed by the Professor, Charles Villiers Stanford, for his address not only praises the *ardor fervidus* and the *languor subtristis* with which Tchaikovsky had interpreted the Slav genius, but comments favourably on his orchestration and his variation technique. For all his nervousness at this ordeal, he liked Cambridge. But he was glad to be home; not even the news of the deaths of some friends could wholly upset his present mood of assurance. Albrecht had died while he was abroad; his old friend Apukhtin was mortally ill; and immediately he had returned he learned of the death of Vladimir Shilovsky. A few years, or even months, previously one such death would have affected him more than all of them did now, Modest writes; whether he had come to terms with death in some way or, which seems more likely, had emerged from a dark phase into a period of calm and confidence, he did not now allow his distress to overwhelm him. He was, Modest is anxious to stress, 'as serene and cheerful as at any period in his existence'.

The symphony continued to absorb most of his energies. Although the actual composition had gone fluently, he was having difficulty over the scoring, spending two days sitting over a couple of pages he could not make come right. He knew he had written something out of the ordinary, and told Bob Davidov that he expected abuse and misunderstanding, but he reiterated to Jürgenson his belief in it and his open pride in being its creator. He found time to revise the Third Piano Concerto (with little enthusiasm), and he reread Nadezhda von Meck's letters; still puzzled by her sudden withdrawal of the subsidy and her friendship, he found the subject now no longer painful, he claimed, but merely irritating and only too typical of woman's deceitfulness. To Modest he wrote begging him to find the subject for an opera. But the scoring of the symphony was the major task, and by 1 September, it was complete.

*P. I. Tchaikovsky, Mus.D.(Cantab.)*

With his last work, Tchaikovsky completes the triptych of symphonies that deal with his obsession with a personal Fate that had always haunted his life. In the Fourth, Fate had been represented by a violent, merciless theme, void of any expressive harmony at first and eventually set aside in the Finale claiming solace in the life of the peasants. In the Fifth, Fate had become Providence, a more sympathetic concept and one accompanied by humanizing harmony, though this, too, proved fundamentally hostile and was subjected to a still less convincing defeat. Tchaikovsky had immediately sensed the hollow nature of that victory, and in his last symphony he finally faces up to the truth about his nature and his failure to master Fate. The despair is at once evident in the theme itself, a simple melodic phrase that attempts to heave itself up painfully and at its second statement is forced to collapse back onto the original note; while beneath it a slowly descending figure provides sorrowful harmony that is matched in the sombre scoring for bassoon and lower strings. It is clearly to be a symphony of defeat. Although Tchaikovsky kept his resolve not to reveal the programme, it is one which is not hard to sense in general outline even without the brief note, probably an early draft, which was found among his papers:

> The ultimate essence of the plan of symphony is LIFE. First part – all impulsive passion, confidence, thirst for activity. Must be short. (Finale DEATH – result of collapse.) Second part love; third disappointments; fourth ends dying away (also short).

There is an essential difference in treatment from that of the two previous symphonies; for even when the Allegro non Troppo sets off, suggesting confidence and activity, it is with a first theme based on the notes of the opening. Not only has the slow Introduction which Tchaikovsky liked all his life to use now been made organic to the symphony, as had been the case with the Fourth and Fifth, but it even colours the thematic material – an admirable example of how in a fine composer new technical procedures and new expressive requirements are part of the same act of the imagination. The second part is clearly recognizable, even without Tchaikovsky's hint, as a love theme. It is one of his most famous, and most beautiful, bearing traces of his beloved *Carmen*'s 'Flower Song' in its expressive contours, yet wholly personal, not least in its scoring for muted strings over morose brass and low woodwind, and its passionate marking (*teneramente, molto cantabile, con espansione*). The answer is a lighter theme in rising scales, but the outcome is the love theme in still more passionate vein, declining into silence. The development opens with an explosion into some of the most violent music Tchaikovsky ever wrote, and it introduces both a melody from the Orthodox funeral service and a shrill gesture of mockery. It is a magnificent movement; he has rallied all his powers, bringing into one superb symphonic act themes that are both technically well adapted to handling of this kind and emotionally fully expressive of what he needed to say.

Even the ensuing waltz movement is no longer escape or a movement of diversion, for by a marvellous stroke it is not in the waltz's essential triple time, three beats to a bar, but quintuple, a limping waltz with its grace somehow maimed. Its lightness of manner presents the necessary contrast to the force of the first movement, yet it continues to expound the subject of the symphony by being unable to achieve the natural pace of dance, and still more subtly by the tune itself, which for all that it is one of Tchaikovsky's most elegant, proves unable to break out of the circle of its obsessively repeated, slightly varied phrases. For the Trio section, this two-bar strain is still further reduced to a one-bar phrase, again varied as a means of keeping it moving yet unable to achieve real freedom.

Nothing could more impressively demonstrate Tchaikovsky's ability, in this crowning work of his career, to bring into a major symphonic experience the waltz that had been part of his whole imaginative make-up, and which he had left marked for ever with his personality; and the same is true of the march which follows. Miniature marches, military marches, formal and informal marches, official marches and toy marches occur throughout his music; here, in the context of the symphony, a funeral march might perhaps be expected. Tchaikovsky is wiser. All the first part of the movement is preparation, lively figuration thrown from one instrument to another across the orchestra, with little shreds of a theme blown to and fro but never grasped until the right dramatic moment, when a rising scale on clarinets at last releases the tension with the full statement of the tune. On the face of it this is a sprightly march; yet it is barren, constructed out of bleak intervals, and for all the merriness of its manner and the lightness of its scoring, essentially empty, and containing within it the same central descending scale that marks the symphony. This is the whole matter of a brilliant movement whose excitement and ever-increasing tension finally explode into a frenzy that is undoubtedly thrilling but that has coldness at its heart.

The answer comes with the heavy phrases of the Finale, Adagio Lamentoso. In the previous year, Tchaikovsky had been profoundly disturbed at the thought of death; there is no reason whatever to suppose that he had a premonition of his own end when he wrote this music, and indeed he was well and content, ready to contemplate plans for new works, but it would be in the nature of the artistic imagination for the experiences of the recent past, once properly absorbed, to become the substance of music. For Russians this movement has come to mean Death; and there can be few listeners who do not sense its mournful finality. It is the ideal structural answer to the pattern of the symphony, and the true conclusion of the hidden programme, which has clearly passed through its several experiences into a final submission to Fate. The opening theme is the same descending scale that has lain at the centre of the symphony's invention; and when the strings manage to force their way up to a climax by a similar heaving process to that of the opening, the woodwind drag the music down again in a long, painfully twisting scale. The descending scale gives a poignant quality to the gentler middle section, which for all its marking *con lenezza e devozione* is shadowed with wistfulness. Though it builds up to a powerful chord and a dramatic pause, the resumption is still more grief-laden and bitter, and the succeeding climaxes desperate. A passage of grave chords over a soft gong stroke leads into the second theme once more, before the symphony moves over the steady throb of double basses into silence.

Never had Tchaikovsky so closely integrated his emotional ideas with his musical material, both in the actual 'lyrical idea' and, which is what makes the symphony a masterpiece, in the handling to which the material is subjected. There is no longer the need for artifice to support the lyrical ideas that were the essence of his invention; here technique and imagination are one, with both musically and emotionally the tragic outcome of the symphony implied in the opening material and then faithfully and inventively carried out. The detail of the programme has remained his secret; but there can be little doubt that what is here composed is a further engagement with the real emotional problem of his life, which he claimed he had successfully turned aside in the Fourth and defeated in the Fifth. There is a total unity in this last of his symphonies which shows that he had finally acknowledged the truth of his condition, that of a passionate and gentle nature doomed only to loneliness and frustration.

As he finished the symphony, news came of Apukhtin's death. It was suggested that Tchaikovsky might compose a setting of the poet's *Requiem* as a memorial; but he refused, observing that he did not wish to take up again so quickly a similar mood to that which he had been expressing, 'and my last symphony (particularly the Finale) is permeated with such a mood.'

On 22 October, Tchaikovsky arrived in St Petersburg for the first performance. He had parted from Kashkin in Moscow in good spirits, saddened though both of them were by the loss of several friends in recent months. Tchaikovsky was full of confidence about the symphony, worrying only that the Finale might have to be reconsidered after performance. He stayed with Modest for the performance, and even the coolness of the orchestra towards the new work did not lower his confidence in it. He still refused to explain its meaning, even to his colleagues; in the interval of the concert, at which the work was received with a good deal of puzzlement, he met Rimsky-Korsakov. 'I asked him,' Rimsky recalled in his *Memoirs*, 'was there not a programme in this work? He replied that indeed there was, but that he didn't want to reveal it.' There remained, however, the question of the title, as Modest has described.

Coming down to morning tea next day, I found Pyotr Ilyich already long since up and with the score of the Sixth Symphony before him. He had agreed to send it to Jürgenson that same day and did not know what title to give it. He did not want to leave it with only a number, nor to call it 'Programme' as he originally thought. 'Why "Programme" when I don't want to give the programme!' I suggested calling it 'Tragic'. That did not please him. I went out of the room, leaving Pyotr Ilyich in a state of indecision. Then suddenly the title 'Pathetic' came into my head. I went back and, I remember as if it were yesterday, I stood in the doorway and uttered the word. 'Excellent, Modya, bravo, *Pathetic!*', and before my eyes he wrote on the score the title by which it has since been known.

It has been a misleading title, especially in English. The Russian word which Modest used is similar, *patetichesky*; it carries more feeling of 'passionate' and 'emotional' in it than the English 'pathetic', and perhaps an overtone, which has largely vanished from our word, of the original Greek, 'suffering'. Certainly the work is Tchaikovsky's symphony of emotional suffering.

On 30 October Tchaikovsky wrote to Jürgenson to say that he would shortly be in Moscow to discuss publication; meanwhile he spent his time going to the theatre or dining with friends. He was, Modest recounts, in good health and spirits, and even managed to laugh at an actor friend's guying of spiritualism and other reminders of death. For his part, he declared, he felt he had a long time to live. But on the morning of the 2nd he failed to appear for breakfast. Modest found him complaining of indigestion and a bad night. However, he went out to see Nápravník, in whose hands the second performance of the symphony was to be, and refused to see a doctor. He ate nothing at lunch, having arrived at a restaurant in a state of upset caused by an unfortunate encounter with a woman who had been blackmailing him over his relationship with her son and now waylaid him with abuse. To his friends' alarm, in view of the current cholera scare, he seized and insisted on drinking a glass of unboiled water. He grew worse during the day, and by evening Modest was sufficiently worried to send for a doctor. Glazunov had called during the afternoon and found Tchaikovsky weak but refusing to admit the possibility of cholera. But when Modest's doctor arrived in the evening he saw at once that matters were serious. Tchaikovsky had begun to feel congestion in his chest, and more than once he repeated, 'I believe this is death.' Dr Bertenson called in his brother, and eventually a third doctor; and the anxious friends spent the night nursing him through the cramps that characterize the early stage of cholera. When not in pain, he begged them to retire for the night, trying to joke with them and thanking them gratefully for the smallest service.

In the morning he felt better and spoke of having been snatched from the jaws of death. But this was the deceptive phase in which the patient feels new strength; and on the third day his depression returned. 'Leave me,' he told the doctors. 'You can do no good. I shall never recover.' He passed into the second stage, and with the failure of his kidneys became delirious, repeating the feminine form of the word for 'accursed one!' (*proklyatya*), which Modest assumes to have referred to Nadezhda von Meck but could equally have meant the blackmailer or perhaps even the disease itself ('cholera' is feminine in Russian). When Alexey Sofronov arrived, hastily summoned from Klin, his master did not recognize him. At last, as had once long ago been tried with his mother, they resorted to the hot bath. It was no use, and his pulse began to fail. A priest was sent for, but finding Tchaikovsky too weak to

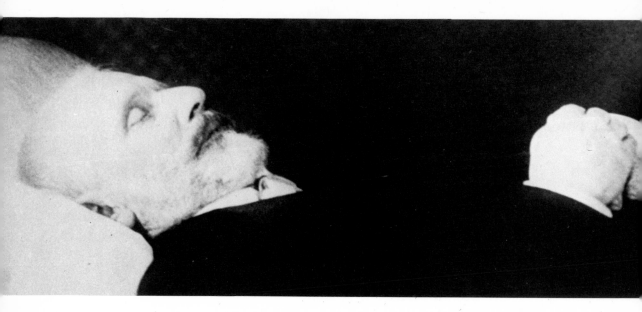

receive the Sacrament, prayed by his bed in loud tones which Tchaikovsky showed no sign of hearing. At three o'clock on the morning of 6 November the gathering round the bed consisted of Modest, his eldest brother Nikolay, Bob Davidov, a cousin and a friend of Bob's, the three doctors and Alexey Sofronov. At the last moment, Modest recalled, a look of 'clear recognition' of them passed across his face; and then he closed his eyes.

# Comprehensive List of Works

## OPERAS

| TITLE | OPUS NO. | SOURCE | LIBRETTIST | COMPOSED | PRODUCED | SINGERS AND CONDUCTOR |
|---|---|---|---|---|---|---|
| *The Voyevoda* | 3 | Alexander Ostrovsky: *A Dream on the Volga* | Ostrovsky and composer (3 acts) | 20 Mar. 1867– summer 1868 | Moscow, Bolshoy, 11 Feb. 1869 | Ludovico Finocchi (Shaligin), Platon Radonezhsky (Vlas Dyuzhoy), Anna Annenskaya (Nastasya), Alexandra Menshikova (Maria), Z. Kronenberg (Praskovya), Alexander Rapport (Bastryukov), Stepan Demidov (Dubrovin), Ivanova (Olyena), Bozhanovsky (Rezvy), Lavrov (Buffoon), Rozanova (Nedviga), Korin (New Voyevoda); cond. Eduard Merten. |
| *Undine* | – | Friedrich de la Motte Fouqué: *Undine* (trans. Zhukovsky) | Count Vladimir Sollogub, originally prepared for Alexy Lvov (3 acts) | Jan.–Feb. 1869 | – | – |
| *The Oprichnik* | – | Ivan Lazhechnikov: *The Oprichniks* | Composer (4 acts) | Feb. 1870– Apr. 1872 | St Petersburg, Maryinsky, 24 Apr. 1874 | Dmitry Orlov (Andrey Morozov), Alexandra Kritikova (Boyarina Morozova), Vladimir Vasilyev (Prince Zhemchuzhny), Wilhelmine Raab (Natalia), Vladimir Sobolyev (Molchan Mitkov), Vasily Vasilyev (Basmanov), Ivan Melnikov (Prince Vyazminsky), Olga Schroeder (Zakharyevna); cond. Eduard Nápravník. |
| *Vakula the Smith* (see also *Cherevichki*) | 14 | Nikolay Gogol: *Christmas Eve* | Yakov Polonsky (3 acts) | Jun.–2 Sept. 1874 | St Petersburg, Maryinsky, 6 Dec. 1876 | Fyodor Komissarjevsky (Vakula), Ivan Matchinsky (Chub), Osip Petrov (Pan Golova – Mayor), Ivan Melnikov (the Devil), Vasily Vasilyev (Panas), Anna Bichurina (Solokha), Wilhelmine Raab (Oxana), Ende [Nikolay Dyerviz] (Schoolmaster), Fyodor Stravinsky (His Royal Highness), Pavel Dyuzhikov (Official); cond. Eduard Nápravník. |
| *Eugene Onegin* | 24 | Alexander Pushkin: *Eugene Onegin* | Composer and Konstantin Shilovsky (3 acts) | May 1877– 1 Feb. 1878 | Moscow, Maly Theatre, 29 Mar. 1879 | Maria Klimentova (Tatyana), Alexandra Levitskaya (Olga), Maria Reiner (Mme Larina), Zinaida Konshina (Filipyevna), Sergey Gilyev (Onegin), Mikhail Medvedyev (Lensky), Vasily Makhalov (Prince Gremin and a Captain), D. B. Tarkhov (M. Triquet and Zaretsky); cond. Nikolay Rubinstein. |
| *The Maid of Orleans* | – | Friedrich Schiller: *Die Jungfrau von Orleans* (trans. Zhukovsky) | Composer (4 acts) | 17 Dec. 1878– 4 Sept. 1879 | St Petersburg, Maryinsky, 25 Feb. 1881 | Maria Kamenskaya (Joan), Vladimir Vasilyev (the King), Wilhelmine Raab (Agnes Sorel), Fyodor Stravinsky (Dunois), Ippolit Pryanishnikov (Lionel), Vladimir Mayboroda (Cardinal), Mikhail Koryakin (Thibaut), Fyodor Sokolov (Raymond); cond. Eduard Nápravník. |
| *Mazeppa* | – | Alexander Pushkin: *Poltava* | Viktor Burenin and composer (3 acts) | Summer 1881– 11 May 1883 | Moscow, Bolshoy, 15 Feb. 1884 | Bogomir Korsov (Mazeppa), Pavel Borisov (Kochubey), Alexandra Krutikova (Lyubov Kochubey), Emilia Pavlovskaya (Maria), Dmitry Usatov (Andrey), Otto Führer (Orlik), Pyotr Grigoryev (Iskra), Alexander Dodonov (Drunken Cossack); cond. Ippolit Altani. |
| *Cherevichki* (revised version of *Vakula the Smith*, also known as *Oxana's Caprices*) | – | Nikolay Gogol: *Christmas Eve* | Yakov Polonsky (4 acts) | Feb.–3 Apr. 1885 | Moscow, Bolshoy, 31 Jan. 1887 | Dmitry Usatov (Vakula), Bogomir Korsov (the Devil), Vladimir Streletsky (Pan Golova – Mayor), Alexander Dodonov (Schoolmaster), Ivan Matchinsky (Chub) Pavel Khokhlov (His Royal Highness), Romuald Vasilyevsky (Master of Ceremonies), Maria Klimentova (Oxana), Alexandra Svyatlovskaya (Solokha); cond. Tchaikovsky. |
| *The Sorceress* | – | Ippolit Shpazhinsky: *The Sorceress* | Shpazhinsky (4 acts) | Sept. 1885– 14 May 1887 | St Petersburg, Maryinsky, 1 Nov. 1887 | Ivan Melnikov (Prince Kurlyatev), Maria Slavina (Princess), Mikhail Vasilyev (Prince), Fyodor Stravinsky (Mamirov), Maria Dolina (Nenila), Emilia Pavlovskaya (Nastasya – Kuma), Nikolay Klimov (Foka), Elena Markovskaya (Polya), Mikhail Koryakin (Kichiga), Vasily Vasilyev (Paysy), Sergey Pavlovsky (Kudma), Vladimir Sobolev (Potap), Grigory Ugrinovich (Lukash); cond. Tchaikovsky. |

| TITLE | OPUS NO. | SOURCE | LIBRETTIST | COMPOSED | PRODUCED | SINGERS AND CONDUCTOR |
|---|---|---|---|---|---|---|
| *The Queen of Spades* | 68 | Alexander Pushkin: *The Queen of Spades* (3 acts) | Modest Tchaikovsky and composer | 31 Jan.–20 Jun. 1890 | St Petersburg, Maryinsky, 19 Dec. 1890 | Nikolay Figner (Hermann), Ivan Melnikov (Tomsky), Leonid Yakovlev (Eletsky), Vasily Vasilyev (Chekalinsky), Hjalmar Frey (Surin), Konstantin Kondaraki (Chaplitsky), Vladimir Sobolev (Narumov), Vasily Efimov (Master of Ceremonies), Alexander Klimov (Zlatogor), Maria Slavina (Countess), Medea Figner (Lisa), Maria Dolina (Pauline), Maria Piltz (Governess), Yulia Yunosova (Maid), Olga Olgina (Prilepa), Nina Fride (Milovsor) cond. Eduard Nápravník. |
| *Yolanta* | 69 | Henrik Hertz: *King René's Daughter* (trans. Zvantsyev) | Modest Tchaikovsky (1 act) | 22 Jul.–27 Dec. 1891 | St Petersburg, Maryinsky, 18 Dec. 1892 | Konstantin Serebryakov (King René), Leonid Yakovlev (Robert), Nikolay Figner (Vaudémont), Arkady Chernov (Ebn-Hakia), Vasily Karelin (Almerik), Hjalmar Frey (Bertrand), Medea Figner (Yolanta), Maria Kamenskaya (Marthe), Alexandra Runge (Brigitte), Maria Dolina (Laure); cond. Eduard Nápravník. |

## BALLETS

| TITLE | OPUS NO. | SOURCE | SCENARIO | DESIGNER | COMPOSED | PRODUCED | DANCERS, PRODUCER AND CONDUCTOR |
|---|---|---|---|---|---|---|---|
| *Swan Lake* | 20 | Original | Vladimir Begichev and Vasily Geltzer (4 acts) | Act 1: Shangin Acts 2 and 4: Karl Waltz Act 3: Gropius | Aug. 1875–22 Apr. 1876 | Moscow, Bolshoy, 4 Mar. 1877 | Pelageia Karpakova (Odette/Odile), Olga Nikolayeva (Princess), Stanislav Gillert (Prince Siegfried), Sergey Nikitin (Benno), Sergey Sokolov (Rotbart), Wilhelm Wanner (Wolfgang), Reinshausen (Stein); prod. Yuly Reisinger; cond. Stepan Ryabov. |
| *The Sleeping Beauty* | 66 | Charles Perrault: *La Belle au Bois Dormant* | Marius Petipa and Ivan Vsevolozhsky (3 acts) | Heinrich Levot, Ivan Andreyev, Mikhail Bocharov, Konstantin Ivanov, Matvey Shishkov | Dec. 1888–1 Sept. 1889 | St Petersburg Maryinsky, 15 Jan. 1890 | Carlotta Brianza (Princess Aurora), Pavel Gerdt (Prince Désiré), Enrico Cecchetti (Fairy Carabosse), Maria Petipa (Lilac Fairy); prod. Marius Petipa; cond. Riccardo Drigo. |
| *The Nutcracker* | 71 | Alexandre Dumas (*père*) after E. T. A. Hoffmann: *Nussknacker und Mausekönig* | Marius Petipa (2 acts) | | Feb. 1891–4 Apr. 1892 | St Petersburg Maryinsky, 18 Dec. 1892 | Felix Kshesinsky (President Silberhaus), Augusta Ogoleit (Frau Silberhaus), Stanislava Belinskaya (Clara), Vasily Stukolkin (Prince), Lydia Rubstova (Marianna), Timofey Stukolkin (Drosselmeyer), Maria and Elizaveta Onegina (the President's relations), Sergey Legat (the Nutcracker), Nikolay Lozhkin (the President's Servant), Antonietta dell'Era (Sugar-Plum Fairy), Pavel Gerdt (Prince Cocliouche), Ivanov (Majordomo); prod. Marius Petipa and Lev Ivanov; cond. Riccardo Drigo. |

## MISCELLANEOUS DRAMATIC MUSIC

| TITLE | DESCRIPTION | SOURCE | LIBRETTO | COMPOSED | PRODUCED |
|---|---|---|---|---|---|
| *Boris Godunov* (lost) | Scene for projected opera | Alexander Pushkin: *Boris Godunov* (Fountain Scene) | ? | 1863–4? | – |
| *The Tangle* (lost) | Couplets | Pavel Fyodorov: *The Tangle* (vaudeville) | ? Original | Dec. 1867 | Moscow, Mme Lopukhin's house, Dec. 1867 |
| *Dmitry the Pretender and Vasily Shiusky* | Incidental music (2 numbers) | Alexander Ostrovsky: *Dmitry the Pretender* | – | By 11 Feb. 1867 | ? |
| *Le Domino Noir* | Recitatives and choruses | Auber: *Le Domino Noir* | – | Oct. 1868 | Moscow, 1868 |
| *Mandragora* | Chorus for projected opera | Sergey Rachinsky: *Mandragora* | Rachinsky | 8 Jan. 1870 | Moscow, 30 Dec. 1870 |
| *The Barber of Seville* | Couplets, 'Vous l'ordonnez' | Pierre Caron de Beaumarchais: *Le Barbier de Seville* | Original, trans. Mikhail Sadovsky | By 24 Feb. 1872 | Moscow, Conservatory, 24 Feb. 1872 |
| *The Snow Maiden* (Op. 12) | Incidental music (19 numbers) | Alexander Ostrovsky: *The Snow Maiden* | – | Mar.–Apr. 1873 | Moscow, Maly (on Bolshoy stage), 23 May 1873 |
| *Le Nozze di Figaro* | Recitatives | Mozart: *Le Nozze di Figaro* | Original, trans. Tchaikovsky | 1875 | Moscow, Conservatory, 17 May 1876 |
| *La Fée* | Cradle song | Octave Feuillet: *La Fée* | Original | 13 Jul. 1879 | Kamenka, Alexandra Davidov's house, Jul. 1879 |
| *Montenegrins Receiving News of Russia's Declaration of War on Turkey* | Music for a tableau | – | – | 8–11 Feb. 1880 | – |
| *The Voyevoda* | Melodrama | Alexander Ostrovsky: *A Dream on the Volga* (Domovoy scene) | Origina | 25–29 Jan. 1886 | Moscow, Maly, 31 Jan. 1886 |
| *Hamlet* (Op. 67b) | Incidental music (16 numbers) | William Shakespeare: *Hamlet* | Original, trans.? | 13 Jan.–3 Feb. 1891 | St Petersburg, Mikhailovsky 23 Feb. 1891 |
| *Romeo and Juliet* | Duet, possibly for projected opera | William Shakespeare: *Romeo and Juliet* | Original, trans. Alexander Sokolovsky | 1893 | – |

# CHORAL WORKS

| TITLE | OPUS NO. | WORDS | SETTING | COMPOSED | PERFORMED |
|---|---|---|---|---|---|
| [Oratorio] | – | ? | ? | 1863–4 | – |
| 'On Going to Sleep' | – | Nikolay Ogarev | Mixed chorus, unacc. (later arr. by composer with orchestra) | ? | 1863–4 |
| *To Joy* | – | Friedrich Schiller: *An die Freude*, trans. Konstantin Aksakov | SATB soloists, mixed chorus and orchestra | Nov. 1865– 10 Jan. 1866 | St Petersburg, Conservatory, 10 Jan. 1866; cond. [?] Anton Rubinstein |
| Cantata for the Opening of the Polytechnic Exhibition in Moscow | – | Yakov Polonsky | Tenor, mixed choir and orchestra | Feb.–Mar. 1872 | Moscow, Polytechnic Exhibition, 12 Jun. 1872; soloist, Alexander Dodonov, cond. Karl Davidov |
| Cantata (hymn) on the Occasion of the Celebration of the 50th Jubilee of O. A. Petrov | – | Nikolay Nekrasov | Tenor, mixed chorus and orchestra | 29 Dec. 1875 | St Petersburg, Conservatory, 6 May 1876; cond. Karl Davidov |
| Liturgy of St John Chrysostom (15 numbers) | 41 | | Mixed chorus, unacc. (arr. by composer for piano, 1878) | 8 Jun. 1878 | |
| 'Evening' | – | Composer (?) | 3-part male chorus, unacc. | By 25 Dec. 1881 | ? |
| Cantata (lost) | – | Pupils of the Patriotic Institute | 4-part female chorus, unacc. | ? Dec. 1881 | ? |
| Vesper Service (17 numbers) | 52 | | Mixed chorus, unacc. | May 1881– 7 Dec. 1882 | |
| *Moscow* (Coronation Cantata) | – | Apollon Maykov | Mezzo-soprano, baritone, mixed chorus and orchestra | 21 Mar.– 5 Apr. 1883 | Moscow, Kremlin, 27 May 1883; cond. Eduard Nápravník |
| Three Cherubic Hymns | – | | Mixed chorus, unacc. (arr. by composer for piano) | Nov. 1884 | |
| Hymn in honour of SS Cyril and Method | – | Composer (on Old Czech melody) | Mixed chorus, unacc. | 18–20 Mar. 1885 | Moscow, Conservatory, 18 Apr. 1885 |
| Six Church Songs | – | Liturgical | Mixed chorus, unacc. (arr. by composer for piano) | Mar.–Apr. 1885 | |
| 'The Pure Bright Flame of Truth' (School of Jurisprudence Song) | – | Composer | Mixed chorus, unacc. | By 9 Oct. 1885 | ? |
| 'An Angel Crying' | – | ? | Mixed chorus, unacc. | 2 Mar. 1887 | ? |
| 'The Golden Cloud Had Slept' | – | Mikhail Lermontov | Mixed chorus, unacc. | 17 Jul. 1887 | ? |
| 'Blessed is He Who Smiles' | – | 'K.R.' [Grand Duke Konstantin (Romanov)] | 4-part male chorus, unacc. | 19 Dec. 1887 | Moscow, Conservatory; cond. V. G. Malm |
| Greeting to Anton Grigoryevich Rubinstein | – | Yakov Polonsky | Mixed chorus, unacc. | 2–12 Oct. 1889 | St Petersburg, Hall of the Society of the Nobility, 30 Nov. 1889; cond. composer |
| 'The Nightingale' | – | Composer | Mixed chorus, unacc. | By 27 Dec. 1889 | Moscow, 25 Dec. 1892; cond. Antony Arensky |
| ''Tis not the Cuckoo in the Dank Pinewood' | – | Nikolay Tsiganov | Mixed chorus, unacc. | By 26 Feb. 1891 | ? St Petersburg; cond. Fyodor Becker |
| 'The Merry Voice Fell Silent' | – | Alexander Pushkin | 4-part male chorus, unacc. | By 26 Feb. 1891 | ? St Petersburg; cond. Fyodor Becker |
| 'Without Time, without Season' | – | Nikolay Tsiganov | 4-part female chorus, unacc. | By 26 Feb. 1891 | ? St Petersburg; cond. Fyodor Becker |
| 'Spring' (lost) | – | ? | Female chorus, unacc. | ? | ? |

# ORCHESTRAL WORKS

| TITLE | OPUS NO. | KEY | COMPOSED | PERFORMED | CONDUCTOR |
|---|---|---|---|---|---|
| Andante ma non troppo, for small orchestra | – | A major | 1863–4 | ? | ? |
| Agitato and allegro, for small orchestra | – | E minor | 1863–4 | ? | ? |
| Little Allegro with Introduction for small orchestra | – | D major | 1863–4 | ? | ? |
| Allegro ma non tanto, for strings | – | G major | 1863–4 | ? | ? |
| Allegro vivo | – | C minor | 1863–4 | ? | ? |
| *The Romans in the Coliseum* | – | ? | 1863–4 | ? | ? |
| *The Storm*: overture to Ostrovsky's drama | 76 | E minor– E major | Summer 1864 | St Petersburg, 7 Feb. 1896 | Alexander Glazunov |
| Overture, for small orchestra (rev. for full orchestra) | – | F major F major | 27 Aug.–27 Nov. 1865 Feb. 1866 | St Petersburg, 26 Nov. 1865 Moscow, 16 Mar. 1866 | Composer Nikolay Rubinstein |
| Characteristic Dances (later rev. as 'Dances of the Serving Maids' in *The Voyevoda*) | – | | Winter 1865 | Pavlovsk, 11 Sept. 1865 | Johann Strauss (jun.) |
| Concert Overture | | C minor | Summer 1865– 31 Jan. 1866 | Voronezh, 1931 | Konstantin Saradzhev |

| TITLE | OPUS NO. | KEY | COMPOSED | PERFORMED | CONDUCTOR |
|---|---|---|---|---|---|
| Symphony No. 1 ('Winter Reveries') | 13 | G minor | Mar.–Aug. 1866 (rev. Dec. 1866) (rev. 1874) | Moscow, 15 Feb. 1868 Moscow, 1 Dec. 1883 | Nikolay Rubinstein Max Erdmannsdörfer |
| Ceremonial Overture on the Danish National Anthem | 15 | D major | 22 Sept.–24 Nov. 1866 | ? | ? |
| Symphonic Poem, *Fate* | 77 | C minor–C major | 22 Sept.–Dec. 1868 | Moscow, 27 Feb. 1869 | Nikolay Rubinstein |
| Overture, *Romeo and Juliet* (after Shakespeare) | – | | 7 Oct.–27 Nov. 1869 (rev. summer 1870) (rev. by 10 Sept. 1880 as 'overture-fantasia') | Moscow, 16 Mar. 1870 St Petersburg, 17 Feb. 1872 Tiflis, 1 May 1886 | Nikolay Rubinstein Eduard Nápravník Mikhail Ippolitov-Ivanov |
| Symphony No. 2 ('Little-Russian') | 17 | C minor | Jun.–Nov. 1872 (rev. Dec. 1879) | Moscow, 7 Feb. 1873 St Petersburg, 12 Feb. 1881 | Nikolay Rubinstein Karl Zike |
| Serenade for N. G. Rubinstein's name-day, for small orchestra | – | | 13 Dec. 1872 | Moscow, Nikolay Rubinstein's flat, 18 Dec. 1872 | |
| Symphonic Fantasia, *The Tempest* (after Shakespeare) | 18 | F minor | 19 Aug.–22 Oct. 1873 | Moscow, 19 Dec. 1873 | Nikolay Rubinstein |
| Symphony No. 3 | 29 | D major | 17 Jun. (or 7 Aug.)–13 Aug. (or 12 Aug.) 1875 (autograph dates differ) | Moscow, 19 Nov. 1875 | Nikolay Rubinstein |
| Slavonic March | 31 | B flat minor–B flat major | 7 Oct. 1876 | Moscow, 17 Nov. 1876 | Nikolay Rubinstein |
| Symphonic Fantasia, *Francesca da Rimini*, after Dante | 32 | E minor | 7 Oct.–17 Nov. 1876 | Moscow, 9 Mar. 1877 | Nikolay Rubinstein |
| Symphony No. 4 | 36 | F minor | May 1877–7 Jan. 1878 | Moscow, 22 Feb. 1878 | Nikolay Rubinstein |
| Suite No. 1 | 43 | D minor D major | 27 Aug. 1878–26 Apr. 1879 | Moscow, 23 Nov. 1879 | Nikolay Rubinstein |
| Italian Capriccio | 45 | A major | 16 Jan.–27 May 1880 | Moscow, 18 Dec. 1880 | Nikolay Rubinstein |
| Serenade, for string orchestra | 48 | G major | 21 Sept.–4 Nov. 1880 | St Petersburg, 30 Oct. 1881 | Eduard Nápravník |
| Ceremonial Overture, *1812* | 49 | E flat major | 12 Oct.–19 Nov. 1880 | Moscow, 20 Aug. 1882 | Ippolit Altani |
| Ceremonial Coronation March | – | D major | 21 Mar.–1 Apr. 1883 | Moscow, Sokolniki, 4 Jun. 1883 | Sergey Taneyev |
| Suite No. 2 | 53 | C major | 9 Jul.–25 Oct. 1883 | Moscow, 16 Feb. 1884 | Max Erdmannsdörfer |
| Suite No. 3 | 55 | G major | Apr.–31 Jul. 1884 | St Petersburg, 24 Jan. 1885 | Hans von Bülow |
| Elegy in honour of I. V. Samarin, for string orchestra | – | G major | 18 Nov. 1884 | Moscow, 28 Dec. 1884 | Ippolit Altani |
| Symphony, *Manfred*, after Byron | 58 | B minor | Apr.–4 Oct. 1885 | Moscow, 11 Mar. 1886 | Max Erdmannsdörfer |
| Jurists' March | – | D major | 17 Nov. 1885 | ? | ? |
| Symphony No. 5 | 64 | E minor | May–26 Aug. 1888 | St Petersburg, 17 Nov. 1888 | Composer |
| Overture-fantasia, *Hamlet*, after Shakespeare | 67 | F minor | Jun.–19 Oct. 1888 | St Petersburg, 24 Nov. 1888 | Composer |
| Symphonic Ballad, *The Voyevoda*, after Mickiewicz | 78 | A minor | Sept. 1890–4 Oct. 1891 | Moscow, 18 Nov. 1891 | Composer |
| Ballet Suite, *The Nutcracker* | 71a | B flat major–D major | Jan.–21 Feb. 1892 | St Petersburg, 19 Mar. 1892 | Composer |
| Symphony No. 6 'Pathetic' | 74 | B minor | 16 Feb.–31 Aug. 1893 | St Petersburg, 28 Oct. 1893 | Composer |

# WORKS FOR SOLO INSTRUMENT WITH ORCHESTRA

| TITLE | OPUS NO. | KEY | COMPOSED | PERFORMED | SOLOIST | CONDUCTOR |
|---|---|---|---|---|---|---|
| Concerto No. 1 for piano | 23 | B flat minor | Nov. 1874–21 Feb. 1875 | Boston, 25 Oct. 1875 | Hans von Bülow | Benjamin Johnson Lang |
| Sérénade mélancolique, for violin | 26 | B flat minor | Jan. 1875 | Moscow, 28 Jan. 1876 | Adolf Brodsky | Nikolay Rubinstein |
| Variations on a Rococo Theme, for cello | 33 | A major | Dec. 1876 | Moscow, 30 Nov. 1877 | Wilhelm Fitzenhagen | Nikolay Rubinstein |
| Valse-Scherzo, for violin | 34 | C major | 1877 | Paris, 20 Sept. 1878 | Stanislav Bartsevich | Nikolay Rubinstein |
| Concerto, for violin | 35 | D major | 17 Mar.–11 Apr. 1878 | Vienna, 4 Dec. 1881 | Adolf Brodsky | Hans Richter |
| Concerto No. 2, for piano | 44 | G major | 22 Oct. 1879–10 May 1880 (rev. Aug.–1 Sept. 1893, Siloti) | Moscow, 30 May 1882 | Sergey Taneyev | Anton Rubinstein |
| Concert Fantasia, for piano | 56 | G major | Jun.–6 Oct. 1884 | Moscow, 6 Mar. 1885 | Sergey Taneyev | Max Erdmannsdörfer |
| Pezzo Capriccioso, for cello | 62 | B minor | 24–31 Aug. 1887 | Moscow, 7 Dec. 1889 | Anatoly Brandukov | Composer |
| Concerto No. 3, for piano | 75 | E flat major | 5 Jul.–15 Oct. 1893 | St Petersburg, 19 Jan. 1895 | Sergey Taneyev | ? |
| Andante and Finale, for piano | 79 | B flat major–E flat major | Begun after 15 Oct. 1893; completed and orchestrated by Taneyev, 1895 | Moscow, 20 Feb. 1896 | Sergey Taneyev | ? |

# CHAMBER MUSIC

| TITLE | OPUS NO. | KEY | COMPOSED | PERFORMED |
|---|---|---|---|---|
| Adagio, for wind octet | – | F major | 1863–4 | ? |
| Allegro, for string quartet, double bass and piano | – | C minor | 1863–4 | ? |
| Adagio molto, for string quartet and harp | – | E flat major | 1863–4 | ? |
| Andante ma non troppo, Prelude for string quintet | – | E minor | 1863–4 | ? |
| Allegretto molto, for string trio | – | D major | 1863–4 | ? |
| Andante molto, for string quartet | – | G major | 1863–4 | ? |
| Allegro vivace, for string quartet | – | B flat major | 1863–4 | ? |
| Adagio, for four horns | – | C major | 1863–4 | ? |
| Allegretto, for string quartet | – | E major | 1863–4 | ? |
| String Quartet (one movement only) | – | B flat major | 27 Aug.–by 11 Nov. 1865 | St Petersburg, Conservatory, 11 Nov. 1865; Konstantin Pushilov, D. Panov, Vasily Bessel, Alexander Kuznetsov |
| String Quartet No. 1 | 11 | D major | Feb. 1871 | Moscow, 28 Mar. 1871; Ferdinand Laub, Pryanishnikov, Ludwig Minkus, Wilhelm Fitzenhagen |
| String Quartet No. 2 | 22 | F major | 30 Jan. 1874 | Moscow, 22 Mar. 1874; Ferdinand Laub, Jan Hřímalý, Yuly Gerber, Wilhelm Fitzenhagen |
| String Quartet No. 3 | 30 | E flat minor | Beginning Jan.– 1 Mar. 1876 | Moscow, 30 Mar. 1876; Jan Hřímalý, Adolf Brodsky, Yuly Gerber, Wilhelm Fitzenhagen |
| *Souvenir d'un lieu cher*, for violin and piano | 42 | | Mar.–May 1878 | ? |
| 1. Meditation | | D minor | | |
| 2. Scherzo | | C minor | | |
| 3. Mélodie | | E flat minor | | |
| Trio, for piano, violin and cello | 50 | A minor | Dec. 1881– 9 Feb. 1882 | Moscow, 23 Mar. 1882; Sergev Taneyev, Jan Hřímalý, Wilhelm Fitzenhagen |
| Sextet, *Souvenir de Florence*, for two violins, two violas and two cellos | 70 | D minor | 1887; 24 Jun.– Aug. 1890; Dec. 1891–Jan. 1892 | St Petersburg, 6 Dec. 1892; Leopold Auer, Emmanuel Krüger, Franz Hildebrandt, Sergey Korguyev, Alexander Verzhbilovich, Alexander Kuznetsov |

# PIANOFORTE MUSIC

| TITLE | OPUS NO. | KEY | COMPOSED | PERFORMED |
|---|---|---|---|---|
| Valse | – | ? | Aug. 1854 | ? |
| Piece (on the theme, 'By the River, by the Bridge'), after Lyadov | – | ? | Sept.–Dec. 1862 | ? |
| Allegro (fragment) | – | F minor | 1863–4 | ? |
| Theme and Variations (9) | – | A minor | 1863–4 | ? |
| Sonata | 80 | C sharp minor | 1865 | ? |
| Two Pieces | 1 | | | |
| 1. Russian Scherzo | | B flat major | 20 Mar. 1867 | Moscow, 12 Apr. 1867; Nikolay Rubinstein |
| 2. Impromptu | | E flat minor | | St Petersburg, 25 Feb. 1893; Schwarz |
| Potpourri on themes from *The Voyevoda* | | | 1868 | ? |
| *Souvenir of Hapsal* | 2 | | Jun.–Jul. 1867 | ? |
| 1. The Castle Ruins | | E minor | | Moscow, 10 Mar. 1868; Nikolay Rubinstein |
| 2. Scherzo | | F major | | |
| 3. Song without words | | F major | | St Petersburg, 14 Nov. 1874; Gustav Kross |
| Valse | 4 | D major | Oct. 1868 | Moscow, 2 Mar. 1886; Anton Rubinstein |
| Romance | 5 | F minor | Nov. 1868 | Moscow, 20 Dec. 1868; Nikolay Rubinstein |
| Valse–scherzo | 7 | A major | 15 Feb. 1870 | ? |
| Capriccio | 8 | G flat major | 15 Feb. 1870 | ? |
| Trois morceaux | 9 | | By 7 Nov. 1870 | |
| 1. Rêverie | | D major | | Moscow, 28 Mar. 1871; Nikolay Rubinstein |
| 2. Polka de salon | | B flat major | | ? |
| 3. Mazurka de salon | | D minor | | Moscow, 28 Mar. 1871; Nikolay Rubinstein |
| Deux morceaux | 10 | | Dec. 1871 | |
| 1. Nocturne | | F major | | Tiflis, 1 May 1886; Gennary Korganov |
| 2. Humoreske | | G major | | Paris, 28 Feb. 1888; Louis Diémer |
| Six Pieces | 19 | | 8 Nov. 1873 | |
| 1. Rêverie | | G minor | | ? |
| 2. Scherzo humoristique | | D major | | ? |
| 3. Feuillet d'album | | D major | | ? |
| 4. Nocturne | | C sharp minor | | ? |
| 5. Capriccioso | | B flat major | | St Petersburg, 18 Dec. 1888; Nikolay Lavrov |
| 6. Thème original et variations (13) | | F major | | Moscow, 10 Mar. 1876; Nikolay Rubinstein |
| Six Pieces on a Single Theme | 21 | | By 12 Dec. 1873 | |
| 1. Prelude | | G sharp minor | | Tiflis, 10 Apr. 1891; F. K. Kessner |
| 2. Fuge à 4 voix | | G sharp minor | | ? |
| 3. Impromptu | | C sharp minor | | ? |
| 4. Marche funèbre | | A flat minor | | St Petersburg, 12 Dec. 1893; Felix Blumenfeld |
| 5. Mazurque | | A flat minor | | ? |
| 6. Scherzo | | A flat major | | ? |
| *The Seasons:* Twelve Characteristic Pieces | 37b | | 1875–6, monthly | ? |
| 1. By the Hearth [January] | | A major | | |
| 2. Carnival [February] | | D major | | |
| 3. Song of the Lark [March] | | G minor | | |

| TITLE | OPUS NO. | KEY | COMPOSED | PERFORMED |
|---|---|---|---|---|
| 4. Snowdrop [April] | | B flat major | | |
| 5. White Nights [May] | | G major | | |
| 6. Barcarolle [June] | | G minor | | |
| 7. Song of the Reaper [July] | | E flat major | | |
| 8. Harvest [August] | | B minor | | |
| 9. The Hunt [September] | | G major | | |
| 10. Autumnal Song [October] | | D minor | | |
| 11. In the Troika [November] | | E major | | |
| 12. Christmas-tide [December] | | A flat major | | |
| March [for the Volunteer Fleet], by 'P. Sinopov' | – | C major | 6 May 1878 | |
| Twelve Pieces of Moderate Difficulty | 40 | | 24 Feb.–12 May 1878 | ? |
| 1. Etude | | G major | | |
| 2. Chanson triste | | G minor | | |
| 3. Funeral march | | C minor | | |
| 4. Mazurka | | C major | | |
| 5. Mazurka | | D major | | |
| 6. A Song without words | | A minor | | |
| 7. In the Village | | A minor | | |
| 8. Valse | | A flat major | | |
| 9. Valse (2nd version) | | F sharp minor | (1st version, 16 Jul. 1876) | |
| 10. Russian scherzo | | A minor | | |
| 11. Scherzo | | D minor | | |
| 12. Interrupted Reverie | | A flat major | | |
| Funeral March (on themes from *The Oprichnik*) (for piano duet) | – | | 19–28 Mar. 1877 | ? |
| *Children's Album* (24 Easy Pieces) | 39 | | ? 26 Feb.–Oct. 1878 | ? |
| 1. Morning Prayer | | G major | | |
| 2. Winter morning | | B minor | | |
| 3. Mama | | G major | | |
| 4. Playing Hobbyhorses | | D major | | |
| 5. March of the Wooden Soldiers | | D major | | |
| 6. The New Doll | | B flat major | | |
| 7. The Sick Doll | | G minor | | |
| 8. The Doll's Funeral | | C minor | | |
| 9. Valse | | E flat major | | |
| 10. Polka | | B flat major | | |
| 11. Mazurka | | D minor | | |
| 12. Russian Song | | F major | | |
| 13. The Peasant plays the Mouth-organ | | B flat major | | |
| 14. Kamarinskaya | | D major | | |
| 15. Italian Air | | D major | | |
| 16. Old French Air | | G minor | | |
| 17. German Air | | E flat major | | |
| 18. Neapolitan Air | | E flat major | | |
| 19. Nanny's Story | | C major | | |
| 20. Baba-Yaga | | E minor | | |
| 21. Sweet Reverie | | C major | | |
| 22. Song of the Lark | | G major | | |
| 23. In Church | | E minor | | |
| 24. The Organ-grinder Sings | | G major | | |
| Grand Sonata | 37 | G major | 13 Mar.–7 Aug. 1878 | Moscow, 2 Nov. 1879; Nikolay Rubinstein |
| Six Pieces | 51 | | Aug.–22 Sept. 1882 | ? |
| 1. Valse de salon | | A flat major | | |
| 2. Polka peu dansante | | B minor | | |
| 3. Menuetto-scherzoso | | E flat major | | |
| 4. Natha-valse (2nd version) | | A major | (1st version, 17 Aug. 1878) | |
| 5. Romance | | F major | | |
| 6. Valse sentimentale | | F minor | | |
| Impromptu – Caprice | – | G major | 2 Oct. 1884 | ? |
| Dumka (Russian rustic scene) | 59 | C minor | 27 Feb.–5 Mar. 1886 | ? |
| Valse – scherzo | – | A major | 28 Aug. 1889 | ? |
| Impromptu | – | A flat major | 2–12 Sept. 1889 | ? |
| 'Aveu passioni' | – | E minor | ? 1892 | |
| Military March (for the 98th Yurevsky Infantry) | – | B flat major | 5 Apr.–17 May 1893 | ? |
| Eighteen Pieces | 72 | | 19 Apr.–4 May 1893 | ? |
| 1. Impromptu | | F minor | | |
| 2. Berceuse | | A flat major | | |
| 3. Tendres Reproches | | C sharp minor | | |
| 4. Danse caractéristique | | D major | | |
| 5. Méditation | | D major | | |
| 6. Mazurka pour danser | | B flat major | | |
| 7. Polacca de concert | | E flat major | | |
| 8. Dialogue | | B major | | |
| 9. Un poco di Schumann | | D flat major | | |
| 10. Scherzo-fantaisie | | E flat minor | | |
| 11. Valse – bluette | | E flat major | | |
| 12. L'espiègle | | E major | | |
| 13. Echo rustique | | E flat major | | |
| 14. Chant élégiaque | | D flat major | | |
| 15. Un poco di Chopin | | C sharp minor | | |
| 16. Valse à cinqtemps | | D major | | |
| 17. Passé lointain | | E flat major | | |
| 18. Scène dansante. Invitation au trépac | | C major | | |
| Impromptu (Momento lirico) (finished by Taneyev) | – | A flat major | ? 1893 | ? |

# SONGS

| TITLE | OPUS NO. | KEY | VOICE | COMPASS | WORDS | COMPOSED |
|---|---|---|---|---|---|---|
| My genius, my angel, my friend | – | C minor | Low | G–E flat | Afanasy Fet, from cycle *To Ophelia* | End 1850s |
| Zemfira's Song | – | A minor | High | E–A | Alexander Pushkin, from *The Gypsies* | End 1850s |
| Mezza Notte | – | G major | High | C sharp–A | Anon., Italian | ? |
| Who Goes? [lost] | – | ? | ? | ? | Alexey Apukhtin | ? |
| Six Songs | 6 | | | | | 27 Nov.–29 Dec. 1869 |
| 1. Do not believe, my friend | | C minor | High | C sharp–F sharp | Alexey Tolstoy | |
| 2. Not a word, O my friend | | E minor | High | D sharp–G | Alexey Pleshcheyev, from Moritz Hartmann's 'Silence' | |
| 3. Both painfully and sweetly | | A major | Medium | B–A | Evdokia Rostopchina, 'Words for Music' | |
| 4. A tear trembles | | G flat major | Baritone | D flat–F flat | Alexey Tolstoy | |
| 5. Why? | | D major | High | D–A | Lev Mey, after Heine, from cycle *Lyrisches Intermezzo* | |
| 6. No, only he who has known (None but the lonely heart) | | D flat major | Medium | C–F | Mey, from Goethe, *Mignon's lied* 'Nur wer die Sehnsucht kennt', from *Wilhelm Meister* | |
| To forget so soon | – | F major/minor | High | E–A flat | Apukhtin | By 7 Nov. 1870 |
| Nature and Love (trio) | – | G flat major | SSA | | Composer | Dec. 1870 |
| Six Songs | 16 | | | | | ? Dec. 1872 |
| 1. Cradle song | | A flat major | High | D sharp–A flat | Apollon Maykov, from cycle, *Modern Greek Songs* | |
| 2. Wait! | | A minor–major | High | D sharp–F sharp | Nikolay Grekov | |
| 3. Accept just once | | C minor | Low | B–F | Fet | |
| 4. O sing that song | | G major | High | D–G | Pleshcheyev, from Felicity Hemans [?], 'Mother! Oh sing me to rest' | |
| 5. Thy radiant image | | F sharp minor–A major | High | E–A | 'NN' [Composer] | |
| 6. Modern Greek Song: 'In Dark Hell' | | E flat major | High | D flat–F | Maykov, from cycle, *Modern Greek Songs* | |
| Take my heart away | – | A minor | Medium | D sharp–F | Fet | By 11 Oct. 1873 |
| Blue eyes of spring | – | A major | Medium | E–F sharp | Mikhail Mikhailov, after Heine, 'Die blaue Frühlingsaugen' | By 11 Oct. 1873 |
| Six Songs | 25 | | | | | Sept. 1874 |
| 1. Reconciliation | | G minor | Medium | A–G | Nikolay Shcherbina | |
| 2. As over the burning ashes | | B minor | High | F sharp–G | Fyodor Tyutchev | |
| 3. Mignon's Song: Knowst thou the land? | | E flat major | High | E–G flat | Tyutchev, after Goethe, 'Kennst du das Land', from *Wilhelm Meister* | |
| 4. The Canary | | G minor | High | C–G | Mey, from cycle, *Octaves* | |
| 5. I never spoke to her | | A major | Low | A–E | Mey, from cycle, *Octaves* | |
| 6. As they kept on saying, 'Fool' | | G minor | Medium | F–F | Mey, 'Song' | |
| I should like in a single word | | D minor | High | E–G | Mey, after Heine, from cycle, *Die Heimkehr* | By 10 Jul. 1875 |
| We have not far to walk | | E major | Medium | C sharp–F sharp | Grekov | By 10 Jul. 1875 |
| Six Songs | 27 | | | | | By 20 Apr. 1875 |
| 1. To sleep | | B flat minor | Medium | B flat–F | Nikolay Ogarev | |
| 2. Look, yonder cloud | | C minor | Low | G–F | Grekov, 'Stanzas' | |
| 3. Do not leave me | | F major | Medium | A–F | Fet, from cycle, 'Melodies' | |
| 4. Evening | | B flat major | Medium | C–F | Mey, after Taras Shevchenko | |
| 5. Was it the mother who bore me? | | E flat major | Medium | B–G flat | Mey, after Adam Mickiewicz, 'Song' | |
| 6. My spoiled darling | | A major | Medium | A–F sharp | Mey, after Mickiewicz | |
| Six Songs | 28 | | | | | By 23 Apr. 1875 |
| 1. No, I shall never tell | | E flat major | High | E flat–A flat | Grekov, after Alfred de Musset's 'Chanson de Fortunio' | |
| 2. The Corals | | F sharp minor | High | F sharp–A | Mey, after V. Syrokomla [Ludwig-Vladislav Kondratovicz] | |
| 3. Why did I dream of you? | | D minor | High | D–G (A ad lib.) | Mey | |
| 4. He loved me so much | | D minor | High | D–A | Anon. [? Apukhtin] | |
| 5. No answer, or word, or greeting | | C minor | Medium | C–F | Apukhtin | |
| 6. The fearful moment | | F sharp minor | High | C sharp–G sharp | 'NN' [composer] | |
| The Underdog [musical joke] | – | ? | | | Composer | 1876 |
| Six Songs | 38 | | | | | 23 Feb.–8 Jun.1878 |
| 1. Don Juan's Serenade | | B minor | Baritone | B–E (F sharp ad lib. | Alexey Tolstoy, from *Don Juan* | |
| 2. It was in the early spring | | E flat major | High | E flat–G | Alexey Tolstoy | |
| 3. Amid the noise of the ball | | B minor | Medium | B–E | Alexey Tolstoy | |
| 4. O, if you could for a moment | | D major | Medium | C sharp–E flat | Alexey Tolstoy | |
| 5. The love of a dead man | | F major | Medium | C–F | Mikhail Lermontov | |
| 6. Pimpinella: Florentine air | | G major | Medium | A–F | Composer, from trad. Italian | |
| Six Duets | 46 | | | | | 16 Jun.–5 Sept. 1880 |
| 1. Evening | | A flat major | S Mezzo | D–A flat; G–A flat | Ivan Surikov | |
| 2. Scottish Ballad: 'Edward' | | A minor | S Bar. | D–A; E flat–F | Alexey Tolstoy, after trad. Scottish ballad | |
| 3. Tears | | G minor | S Mezzo | C–A flat; A–F | Tyutchev | |
| 4. In the garden, near the ford | | A major | S Mezzo | E–G sharp; G sharp–E | Surikov, after Shevchenko | |
| 5. Passion spent | | F minor | ST | D–A flat; E flat–B double flat | Alexey Tolstoy | |
| 6. Dawn | | E major | S Mezzo | E–A; G sharp–E | Surikov | |
| Seven Songs | 47 | | | | | Jul.–Aug. 1880 |
| 1. If only I had known | | C minor | High | D–A flat | Alexey Tolstoy | |
| 2. Softly the spirit flew up to heaven | | E major | High | E–G sharp | Alexey Tolstoy | |
| 3. Dusk fell on the earth | | F major | High | E–F | Nikolay Berg, from Mickiewicz, 'Morning and Evening' | |

| TITLE | OPUS NO. | KEY | VOICE | COMPASS | WORDS | COMPOSED |
|---|---|---|---|---|---|---|
| 4. Sleep, poor friend | | G flat major | Medium | D flat–E | Alexey Tolstoy | |
| 5. I bless you, forests | | F major | Baritone | C–F | Alexey Tolstoy, from *John Damascene* | |
| 6. Does the day reign? | | E major | High | D sharp–A | Apukhtin | Orch. composer, 24 Feb. 1888 |
| 7. Was I not a little blade of grass? | | F sharp minor | High | D–A | Surikov, 'Little Russian Song' | Orch. composer 7 Oct. 1884 |
| Sixteen Songs for Children | 54 | | | | | 28 Oct.–15 Nov. 1883 (except for No. 16) |
| 1. Granny and grandson | | A minor | High | D–E | Pleshcheyev | |
| 2. The little bird | | G major | High | D sharp–F | Pleshcheyev, from the Polish (in his collection *The Snowdrop*) | |
| 3. Spring ('The grass grows green') | | G major | High | D–G | Pleshcheyev, from the Polish, 'Country Song' | |
| 4. My little garden | | G major | High | E–F sharp | Pleshcheyev | |
| 5. Legend | | E minor | High | D–E | Pleshcheyev, from the English | Orch. composer, 14 Apr. 1884, arr. for mixed choir, 27 Dec. 1889 |
| 6. On the bank | | C major | High | E flat–E | Pleshcheyev, from the English | |
| 7. Winter Evening | | C minor | High | D–G | Pleshcheyev | |
| 8. The Cuckoo | | G major | High | B–G | Pleshcheyev, after Christian Gellert | |
| 9. Spring ('The snow is already melting') | | F major | High | E–F | Pleshcheyev | |
| 10. Lullaby in a storm | | F minor | High | E–F | Pleshcheyev | |
| 11. The Flower | | F major | High | E–F | Pleshcheyev, after Louis Ratisbonne | |
| 12. Winter | | D major | High | D–E | Pleshcheyev | |
| 13. Spring Song | | A major | High | E–E | Pleshcheyev | |
| 14. Autumn | | F sharp minor | High | F sharp–E | Pleshcheyev | |
| 15. The Swallow | | G major | High | D sharp–E | Surikov, after Teofil Lenartowicz | |
| 16. Child's Song | | A minor | High | E–E | Konstantin Aksakov | By 19 Jan. 1881 |
| Six Songs | 57 | | | | | Nov. 1884 (except for No. 1) |
| 1. Tell me, what in the shade of the branches | | E major | High | D sharp–A | Vladimir Sollogub | Early or mid-1884 |
| 2. On the golden cornfields | | F minor | Baritone | D–G flat | Alexey Tolstoy | |
| 3. Do not ask | | D minor | Medium | A–G | Alexander Strugorshchikov, after Goethe, 'Heiss mich nicht reden', from *Wilhelm Meister* | |
| 4. Sleep! | | F major | Medium | B–F | Dmitry Merezhkovsky | |
| 5. Death | | F major | High | D–G | Merezhkovsky | |
| 6. Only thou | | G major | Low | A–F sharp | Pleshcheyev | |
| Twelve Songs | | | | | | 31 Aug.–20 Sept. 1886 |
| 1. Last night | | A flat major | High | E flat–A flat | Alexey Khomyakov, 'Nachtstück' [*sic*] | |
| 2. I'll tell you nothing | | E major | High | E–F sharp | Fet, 'Song', from cycle *Melodies* | |
| 3. O, if you knew | | E flat major | High (written for tenor, but transposition for baritone suggested by composer) | E flat–A flat | Pleshcheyev | |
| 4. The Nightingale | | C minor | High | G–A flat | Alexander Pushkin, after Vuk Stefanović Karadzić | |
| 5. Simple words | | F major | Medium | D–F | 'NN' [Composer] | |
| 6. Frenzied nights | | G major | High | D–A flat | Apukhtin | |
| 7. Gypsy's Song | | E minor | High | D–F | Yakov Polonsky | |
| 8. Forgive | | F major | High | C–A | Nikolay Nekrasov | |
| 9. Night | | G minor | High | D–G | Polonsky | |
| 10. Behind the window in the shadow | | F major | High | D–A | Polonsky, 'Challenge' | |
| 11. Exploit | | G minor | Baritone | C–G | Alexey Khomyakov | |
| 12. The mild stars shone for us | | F major | Medium | C–G flat | Pleschceyev, 'Words for music' | |
| Six Songs, to words by K.R. | 63 | | | | Grand Duke Konstantin (Romanov) | Nov.–Dec. 1887 |
| 1. I did not love you at first | | B flat major | High | F–F | | |
| 2. I opened the window | | F major | Medium | D–F | | |
| 3. I do not please you | | C major | Medium | D–F | | |
| 4. The first meeting | | E flat major | High | E flat–G | | |
| 5. The fires in the room were already out | | E major | High | E–F sharp | | |
| 6. Serenade ('O child, beneath thy window') | | G major | High | D–A | | |
| Six Songs, to French texts | 65 | | | | | Summer–22 Oct. 1888 |
| 1. Sérénade | | D major | Medium | B–F sharp | Édouard Turquéty, 'Aurore' | |
| 2. Déception | | E minor | Low | A–E | Paul Collin | |
| 3. Sérénade | | B flat major | Medium | D–F | Collin | |
| 4. Qu'importe que l'hiver | | D minor | Medium | C–F | Collin | |
| 5. Les larmes | | G major | Medium | D–E | Auguste-Malvine Blanchecotte | |
| 6. Rondel | | G major | Medium | D–E | Collin | |
| [Musical joke: plea to composer's nephew Vladimir Davidov] | | | | | Composer | 1892 |
| Night (quartet, based on music of Mozart's C minor Fantasia, K.475) | | B flat major | SATB | | 'NN' [Composer] | 15 Mar. 1893 |
| Six Songs, to poems by D. M. Rathaus | 73 | | | | Daniel Rathaus | 5–17 May 1893 |
| 1. We sat together | | E major– C sharp minor | High | E–G sharp | | |
| 2. Night | | F minor | High | C–G flat | | |
| 3. In this moonlight | | A flat major | High | D–A flat | | |

## ARRANGEMENTS OF WORKS BY OTHER COMPOSERS

| COMPOSER | WORK | ORIGINAL | ARRANGEMENT | COMPOSED |
|---|---|---|---|---|
| Beethoven | Sonata in D Minor (Op. 31, No. 2). First movement | Piano | Orchestra (four versions) | ?1863 |
| Beethoven | Sonata in A major (Op. 47) ('Kreutzer'). First movement | Piano and violin | Large orchestra | 1863–4 |
| Weber | Sonata in A flat (J 199). Scherzo Menuetto | Piano | Orchestra | 1863 |
| Schumann | Études Symphoniques. Adagio and Allegro brillante | Piano | Orchestra | 1864 |
| Gung'l | 'Le Retour', waltz | Piano | Orchestra | 1863–4 |
| Kral | Ceremonial March | Piano | Orchestra | May 1867 |
| Dargomizhsky | 'Little-Russian Kazachok' | Orchestra | Piano | 1868 |
| Tarnovsky | Song, 'I remember all', arranged by Dubuque | Piano | Piano Duet | 1868 |
| Dubuque | 'Maria-Dagmar', polka | Piano | Orchestra | 1869 |
| – | Fifty Russian Folksongs | Voice: 1–25 from collection of Konstantin Villebois, 26–50 from collection of Balakirev, except for No. 47, coll. by composer | Piano duet | 1–25: ?Summer 1868 26–50: by 7 Oct. 1869 |
| Anton Rubinstein | *Ivan the Terrible* | Orchestra | Piano duet | 18 Oct.–11 Nov. 1869 |
| Anton Rubinstein | *Don Quixote* | Orchestra | Piano duet | 1870 |
| Stradella | 'O del mio dolce' | Voice and piano | Voice and orchestra | 10 Nov. 1870 |
| Cimarosa | Trio, 'Le faccio un inchino', for Carolina, Elisetta and Fidalma, from Il Matrimonio Segreto' | SS Mezzo and piano, in form available | SS Mezzo and orchestra | 1870 |
| Dargomizhsky | 'The golden cloud had slept' | 3 voices and piano | 3 voices and orchestra | 1870 |
| Weber | Sonata in C major (J 138). Perpetuum mobile | Piano | Piano, left hand | 1871 |
| Prokupin (coll.) | 66 Russian folksongs | Voice | Voice (edited) | 1–33: 1872 34–66: 1873 |
| Mamontova (coll.) | Children's Songs | Voice | Voice and piano | 1–24: by 7 Sept. 1872 25–43: by May 1877 |
| Haydn | 'Gott erhalte den Kaiser' | 4 voices | Orchestra | By 24 Feb. 1874 |
| Schumann | Ballade vom Haideknaben (Op. 122, No. 1) | Declamation and piano | Declamation and orchestra | 11 Mar. 1874 |
| Liszt | 'Es war ein König in Thule' | Voice and piano | Voice and orchestra | 3 Nov. 1874 |
| (Trad.) | 'Gaudeamus igitur' | Melody | 4-part male chorus and piano | 1874 |
| Bortyansky | Complete Church Music | Choir | Choir (edited) | 3 Jul.–8 Nov. 1881 |
| Glinka | 'Slavsya', from *A Life for the Tsar* | Arr. as couplets | Mixed chorus orchestra | 9–16 Feb. 1883 |
| Lvov | 'God save the Tsar' (national anthem 1833–1917) | Chorus and piano | | |
| Mozart | 1. Gigue (K 574) 2. Minuet (K 355) 3. Ave verum (K 618), arr. Liszt 4. Variations on 'Unser dummer Pöbel meint', from Gluck's *Der Pilger von Mekka* (K. 455) | Piano Piano Orchestra Piano | Orchestra, as Suite No. 4, *Mozartiana* | 29 Jun.–9 Aug. 1887 |
| Laroche | Fantasy Overture, *Karmosina* | Piano | Orchestra | 27 Aug–27 Sept. 1888 |
| Mozart | 'Night' [see Songs, 1893] | | | |
| Menter | Ungarische Zigeunerweisen | Piano | Piano and orchestra | 1893 |

## LITERARY WORKS AND MISCELLANEOUS WRITINGS

Translation of François Gevaert's *Traité d'Instrumentation* (1863), from French: 1865

Translation of Urbain's Cavatina, 'Une dame noble et sage', from Meyerbeer's *Les Huguenots*, from Italian: by 5 Jun. 1868

Translation of Schumann's *Musikalische Haus- und Lebensregeln*, from German: by Jul. 1868

Translation of J. C Lobe's *Katechismus der Musik* (1851), from German: by 20 Nov. 1869

Translations of Anton Rubinstein's *Persische Lieder* (Op. 34), from F. von Bodenstedt's German translation of Mirza Shafi: by 24 Dec. 1869

Translations of two of Anton Rubinstein's songs (Op. 32, Nos. 1 and 6), from German: ?1870–1

Translations of two of Anton Rubinstein's songs (Op. 33, Nos. 2 and 4), from German: ?1870–1

Translations of Anton Rubinstein's Six Songs (Op. 72), from German: ?1870–1

*Guide to the Practical Study of Harmony*: completed 14 Aug. 1871

Translations of Anton Rubinstein's Six Songs (Op. 76), from German: ?1871

Translations of three of Anton Rubinstein's songs (Op. 83, Nos. 1, 5 and 9), from German: ?1871

*A Short Manual of Harmony, adapted to the study of religious music in Russia*: 1874

Translation of Mozart's *Marriage of Figaro*, from German: 1875

Translations of five Italian songs by Glinka: by 27 Dec. 1877

Translation of Glinka's *Prayer*, for quartet: 1877

Translation of Handel's *Israel in Egypt* (with Taneyev): 1886

Editing and correction of musical terms in Vols. 2 and 3 in *Dictionary of the Russian Language*: Oct. 1892–3

Diaries: 1858–9 (destroyed by accident, 1866); 1873; 1882 (lost); 1884; 1885 (lost); 1886; 1887; 1888 (*Diary of My Tour*); 1889; 1890; 1891.

Critical writings and reviews (see full list in Dombayev)

Autobiography (incomplete, lost)

Juvenile writings and poems

# Select Bibliography

In this very brief selection of the most important books on Tchaikovsky I have included Russian works as well as English, for the benefit of those increasing numbers of readers familiar with the language who may be interested in the original versions of much material of which I have made use. The many important monographs, memoirs or articles essential to the serious student are not here included, but good, full, if inevitably now out-of-date lists may be found in Weinstock's book and Abraham's symposium.

*Polnoye Sobraniye Sochineny (Complete Collected Works)*
  The standard complete edition of the music, with full and efficient prefaces. As part of this enterprise, there is currently appearing a new edition of the complete writings and letters, excellently annotated but unfortunately marred by bowdlerization.

Nikolay Kashkin: *Vospominaniya o P. I. Tchaikovskom (Recollections of P. I. Tchaikovsky)*, Moscow, 1896

Pyotr Jürgenson: *Catalogue Thématique des Oeuvres de P. Tchaikovsky*, Moscow, 1897; reprinted, London, 1965
  A list of Jürgenson's Tchaikovsky publications, with incipits.

Pyotr Tchaikovsky: *Musikalniye Feletoni i Zametki (Musical Articles and Reviews)*, Moscow, 1898
  Writings of the years 1876–88, including the Bayreuth articles and the 1888 tour diary; with an introduction by Herman Laroche.

Modest Tchaikovsky: *Zhizn Petra Ilyicha Tchaikovskovo (The Life of Pyotr Ilyich Tchaikovsky)*, 3 vols, Moscow, 1900–2; trans. German, Paul Juon, 2 vols, Moscow and Leipzig, 1900–2; abridged trans. English, Rosa Newmarch, 1 vol., London, 1906
  Defensive and in some essential respects misleading, but the basic source work; Newmarch's version is abbreviated and often inaccurately translated.

Rosa Newmarch: *Tchaikovsky*, London, 1900
  Outdated, but useful for its copious quotation of Kashkin's *Recollections* and for its inclusion of a translation of the 1888 tour diary. Revised without the author's co-operation, incorporating new material, by Edwin Evans in 1907.

Pyotr Tchaikovsky (ed. Ippolit Ilyich Tchaikovsky): *Dnevniki Petra Ilyicha Tchai-kovskovo (The Diaries of Pyotr Ilyich Tchaikovsky)*, Moscow, 1923; trans. and ed. Vladimir Lakond, New York, 1945
  Covers the years 1873–91.

Pyotr Tchaikovsky: *Perepiska s N. F. von Meck (Correspondence with N. F. von Mecke)*, 3 vols, Moscow–Leningrad, 1934–6
  Much the most important collection of letters, well edited and annotated.

Gerald Abraham: *Tchaikovsky: a short biography*, London, 1944: revised version of essay in *Masters of Russian Music*, London, 1936

Pyotr Tchaikovsky: *Perepiska s P. I. Jurgensonom (Correspondence with P. I. Jürgenson)*, 2 vols, Moscow-Leningrad, 1938 and 1952

Vasily Yakovlev (ed.): *Dni i godi P. I. Tchaikovskovo: Lyetopis zhizni i tvorchestva (Days and Years of P. I. Tchaikovsky: annals of life and work)*, Moscow–Leningrad, 1940
  Cast in the form of a diary with an entry for every day of interest, together with extracts from letters, diaries, reviews, books, etc; well edited and fully indexed.

Herbert Weinstock: *Tchaikovsky*, New York, 1943
  Based on published Russian material, and well detailed biographically; little attention to the music.

Gerald Abraham (ed.): *Tchaikovsky: a symposium*, London, 1945
  Contains a useful survey of the songs by Arnold Alshvang and admirable discussions of the symphonies by Martin Cooper and the operas by Dr Abraham himself; the latter essay, however, is better consulted in the revised version, incorporating new material, in his *Slavonic and Romantic Music*, London, 1968.

Pyotr Tchaikovsky: *Pisma k Blizkim: Izbrannoe (Letters to Relations: Selection)*, Moscow, 1955

G. Dombayev: *Tvorchestvo Petra Ilyicha Tchaikovskovo (The Works of Pyotr Ilyich Tchaikovsky)*, Moscow, 1958
  A complete, well-organized list of works, with copious relevant quotations from letters and contemporary documents, as well as appendices with lists of first per-formances, librettists, bibliography, etc. An essential reference book.

Pyotr Tchaikovsky: *Tchaikovsky i Zarubezhnye Muzikanty: Izbrannye Pisma Inostrannykh Korrespondentov (Tchaikovsky and Foreign Musicians: Selected Letters of Foreign Corre-spondents)*, Leningrad, 1970

Edward Garden: *Tchaikovsky*, London, 1973
  A recent replacement of Edwin Evans's 1906 volume in the Master Musicians series.

# List and Sources of Illustrations

*The following abbreviations have been used:*

APN – Novosti Press Agency, archives or as stated
APN Glinka – Novosti Press Agency, from the M. I. Glinka State Central Museum of Musical Culture, Moscow
APN Klin – Novosti Press Agency, from the Tchaikovsky House-Museum at Klin
Bib. Nat. Paris – Bibliothèque Nationale, Paris
ILN/LEA – From *The Illustrated London News*, photograph by London Electrotype Agency
Klin – From the Tchaikovsky House-Museum, Klin
Mansell – The Mansell Collection, London
Mary Evans – The Mary Evans Picture Library, London
RTHPL – The Radio Times Hulton Picture Library, London
SCR – The Society for Cultural Relations with the U.S.S.R.
VK – Photograph by Victor Kennett

# Index

Numbers in *italics* refer to illustrations. 'T'=Tchaikovsky

# Frolovsky – von Meck

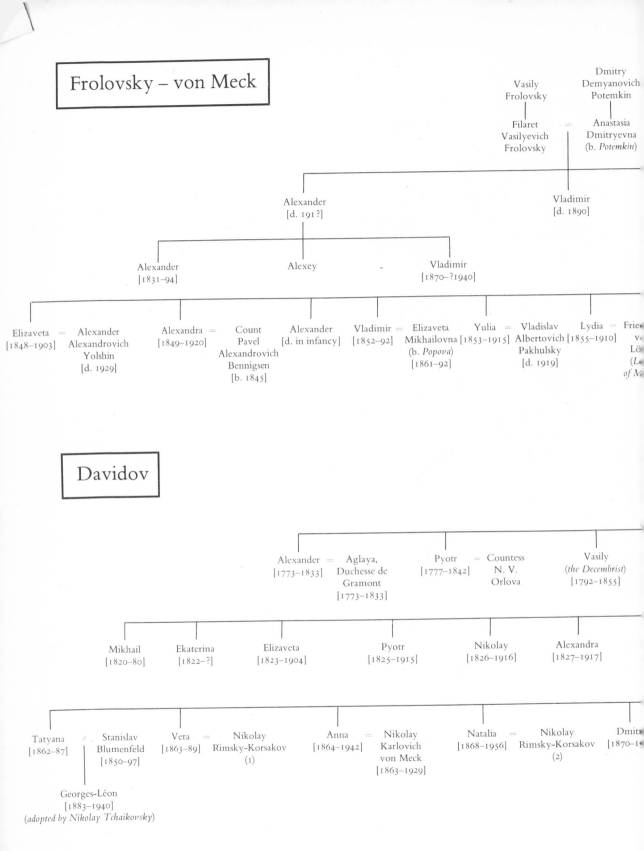

Vasily Frolovsky

Dmitry Demyanovich Potemkin

Filaret Vasilyevich Frolovsky = Anastasia Dmitryevna (b. *Potemkin*)

Alexander [d. 191?]

Vladimir [d. 1890]

Alexander [1831–94]

Alexey

Vladimir [1870–?1940]

Elizaveta [1848–1903] = Alexander Alexandrovich Yolshin [d. 1929]

Alexandra [1849–1920] = Count Pavel Alexandrovich Bennigsen [b. 1845]

Alexander [d. in infancy]

Vladimir [1852–92] = Elizaveta Mikhailovna (b. *Popova*) [1861–92]

Yulia [1853–1915] = Vladislav Albertovich Pakhulsky [d. 1919]

Lydia [1855–1910] = Frie... v... Lö... (L... of M...

# Davidov

Alexander [1773–1833] = Aglaya, Duchesse de Gramont [1773–1833]

Pyotr [1777–1842] = Countess N. V. Orlova

Vasily (*the Decembrist*) [1792–1855]

Mikhail [1820–80]

Ekaterina [1822–?]

Elizaveta [1823–1904]

Pyotr [1825–1915]

Nikolay [1826–1916]

Alexandra [1827–1917]

Tatyana [1862–87] / Stanislav Blumenfeld [1850–97]

Vera [1863–89] = Nikolay Rimsky-Korsakov (1)

Anna [1864–1942] = Nikolay Karlovich von Meck [1863–1929]

Natalia [1868–1956] = Nikolay Rimsky-Korsakov (2)

Dmit... [1870–1...

Georges-Léon [1883–1940] (*adopted by Nikolay Tchaikovsky*)